CHURCH VESTMENTS

By the same author

COSTUME AND FASHION

Vol. I. The Earlier Ages (to 1066)
Vol. II. Senlac to Bosworth (1066–1485)
Vol. III. The Tudor Period
(*in two books*)
Vol. IV. The Stuarts
(*in preparation*)

PLATE I (*see page* 22)

Christ the Teacher

CHURCH VESTMENTS
THEIR ORIGIN & DEVELOPMENT

BY HERBERT NORRIS

ILLUSTRATED WITH
EIGHT PAGES OF PHOTOGRAPHS
AND WITH EIGHT COLOUR PLATES
AND BLACK & WHITE DRAWINGS
BY THE AUTHOR

LONDON
J. M. DENT & SONS LTD

J. M. DENT & SONS LTD.
Aldine House · Bedford St. · London

Made in Great Britain
by
The Temple Press · Letchworth · Herts
First published 1949

Dedicated to the Memory of
A. D. D. M.
Lieut. 1/10th Gurkha Rifles.
Born 1926.   Killed on Active Service 1946.

CONTENTS

LIST OF ILLUSTRATIONS

IN COLOUR AND HALF-TONE

IN BLACK AND WHITE

INTRODUCTION

THIS book has grown, at the request of numerous readers, out of Volume I of the author's *Costume and Fashion*. It therefore deals with the classical garments which were the ancestors of the church vestments, and with their subsequent development to a time approximating to 1400—though fifteenth-century examples have been used where desirable, e.g. when a definite point of development is reached. To give colour to the narrative and descriptions various details of customs and events have been inserted where appropriate. Such digressions are usually indicated by sub-headings. There has been no systematic treatment of ritual, and for specialized subjects like monastic dress the reader must refer to the standard treatises.

The book should be useful professionally to the historian and ecclesiastic on the one hand, and to producers of plays and films (if sufficiently keen on period accuracy) on the other, besides being of interest to the general reader.

The numerous illustrations form a special feature of the work. These have all been taken from the originals, where possible; to make them more directly useful to the student they are not exact reproductions, but have been redrawn by the author so as to bring out their essential features. It is well known that artists (sculptors, carvers, metal workers, painters) of the Middle Ages often represented Biblical characters in the dress of their own day, thus providing an exceptionally useful source: though there is always the possibility that the artists may have been mistaken in their ideas—which nevertheless must be accepted in the absence of good reason to the contrary.

Much attention has been given to accurate dating, and the various sections are arranged in chronological order as far as possible: it is hoped that in this way it has been made easy for the student to discover the date of a particular example with ease and certainty: that a subject appears, e.g. in an illumination of the twelfth century, must not be taken as proving that it came into existence at the time when the MS. was written—it may well date from the previous century or even earlier.

The order in which the various vestments are treated is the approximate order of their emergence with liturgical significance: hence the alb comes first, not for alphabetical reasons, but because it is without doubt the first garment actually to become a vestment.

It has been the aim to keep colour plates in chronological order, and also to show the increasing elaboration of vestments. This arrangement necessitates some of them being placed at a distance from their descriptions: but in such cases the page number of the descriptions is given.

Owing to the greatly inferior quality of post-war materials, especially water-colour paints, it has not always been found possible to produce the exact shade required in the colour plates.

In conclusion, attention may be drawn to certain conventions in the text. Square brackets [ ] in quotations are explanatory insertions of the author: other languages have usually been translated into English. When a garment is mentioned for the first time, or when it first becomes a vestment, the name is printed in SMALL CAPITALS. Prices mean little unless the value of money in terms of purchasing power is known. Titles are not used earlier than the time at which they came into use, e.g. archbishops in the fourth century and pope in the fifth.

The reader who is unfamiliar with the general trend of Church history is advised to refresh his memory by frequent reference to the brief sketch which follows: and when similarly he is uncertain about titles he should consult the section dealing with this matter.

I wish to express my sincere thanks to all those who have so kindly helped me in this work. To the directors of museums and libraries from whom much valuable information has been gained. To Dr. A. Sharman Beer, F.R.S., Edinburgh, for his indefatigable attendance during the indisposition which interrupted my work: I also thank him very heartily for the translations of many Greek and German passages. To my sister, Mrs. Norman Mason, whose domestic help enabled me to concentrate on the development of this book. For their excellent spade-work on the illustrations I am much indebted to Mrs. Margery Paterson and Miss Myrtle Doye. To Mrs. Helen Lowndes, who converted the original figure numbers into those used in the text. To the Rev. Father G. Watts, for his much-sought advice and goodwill, and to Mrs. Margaret Wheeler for her assistance in many ways.

To Messrs. J. M. Dent & Sons Ltd. I am greatly beholden. They have constantly been most sympathetic and helpful to me during the compilation of this publication.

It is a very great pleasure for me again to express my gratitude to the Rev. J. Howard Brown for his translations from the Latin and French. His thoroughness, patience, corrections, and aid in the construction and editing of my manuscript have been a tremendous asset for which I am indeed most appreciative and truly grateful.

HERBERT NORRIS.

THAME, OXON,
March 1949.

AUTHORITIES QUOTED

St. Æthelwold
  Benedictional (c. 975–80)
Lady Alford
  Needlework, 1886
C. F. Allnutt
  Cathedra Petri, 1878
Archaeologia
E. G. Cuthbert Atchley, L.R.C.P.,
  M.R.C.S.
  Ordo Romanus Primus

T. A. Beck
  Annales Furnesienses, 1844
The Venerable Bede
  Ecclesiastical History (VIII century)
Rev. W. K. R. Bedford
  Hospital of Knights of St. John, 1882
Benedictine Monks of St. Augustine's
  Abbey, Ramsgate
  A Book of Saints, 1921
Bibles
  Bible of Charles the Bald (IX century)
  St. Edmundsbury Bible (XII century)
Brasses
Joseph Braun, S.J.
  Die Liturgische Gewandung, 1907
Burlington Magazine

Canons of Councils
Catalogues
  B.M. Catalogue of early Christian Antiquities
  V. and A. Museum Catalogue
Catholic Encyclopaedia
Catholic Encyclopaedia Dictionary, 1921
C. P. S. Clarke, Canon, M.A.
  Short History of the Christian Church, 1939
George Clinch, F.S.A. Scot., F.G.S.
  English Costume, 1909
Convocation of Canterbury, 1908
F. Warre Cornish, M.A., and Sir William
  Smith
  Greek and Roman Antiquities, 1898

Daremberg and Saglio
  Dictionnaire
Canon Percy Dearmer, D.D.
  Ornaments of Ministers, 1920
Herbert Druitt
  Monumental Brasses, 1906

Alfred Edersheim, M.A. Oxon., D.D., Ph.D·
  Life and Times of Jesus the Messiah, 1907
Effigies
Encyclopaedia Britannica

Otto von Falke
  Decorative Silks, 1922

John Farrow
  Pageant of the Popes, 1943
H. W. Fincham
  Order of Hospital of St. John, 1915
Adrian Fortescue, D.D.
  Vestments of the Roman Rite, 1912
A. C. Fox-Davies
  Ecclesiastical Heraldry
Gilbert French
  Notes on the Nimbus, 1854
Frescoes

Walter E. Gawthorp, F.S.A., Scot.
  Brasses, 1923
Edward Gibbon
  Decline and Fall of the Roman Empire,
  1776–88
John Gwillim
  Display of Heraldry, 1610

Sir Paul Harvey
  Companion to Classical Literature, 1937
Sir William Hope and E. G. Cuthbert
  Atchley
  English Liturgical Colours

Illuminated MSS.

Dom Raymund James
  Origin and Developments of Roman Liturgical
  Vestments, 1934
  Orate Fratres
P. W. Joyce, LL.D., M.R.I.A.
  History of Ancient Ireland, 1903

Rudolfo Lanciani
  Pagan and Christian Rome, 1892
Liber Pontificalis
Liber Vitae (XI century)
Walter Lowrie, M.A.
  Christian Art and Archaeology, 1901

R. A. S. Macalister, M.A.
  Ecclesiastical Vestments, 1896
Joseph McCabe
  Empresses of Rome, 1911
  Empresses of Byzantium, 1913
Rev. Wharton B. Marriot, M.A., F.S.A.
  Vestiarium Christianum, 1868
Rabanus Maurus
  De Institutione Clericorum (IX century)
Dr. Eric G. Millar
  Early English Illuminated MSS., 1926
J. R. H. Moorman
  Church Life in England in the XIII Century,
  1946

Order of Crowning (XIV century)

xiii

MATTHEW PARIS
  Historia Maior (XIII century)
J. R. PLANCHÉ, Somerset Herald
  Encyclopaedia of Costume, 1876
PONTIFICALS
PSALTER OF QUEEN MARY TUDOR (early XIV
  century)

DOM E. A. ROULIN, O.S.B.
  Vestments and Vesture, 1933

SACRAMENTARIES
SCULPTURE
SHORTER OXFORD ENGLISH DICTIONARY, 1933
WILLIAM SMITH, D.C.L., LL.D., and SAMUEL
  CHEETHAM, M.A.
  Christian Antiquities, 1876
F. M. STENTON
  Anglo-Saxon England, 1943
MARGARET STOKES
  Early Christian Art in Ireland, 1887
WALAFRID STRABO
  De Rebus Ecclesiasticis (IX century)

CHARLES TEXIER and R. P. PULLAN
  Byzantine Architecture, 1864
REV. JAMES HENTHORN TODD, D.D.
  Life of St. Patrick, 1864

E. VIOLLET-LE-DUC
  Mobilier Français, 1858–75

HENRY OFFLEY WAKEMAN, M.A.
  History of the Church of England, 1898
THE WALPOLE SOCIETY, vol. xiv, 1925–6
RIGHT REV. J. W. C. WAND, D.D., Bishop of
  London
  History of the Early Church, 1937
ALBERT WAY
  The Flabellum in *Archaeological Journal*,
  vol. v
J. WICKHAM-LEGG, D.D., F.S.A.
  Inventory of Westminster in *Archaeologia*, lii
MGR. JOSEPH WILPERT
  *Mosaics, Paintings, Christian Art, and
  Archaeology*, 1917

BRIEF HISTORICAL DATA

B.C.
753. Traditional foundation of Rome.
600. Classic Age in Greece begins.
509. Republican Rome.
428. Plato born.
384. Aristotle born at Stagira.
146. End of Greek independence.
55-4. Roman invasions of Britain under Julius Caesar.
51. Roman conquest of Gaul complete.
37. Herod the Great, King of Judaea.
27. Augustus Caesar made first Roman emperor.
6. Jesus Christ, the Messiah, born.
4. Death of Herod.

A.D.
43. Roman conquest of Britain.
61. Defeat and death of Boadicea.
64. The Emperor Nero burns Rome, and accuses the Christians of the crime. The cause of the first persecution.
67. St. Peter and St. Paul martyred.
69. St. Andrew said to have been martyred, 3rd November.
70. Destruction of Jerusalem by Titus.
117. Hadrian emperor: Roman Empire reaches greatest extent.
161. Marcus Aurelius emperor.
256. Arius, a priest of Alexandria, born. The Arian heresy was condemned at the Council of Nicaea, 325.
284. Diocletian emperor. The era of martyrs.
285. The martyrdom of St. Alban.
290. The martyrdom of St. George.
303. Edict of Diocletian, forbidding the cult of Christianity under severe punishment.
306. Constantine the Great, emperor.
312. Constantine converted to Christianity.
313. Edict of Toleration and Edict of Milan.
323. Christianity becomes the religion of the Roman state.
325. First Oecumenical Council of the Christian Church in Nicaea.
328. St. Helena, the Empress Mother, makes a pilgrimage to the Holy Land. Constantine finds the Holy Sepulchre and builds a church over it.
330. Foundation of the new Byzantium, named after the founder—Constantinople.
361. The Emperor Julian the Apostate attempts to repress Christianity.
364. Division of empire: Valentinian I (West), Valens (East).
380. Theodosius the Great, Emperor of the East, issues his famous Imperial Edict, *De Fide Catholica*, declaring the official religion of the Roman state to be 'that doctrine which St. Peter had preached and of which [Pope] Damasus was supreme.'

A.D.
391. Decree of Theodosius I against paganism.
IV-V century. St. Patrick. Date of birth uncertain.
410. Visigoths under Alaric capture Rome.
451. Council of Chalcedon.
452. Attila attacks Rome—is persuaded to retreat by Pope Leo the Great.
454. Death of Attila the Hun, 'The Scourge of God.'
455. Rome besieged and pillaged by the Vandals and Moors under Genseric.
472. Rome taken by assault by Ricimer, a chief of the Suevi.
476. Odoacer, a barbarian, taxes Rome and forces the Senate to abolish the Imperial sovereignty in the West. Assumes the title of King of Italy. End of the Roman or Western Empire.
481. Clovis, King of the Franks. Saluted by Pope Anastasius II as the most Christian king.
496. Conversion of the Franks under Clovis.
519. St. David, first Archbishop of St. Davids.
529. St. Benedict founded the Benedictine Order at Monte Cassino.
597. St. Augustine, prior of the monastery founded by Gregory, its first abbot, upon the Caelian Hill (San Gregorio) is sent by Gregory, now raised to the papacy, to convert the Anglo-Saxons.
638. Jerusalem captured by Moslems under Omar.
716. St. Boniface, an Anglo-Saxon, sent by Pope Gregory II to evangelize Germany.
732. Battle of Tours: Charles Martel defeats Moslems.
735. Death of Venerable Bede.
800. Charlemagne crowned Holy Roman Emperor by Pope Leo III in the Basilica of St. Peter, Rome.
1012. Martyrdom of Archbishop Ælfheah at Canterbury.
1066. Battle of Hastings.
1099. Crusaders capture Jerusalem: recaptured by Saladin, 1187.
1170. Murder of Thomas à Becket at Canterbury.
1214. Roger Bacon born.
1215. Magna Carta.
1225. Thomas Aquinas born.
1265. Dante Alighieri born.
1340. Geoffrey Chaucer born.
1378. Beginning of the Great Schism in the West.
1417. End of the Great Schism in the West.
1453. Wars of Roses in England until 1461.
1453. The ninth siege and capture of Constantinople by the Turks under Mohammed II. The Crescent had apparently triumphed over the Cross.

JESUS CHRISTUS

The original of this portrait of Christ was discovered by the Italian antiquary
Antonio Bosio (1575–1614)—'the Columbus of Subterranean Rome'—in a
chapel of the catacomb of Callistus, made for the body of St. Callistus I, Bishop
of Rome (217–22), though this 'Bishop of Bishops' was not buried there.
It was probably painted on a wood panel, a method adopted by the Greek
artists of the Alexandrian Age (338–146 B.C.); and is thought to date from the
end of the first or the early second century A.D.

This precious painting unhappily no longer exists, and it is fortunate that
Bosio made a drawing of it before it disappeared.   The above is a reproduction
of a sixteenth-century engraving of it, in the style of this period, but doubtless
incorporating the features of the original.

BRIEF SKETCH OF THE HISTORY OF THE CHRISTIAN CHURCH TILL 1500

CHRISTIANITY is a historic religion, based on the life and teaching, as on the incarnation and resurrection, of Jesus Christ. It was from the first a missionary religion, and demanded a high moral standard from its converts living in a heathen world: for though the first Christians, like St. Peter himself, were of course Jews, these were soon greatly outnumbered by Gentiles as a consequence of the travels of St. Paul. So long as it was confused with Judaism, Christianity shared in the protection of the latter as an official religion: but as the difference between them became evident, and especially when Christians refused to make any terms with emperor worship, the conflict between Church and State became inevitable, and persecutions began, associated with the names of the Emperors Nero and Domitian.

There was, so far, little material inducement to accept Christianity, but it so steadily advanced in numbers and influence that the Emperor Decius (250) and the Emperor Diocletian (303) made determined attempts to suppress it. This was the great era of the Christian martyrs: but even at this late date no one could have foreseen that the Emperor Constantine the Great (313) would grant complete religious toleration, still less that the eastern Emperor Theodosius the Great (380) would make Christianity the one legal religion.

From this troublous period the Church emerged a united body, with a central authority and a complete system of dogma. The orders of bishops, priests, and deacons had developed from the second century onwards. By the fifth the Bishop of Rome had been accorded primacy in the West, with the title 'Pope'; and the necessity of deciding what was orthodox belief, as against the various heresies that arose, led to the calling of the Great General Councils (Nicaea 325, Chalcedon 461), whose decisions, embodying the creeds, were binding on the whole Church.

.   .   .   .   .

When, under the barbarian onslaughts of the fifth century, the western empire began to disintegrate, and Rome itself was captured and sacked, the Church had to face a new problem, and mass conversions took place, resulting in a lowering of standards: it was now a necessity to profess Christianity, and the adherence of many was often merely nominal. But by contrast with the chaos of kingdoms and dynasties which followed the collapse of the Roman Empire, the Christian Church had provided for five centuries an unbroken unity, a rallying point for men of goodwill, and a central figure who might command the loyalty and devotion of all men. Such a man was Pope Gregory the Great (590–604): and from this time onwards the Christian faith spread west and north to the confines of the known world under the influence of devoted missionaries like St. Augustine of Canterbury (597). Of more immediate importance were the baptism of the Franks under Clovis (496), and the work of St. Boniface in Germany (716): and so it was a Christian monarch, Charles Martel, who (732) stemmed the Moslem invasion at the Loire by his victory at Tours.

Amid the general decay of civilization men began to strive to live the good life by a retreat from the world.   Such asceticism began with St. Anthony and the Egyptian hermits early in the fourth century: in the more rigorous climate of Europe this movement took the form of living in houses under vows of poverty, obedience, and chastity (in contrast to the prevailing vices of the age), and it was St. Benedict in Italy who (c. 580) founded the first monasteries.   There a life of contemplation could be lived, to which manual work was soon added as a necessary corrective: yet baser elements intruded themselves from the first.   Nevertheless it was the monasteries which kept learning alive during the Dark Ages, as it was the Papacy which preserved the continuity of the Church.

When, in 800, Pope Leo III crowned Charlemagne, he called into being the Holy Roman Empire, an attempt to unite the western nations into a world federation of Christians: and there began to arise in men's minds the conception of sharing spiritual and temporal power between pope and emperor.   Thereafter occurred a long struggle for precedence: but soon Rome was no longer the patronized but the patron, and it was Hildebrand (Gregory VII, 1073–85) who established the supremacy of the papacy, and laid the foundations of its temporal power and wealth, compelling even the emperor himself (Henry IV) to do penance.   The associated problem of investiture remained: it was essential that the allegiance of bishops should be detached from lay rulers, and the struggle ended in the triumph of the pope and ecclesiastical freedom at the Concordat of Worms (1122).

·   ·   ·   ·   ·   ·   ·

The Eastern (Byzantine) Empire, which had separated from the West during the fourth century, held together when the West collapsed: the nominal adherence of the Church in the East, however, persisted as a sort of formal unity until 1054.   Conditions had diverged from the first, and disputes over matters like the appointment of bishops, the use of unleavened bread, and the marriage of priests widened the breach, until the matter came to a head over the determination of Rome to add the word 'filioque' to the creed, and the final severance took place.   It was from the East that Russia was evangalized: and though shrunken and enfeebled the eastern empire remained as a bulwark against Islam until the Turks captured Constantinople in 1453.

With the avowed aim of recovering the Holy Land from the infidel (who interfered with pilgrimages), the first Crusade was originated (1099) by Pope Urban II: but though the Christian kingdom of Jerusalem lasted almost a century, and though crusade followed crusade well into the thirteenth century, their ultimate importance was rather the opening of the East for trade.   No doubt the primary purpose was to turn the quarrelsome nature and fighting instincts of the time to pious uses: but they also served to divert attention from the disputes of pope and emperor, and incidentally to increase the prestige of the papacy.

As increasing worldliness crept in, attempts were made, about 1100, to restore the monastic rule: the Benedictine rule was reformed by St. Bernard, Bruno founded the Carthusians, and the Cistercians also attempted to stem the growing laxity.   But nothing could stop the accumulation of wealth by the monasteries: and hence early in the thirteenth century there was a second wave of reform in an attempt to restore absolute poverty.   So began the mendicant orders or friars—Franciscans in 1210, Dominicans in 1215—who lived in the world and preached from village to village: but the same fate overtook them. In fact the history of monasticism, like that of so many human institutions, has, down to our own day, been an alternation between decay and resurrection.

Meanwhile under Pope Innocent III (1198–1216) the papacy had reached the height of its power and influence, claiming the complete subjection of the State to the Church, including the right to appoint and depose monarchs. In the exercise of this claim the powers of excommunication and interdict were so frequently abused as to demonstrate their ultimate futility. But it was the concurrent wealth of the Church which caused the greatest dissatisfaction, worldly lives contrasting strongly with pious pretensions. This dissatisfaction was certainly in part the cause of the heresies which sprang up during the later Middle Ages, e.g. the Albigenses (thirteenth century) and the Waldenses (fourteenth century). The suppression of these heresies brought into being the ecclesiastical machinery for combating error which reached its highest point of development in the Spanish Inquisition.

With the death (1303) of Pope Boniface VIII any hope of realizing universal temporal power disappeared: French influence compelled the popes to go into exile for seventy years on their estates at Avignon. No sooner had the return to Rome taken place (1377) than the French cardinals appointed an anti-pope, and so to the scandal of Christendom began the forty-year 'Great Schism.' Such a split in the solidity of the Church was not to be retrieved: the hope of peace on earth faded, and so perished—for the time—the great ideal of the divine government of the world.

Attempts now at suppression and now at internal reform were made, but a larger movement was gathering momentum. Its roots are traced in the teaching of Wycliff (d. 1384) and his translation of the Bible; his doctrines spread to Europe, and in the fifteenth century reached Bohemia, where John Huss was burned as a heretic (1415). The chief feature of this reform movement was its basing of doctrinal truth on the private interpretation of the Scriptures; the beginning of its final phase is usually dated from Martin Luther's denunciation of the traffic in indulgences in 1517. So began a rift, between Rome and the northern protestant countries, which the doctrinal assertions of the Council of Trent (1545–63) made seemingly final.

TITLES OF ECCLESIASTICS

THERE are seven separate degrees of holy orders in the Western Church:

Minor orders: Doorkeeper or porter, lector or reader, exorcist, acolyte (see page 28 and Figs. 26–30).

Major or sacred: Subdeacon, deacon, priest; bishops have the plenitude of the priestly power, while archbishops, patriarchs, and pope are degrees within the episcopate.

The cardinalate is an office, not an order; the same is true of abbacies, canonries, and other prelatures.

Thus work does not deal with these orders as such: but their titles (whether Latin or English) are relevant to the dress and ornaments of those who possess them, therefore some account of the origin of these titles will now be given.

'Deacon' and 'priest' belong to the first century: 'bishop' to the second: 'subdeacon' to the third: 'canon' to the third or fourth: 'abbot' and 'archbishop' date from the fourth: 'pope' from the fifth: 'cardinal' first appears in the ninth.

These titles, like church vestments, have developed as a rule by giving specialized meanings to everyday words in use in classical Greek. Moreover, several of them were in wide general use before becoming restricted to a much smaller number of ecclesiastics.

1. DEACON: I CENTURY

Thus 'diakonos' means commonly a servant or waiting-man, but the derivation implying one who is dusty through running is now discredited. The New Testament writers, e.g. St. Paul, use it to mean a servant or minister of the Church, as in 1 Timothy iii. 8: 'Deacons in like manner must be grave, not double-tongued, not given to much wine, not greedy of filthy lucre.' Note that the 'seven men of honest report' [1] are not actually called deacons.

Drawings of a deacon in his vestments:

> XIII century, Fig. 64, Plate IX, Plate VIII, Fig. 229.
> XIV   „   Fig. 66.
> XV   „   Plate XV.

2. SUBDEACON: III CENTURY

The office of subdeacon no doubt arose out of the growing needs and organization of the Church, and cannot—in the West—be traced further back than the third century, when it is mentioned by St. Cyprian. His duty at first was to assist the deacon: but his special duties soon became better defined, and related to the doorkeeper, the water for washing the priest's hands, and the bringing and returning of the altar vessels—hence there were delivered to him at ordination an empty paten and chalice, and an empty pitcher, a basin, and a towel. The practice of the subdeacon reading the epistle began in the seventh or eighth century. Celibacy was imposed by degrees, and with it came promotion from the highest of the minor orders to the lowest of the major. In modern times his vestments are the tunicle and maniple.

A subdeacon is shown:

> X century, Fig. 26.
> XIII   „   Fig. 63.

3. PRIEST: I CENTURY

Etymologically 'priest' derives from the Greek 'presbuteros,' which means an older man, usually in an honoured sense, i.e. in reference to the wisdom of age, like our word 'alderman.' In the New Testament (first century A.D.) it is translated 'elder,' [2] and in all cases where it occurs the reference is always to disciplinary functions and never in connection with worship.

The usual word translated 'priest' in the New Testament is 'hiereus,' meaning one whose function is to offer a sacrifice, whether Jewish or heathen. It is not there used of an individual Christian minister, but is applied indiscriminately to all Christians. The two words 'presbuteros' and 'hiereus,' elder and priest, were thus at first quite distinct: but later on they became merged. This usage had become fairly general by

---

[1] Acts vi. 3.
[2] Acts xi. 30.

the beginning of the third century, and is universal from the fifth, whence 'hiereus' is invariably applied to those officers of the Church formerly known as 'presbyters.'

Drawings of priests in vestments:

XIII century, Fig. 65.
XIV   ,,   Fig. 106, Plate IX.
XV   ,,   Fig. 115.

4. BISHOP: II CENTURY

The Greek word 'episkopos' means one who watches over, and hence an overseer, superintendent, or guardian. It is a common word in classical Greek, and is used especially for various municipal officers, and of the intendants sent by the Athenians to subject states. It is also used in the Greek Old Testament for minor officers, commissioners, and taskmasters: and in the New Testament five times, being there substantially equivalent to 'presbuteros.'

During the apostolic age the two terms are interchangeable.

The title 'bishop' [1] first appears in the epistles of St. Ignatius of Antioch (A.D. 50–114), who urges obedience to the bishops.

The earliest reference to the existence of episcopacy in England bears the date 314. This alludes to Restitutus Bishop of London, who, with the Bishops of York and Lincoln and their several priests and deacons, attended the Council of Arles.

The following figures show bishops in vestments:

VI century, Fig. 81, Plate IV.
X   ,,   Fig. 95.
XI   ,,   Fig. 96.
XIII   ,,   Plate VIII.
XIV   ,,   Plate III.
XV   ,,   Plate XIII, Fig. 115.

5. CANON: III OR IV CENTURY

This is a term of wide application, the underlying idea being regularity of some kind. As applied to clerics, the primary meaning (third or fourth century) is the staff of clergy serving a particular church: who were so called either because bound by canon law, or because enrolled on a list of Church officers. In these days this sense has descended to the clergy living within the precincts of a cathedral as members of the cathedral chapter, with the right to a stall in the cathedral choir. Many of them are vicars or rectors of important parishes in the diocese.

But in the fifth century bishops began to expect a high degree of austerity from their clergy, and so regular establishments of canons were formed who lived in clergy houses under discipline. The foundation of such semi-monastic orders of canons is attributed to an archbishop of Metz of the eighth century: such canons regular were at first priests bound by their vows of poverty and obedience.

This rule as originally conceived proved too drastic, and by the eleventh century a looser rule had become firmly established. Thus the Augustinian canons were founded by Ivo of Chartres, and this order was introduced into England early in the twelfth

---

[1] 1 Peter ii. 25: 'For ye were going astray like sheep; but are now returned unto the Shepherd and Bishop [originally Overseer] of your souls.' See also 1 Timothy iii. 1.

century: they were known as black canons, from their black cloaks, and had over 150 houses in England and Wales at the dissolution. The white canons (Premonstratensians) were founded by St. Norbert (1134), and at the same period had thirty English houses. Canons regular thus occupied an intermediate position between the monks on the one hand and the secular clergy on the other.

Full-length drawings of canons:

XIV century, Fig. 235.
XV   „   Plate XIV, Fig. 250.

6. ABBOT: IV CENTURY

The Hebrew 'ab'=father, passed into the Latin of the Vulgate [1] as 'abbas,' and so came to mean, in medieval Latin, the head of an ecclesiastical community, whence our word 'abbot' through the Anglo-Saxon. It originally denoted an elderly monk. It dates from the beginnings of monachism in the early fourth century, and particularly from the rise of the Benedictines in the sixth: by which time it indicated exclusively the superior of a monastery, and the Abbot of Monte Cassino received the title 'Abbas Abbatum' as head of the Benedictine monasteries. By virtue of their office such abbots attended imperial and royal councils.

As monastic orders multiplied new titles—such as majors, priors, guardians, rectors, etc.—came into use, but all these prelates have, of course, no jurisdiction outside their own orders.

It was in 1063 that the first *mitred* abbot, so far as is known, was invested by Pope Alexander II (1061–73): he was the Abbot of St. Augustine's, Canterbury—Egelsinus by name—and the mitre signified that his monastery was not subject to the jurisdiction of the bishop. Mitred abbots rank equally with bishops, and consequently are entitled to use all pontificalia. A list of these ceremonial ornaments will be found on page 8.

It must be realized that from the eighth and ninth centuries there were lay abbots, the dignity being conferred by sovereigns more especially on their own relatives and partisans. This was notoriously the case with the Carlovingians.

An abbot in full vestments wore the same as a bishop. Plate III shows an abbot of the thirteenth century in simpler vestments because he is receiving an archbishop, but he carries a pastoral staff. A monk and an anchorite of the fourteenth century are shown in Plate III and in Plate II respectively.

7. ABBESS

The superior of an abbey of nuns was as much a feudal lord as an abbot, with the same powers over her domains and tenants. The influence of the abbess was extensive, and some of them were from time to time summoned to royal councils.

For a thirteenth- and fourteenth-century abbess, a nun, and an anchorite see Plate II.

8. ARCHBISHOP: IV CENTURY

When bishops met in the early councils of the Church, i.e. from about the latter half of the second century, the chairman who presided would be chosen from amongst those

---

[1] The Latin version of the Bible in common use in the Catholic Church, made about 400.

held in the highest esteem by the others: or he might be the bishop of the diocese in which the council was held. On such a bishop his fellow bishops would naturally bestow the title 'arch-bishop.' This title is said to have been first assumed permanently by St. Athanasius, Bishop of Alexandria (326–73): the first Bishop of Rome to take the title of Archbishop of Rome was St. Anastasius I (398–401).

By this time the organization of the Church had become more complex, and the empire was divided into provinces, each containing several dioceses: so that in course of time each had its patriarch, at first called an archbishop.

Plate III. shows a bishop, an archbishop, an abbot, and monks.

For the vestments of archbishops see:

XI century, Fig. 96.
XII „ Plate VII, Fig. 252.
XIII „ Fig. 204.
XIV „ Plate III.
XV „ Plate XV.

9. THE POPE: V CENTURY

When the supremacy of the Bishop of Rome over other bishops of the Christian Church became generally accepted has been a matter of much dispute, as has also the time at which the title of pope was first used in the West. Accordingly the title is not used in this book before the fifth century: the universal acceptance of the papal supremacy begins in the early seventh century.

The facts appear to be as follows:

In ecclesiastical use the Greek word 'papas' (=father) was first used of his teacher by a convert, as being his spiritual father whose name he often adopted. It was thus of wide and varied application before it became, in the third century, the prerogative of bishops. Later it was restricted to the Bishop of Rome in the West and to certain patriarchs in the East; until finally it was claimed exclusively by the Bishop of Rome, apparently about the end of the fifth century.

Eventually the use of the title for any other dignitary was formally forbidden by Gregory VII (Hildebrand) in the Council of Rome, 1073.

So far as can be ascertained, the form of address 'Your Holiness' dates from 401, when it was used by St. Augustine of Hippo to St. Innocent I (401–17). The first pope to be acclaimed 'Vicar of Christ' was apparently St. Gelasius I (492–6), at the Second Council of Rome, 495.

St. Innocent I (401–17) boldly asserted the supremacy of Rome—'Pontifex Maximus' —claiming that its authority was derived from St. Peter as chief of the apostles and founder of the see: and this claim appears to have been generally conceded; but it was under St. Leo the Great (440–61) that the Petrine prerogative first received definite statement; and under his successor St. Hilary (461–8) these claims were pressed in the provinces: it was St. Gregory the Great (590–604) who secured almost universal recognition. This was natural enough amongst the western nations, including England, who owed their conversion to Rome: and its acceptance in the East was helped by the loss of Syria and Egypt, and especially of Jerusalem itself, to the Saracens.

Henceforward the political aspect became inextricably intertwined with the ecclesiastical.

The vestments worn by popes of the eleventh century on ceremonial occasions are shown in Plates V and VI and Fig. 145.

10. CARDINAL: IX CENTURY

'Cardinal' derives ultimately from the Latin 'cardo,' a hinge, meaning therefore something (or someone) on which something else hinges, i.e. of primary importance, with the implied idea of fixity. Thus it was first used indiscriminately for the presbyters and deacons of churches to which a cure of souls was attached. By the ninth century the term was in general use in this sense.

By the eleventh century there were cardinal bishops, seven of whom (Ostia, Porto, St. Rufina, Albano, Sabina, Tusculum, and Praeneste) were, with the cardinal presbyters and deacons, formed into a college for the election of future popes by Pope Nicholas II (1059–61).

The same honours as were accorded to bishops were given to cardinals; they could, for example, celebrate mass in the same vestments, including mitre and crozier.

The resistance of the palatine cardinals, who were personally attached to the pope and lived in the Lateran, prevented the definite organization of the sacred college till Pope Alexander III (1159–81) gave the exclusive right of electing the pope to the cardinals.

A cardinal of the thirteenth and fourteenth centuries in full robes is shown in Fig. 237.

VESTMENTS IN GENERAL

SOME general statements about the wearing of the various vestments by these different orders of clergy may now be given, in anticipation.

All ranks wore the alb, and all major orders the maniple. All those above subdeacon wore amice and stole. All above deacon the chasuble: subdeacons were distinguished by the tunicle, deacons by the dalmatic; and both these vestments were added to the outfit of the bishop.

Buskins, sandals, mitre, gloves, ring, and staff were peculiar to bishops, and to certain abbots to whom they had been expressly granted by the pope: cardinals also had the right to them.

To these vestments archbishops added the pallium. The pope dispensed with the pastoral staff, but reserved the orale and—in later times—the subcingulum (girdle) for his exclusive use.

NOTE. The ceremonial ornaments proper to a bishop are called pontificalia. As mentioned above, they consist of a pectoral cross and ring (worn always); mitre and pastoral staff (used when pontificating, and at pontifical mass): buskins, sandals, gloves: tunicle and dalmatic, worn under the chasuble. The throne is also included among the pontificalia.

Early vestments were derived from the everyday dress of ordinary people—thus the ancestor of the alb was the garment universally worn by the men of classic Greece of the last six centuries B.C., and called the chiton. No distinctive dress was worn by the early clergy: they wore the usual everyday garb of the people, and their costume differed only in some details, if at all, from that of ordinary folk. Their natural impulse would be to insist on a certain measure of refinement, beauty, and dignity: and so they arrayed themselves in the best garments they possessed for the service of God. The officiant from primitive times thus wore his best clothes, both from motives of reverence, and also as an expression of rejoicing.

When the classical Roman dress began to be superseded by the barbarian type, the conservativeness of religion asserted itself by retaining these old-fashioned garments for the minister after laymen had abandoned them: and in consequence the celebrant at the eucharist came to wear clothes which were no longer in secular use. So it came about that the ordinary civil costume of the well-dressed layman of the first century A.D. acquired sacerdotal significance as an ecclesiastical vestment. That this has happened over and over again will be evident from the following pages.

One curious consequence of the unfamiliarity of the minister's clothes has been the evolution of quaint symbolical explanations of their meaning. Such explanations are entirely artificial and fanciful: they may be reasons for continuing their use, but hardly for wearing them in the first instance.

In early times the vestments of the Greek or Eastern and the Roman or Western Church were closely similar: but differences soon developed, and these must be borne in mind when dealing with any particular case.

It must not be deduced from the frequently elaborate examples described that every parish in England or on the Continent was provided with vestments on a luxurious scale. In many cases they would be shabby or even threadbare—often they would be absent altogether.

The large number of names used by early Christian (as well as modern) writers for the same vestment is very troublesome, and leads to misunderstandings. An attempt has been made to clarify this by giving the chief word used and to follow it at once by its various synonyms.

1. THE ALB

Chiton: Kolobus—Tunica—Colobium—Tunica Talaris—Subucula—Tunica Alba.
Also *Clavi* and *Girdle*

The alb has its origin in these six garments worn by the people. Therefore a description of each is given.

THE CHITON

VI CENTURY B.C.

THE garment universally worn by men of classic Greece of the first six centuries B.C. was called the CHITON. In shape this was simply a rectangular piece of linen or woollen fabric, folded round the body, the top edges fastened together by pins or buttons on the shoulders, Fig. 1, and girded at the waist. The man in Fig. 2 has undone one of the buttons to free his arm while working, a usual habit. The two ends which came at one side or the other had the edges usually finished off with a fringe,

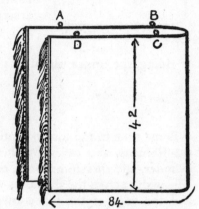

Fig. 1. Diagram of Early Chiton

the raw edges left in the weaving. This fringe is generally translated as 'tasselled' (see Homer's *Odyssey*, xix. 242).

As time went on the open side was sewn up, converting the garment into a cylinder, which was fastened on the body as described above.

The short chiton, to the knees, was worn for the most part by young men; older men and high dignitaries preferred the long chiton which reached to the feet. It was also a garment of ceremony.

Fig. 2.
Greek of the V Century B.C.

THE KOLOBUS

IV CENTURY B.C.

Another form of the chiton came into use about the beginning of the fourth century, and was known as the KOLOBUS.

In shape it was as previously a cylinder, but with this difference: instead of being buttoned the edges of the top part were sewn together on the shoulders, leaving an opening in the middle for the head, and sufficient space at *the sides* for the arms to pass through (Fig. 3). When the kolobus was girded it had the appearance of the older chiton, the distinction being that the arms emerged at the top edge of the chiton, whereas in the kolobus they passed through the openings at the sides, Fig. 4. The name kolobus refers to what might be mistaken for *short* sleeves reaching to just above the elbows. A superior type of kolobus was woven in one piece, with the three openings or slits for the head and arms left in the weaving.

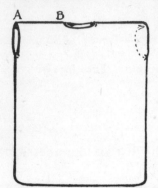

Fig. 3. Diagram of Kolobus

THE TUNICA

During the period of republican Rome the Greek chiton was adopted by the Romans and given the Latin name TUNICA. At first its shape and material were the same as described under the chiton. It was girded at the waist, and the length of the skirt part was regulated by pulling the material above the girdle. For vigorous exercise, or riding, the tunica would be girded higher than for normal wear.

THE COLOBIUM

Some time in the fourth century B.C. the kolobus of the Greeks was also adopted by the Romans, and called by them the COLOBIUM. The garment was still shaped as a cylinder, and therefore closed, and consequently was put on by passing it over the head. The width across the shoulders varied, the greater the distance between the neck opening and the edge of the top corner—see AB and BA in Figs. 3 and 4—the more of the upper arm was covered, thus giving the misleading impression of a draped sleeve almost to the elbow or even below it.

The difference, a slight one, between the tunica and colobium was, that the former had no sleeves, whereas the latter had the shoulder part cut long enough for the material to fall in folds over the upper arms. The Romans had a great aversion to anything in the nature of a long or close arm covering, because these (like trousers) were a characteristic of barbarian dress.

Fig. 5 is a well-dressed young man, a patrician of republican Rome. He wears a shortened edition of the colobium, reaching only to the knees, and decorated with bands of check embroidery down the front, round the armhole openings and neck (unseen) and edging of the bottom hem. The figure shows to advantage the wearing of this simple yet effective garment, and also the hang of the cloak.

THE TUNICA TALARIS

The tunic when it reached the feet was known as the TUNICA TALARIS; and when more than one tunica,

Fig. 4. Roman wearing Colobium,
IV Century B.C.

Fig. 5. A Patrician of Republican and Imperial Rome

short or long, was worn, the under one (of wool) was the same shape as the outer, and called TUNICA INTERIOR or SUBUCULA.

The materials from which tunicae were made were not at this time entirely limited to linen (tunica linea) or wool (tunica lanea), but sometimes, especially in warm climates, of cotton, and occasionally of silk by the wealthy.

THE GIRDLE
(Subcingulum, subcinctorium, zona)

This article of dress is essentially utilitarian, and sometimes ornamental. It always has been used to confine garments round the waist, and dates back to very early times. It was worn by all classes from emperor to peasant.

Girdles and belts worn by the classic Greeks were, besides being very simple, generally a narrow band of material like a modern ribbon, ornamented with gold, and often with semi-precious stones. The Romans copied these ideas of decoration. Ordinary girdles worn by the masses were made of cord, often knotted, of plaited strips of linen, or of leather. Amongst the best-dressed people, it was considered slovenly to appear in public in an ordinary tunica *without* a girdle, but it was dispensed with in private for comfort.

Perhaps the first reference to a girdle in an authoritative sense is found in the sixth-century A.D. Rule of St. Benedict, wherein it is ordered that monks must not set aside their girdles even when they had retired for the night.

The earliest allusion to the girdle in any ecclesiastical sense is made by St. Germanus, Patriarch of Constantinople (715; died in exile 733), who says the napkin should be attached to the girdle of a deacon. Not until the eighth century did the girdle become recognized as part of Christian vestments. After this time, although partly hidden ('subcingulum') by the alb which was pulled out over it, the girdle was decorated with gold and precious stones in a variety of ways.

In the early ages a pocket was formed by the folds of the tunica drawn up by the waist girdle.

The pouch, 'pera,' was known to the Greeks and to the Romans, whose 'bulga' or leather purse was attached to the girdle or slung over the shoulder or arm. The peasant in Fig. 73 is carrying such a pouch, which no doubt contains his midday meal.

When our Lord instructs His disciples (Mark vi. 8) 'that they should take nothing for their journey, save a staff only; neither *scrip*, neither bread, neither money in their purse,' He means that they must take no food—which Jews were accustomed to do on a journey to ensure its ceremonial cleanliness, carrying it in a 'scrip,' i.e. wallet slung over the shoulder—nor must they have any money in the folds of the girded tunica ('purse').

Continued on page 17.

Nun

PLATE II *(see page* 6)
Abbess

British Museum. By kind permission of the Governors
Anchorite

THE TUNICA ALBA
A.D. I CENTURY

No change in the shape or colour of the tunica or colobium took place during the first century A.D.   It was universally of white, and on that account called the TUNICA ALBA.

The CLAVUS [1] stripes appeared on the kolobus in Greece about the fourth century B.C., but purely as a decoration.   They were vertical, usually one over each shoulder, up the front and down the back, woven or sewn on to the garment.   These ornamented the costumes of the 'camilli' and 'camillae,' an association of youths and maidens employed to *minister* in religious rites and ceremonies.

The tunica, when worn by senators of the Roman republic, had one broad stripe of red set down the centre front.   This was the 'latus clavus,' and was about 3 or 4 inches in width.   Men of the Equestrian order decorated their tunicae with two stripes about 1½ inches or 'two fingers' wide.   These were known as 'angusti clavi.'

The tunica on which these stripes were applied was usually un-girded; the punctilious Quintilian (A.D. 35–95, both dates approximate) advises that 'if the tunica has the latus clavus, it is better to wear it without a girdle' to avoid breaking the perpendicular lines, 'but it is not so convenient.'

At the end of the first century A.D. the angustus clavus lost its significance as a badge of rank, since it was universally used as a fashionable adjunct to the tunica in general, and also because it was worn by women.

A.D. II AND III CENTURY

The tunica talaris and the long colobium, which were now looked upon as the same garment, were much worn by men of the upper class during the second and third centuries of the Christian era.   They conferred a special dignity upon the wearer because their length made it impossible for him to do any labour; and being the characteristic garb of learned men found great favour.

Despite the Roman dislike of long sleeves, they were added to the tunica and colobium in A.D. 270.   It is recorded that the Emperor Aurelian (270–5) on his election presented novel gifts of 'tunicae with long sleeves' to the people. After this the tunica and colobium, with long sleeves, were in general use among the upper and lower classes of imperial Rome. These sleeves are shown in Fig. 6.   The construction of this garment, known as a 'tunica manicata alba,' continued to follow the lines of the originals, and the opening for the head was still retained; but often the width of the material was gathered

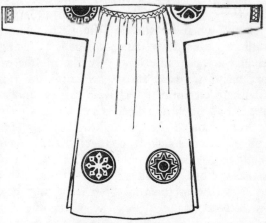

Fig. 6. Roman Tunica

[1] Clavus=a nail, and also a stripe.   The meaning has developed from the original sense of the nail to the long and narrow stripe.

B

into a narrow neck-band, and occasionally it opened a little way down the front, where it was fastened by a fibula or pin, or by buttons and loops.

Long sleeves could, of course, be sewn into the arm-holes, but it was still customary for the garment to be cut in one piece with the sleeves.

The materials used were, as previously, linen and wool, and for the first time, about 265, a new fabric is referred to. It is recorded that the Emperor Gallienus (260–8) made a gift to his eventual successor Claudius (268–70) of an 'Alba Subserica.' This was a tunica of semi-silk, a woven mixture of silk with wool or cotton, and known as subserica. Undergarments, the tunica interior or subucula, previously of woollen material, were now also made of linen.

The clavi which decorated the tunica alba disappeared when the dalmatica (see p. 43) came into use in the third century, and was worn over the tunica, so hiding them from sight.

Those who had adopted the new faith, including women, of course wore the costume of the people in general, so naturally they had their tunicae and stolae embellished with the clavi because it was conformable with the usual practice. The same must have applied both to the Founder and also to ministers of Christianity.

With regard to the upper-class Christian who had been for generations accustomed to rich clothing, decoration, and the brilliant society of imperial Rome it is understandable that they were not 'faithful' enough to relinquish these quite innocent vanities

However, holy writers of the time hurled vituperative language against the 'gay clothing,' luxurious display of dress, and 'immodest apparel' of Christian men and women. After all, God gave fabrics, metals, and precious stones, so why should they not be used for His glorification?

IV CENTURY

The Edict of Toleration published by the Emperor Galerius (305–6), and the Edict of Milan issued by Constantine the Great (306–37) in 313, were followed by a decree of Sylvester, Bishop of Rome (314–36) ordaining that the tunica talaris should be worn by deacons when assisting at the altar. The intention clearly is that he is to wear his ordinary everyday garments, but is to change into a clean tunica for the purpose, and change it again after use. In the middle of this century the overseers of the Church, or 'bishops,' wore three garments—the tunica talaris being one of them—simply as adequate clothing, which was the common everyday dress of the common people: as yet it had no significance whatever in Church ritual.

In a canon of the Council of Carthage (c. 400) we meet with the first use of the word ALB in an ecclesiastical connection. It may well be one of the earliest regulations ever made to govern the ritual usage of a vestment: the Latin word, *vestimenta*, meaning the articles of ordinary clothing. Not only does this canon ordain that an alb is to be used by a deacon at the time of mass as well as of the lesson, but it further prohibits him from wearing the alb except when officiating. This implies that bishops and priests could wear a long white tunica, the prototype of the alb, for everyday dress: but that this was forbidden to deacons. The canon was necessitated on account of the prevailing tendency of the minor clergy to wear their official dress in the streets: the dress was the same, whether for every day or for service, but the deacon is to wear a *clean* garment in Church, and change it afterwards.

St. Jerome (Hieronymus), doctor of the Church (341 or 342–420), translator of the Vulgate, writer of the history of the early Latin Church, confidential adviser of St. Damasus, Bishop of Rome (336–84), enlightens us as to the difference between the garments worn by the clergy when officiating in church, and those used by them for everyday wear. His translated words are: 'The Holy Religion has one dress for Divine Service and another for everyday use': also 'we ought not to enter the Holy of Holies in soiled everyday clothes, but with a clean conscience and with clean clothes to administer the mysteries of the Lord' (see Ezek. xlii. 14, xliv. 19).

The earliest illustration of a bishop is to be found in the partly destroyed mosaic of St. Ambrose (340–97) in the Church of St. Ambrogio, Milan, put up soon after his death. In this he is shown wearing the tunica alba, dalmatic, paenula, and shoes. It is interesting to note that St. Ambrose was elected by the people Bishop of Milan in 374. He is also renowned for his influence in the development of Church music, which he introduced into his diocese about the year 386.

VI CENTURY

Recognition of a distinctive dress or uniform for the minor clergy was not an accepted practice until the later part of the sixth century.

The First Council of Narbonne, which took place in 589, definitely confirms that the tunica talaris or colobium, i.e. the alb, was by this date an official dress. It enacted that 'neither deacon nor subdeacon, nor yet the lector, shall presume to put off his *alba* till after mass is over.' This firmly establishes the fact that the alb was by this time regarded as a vestment.

VII CENTURY

The alb, together with the planeta and orarium or stole, is mentioned in the records of the Fourth Council of Toledo, 633, thereby confirming that these vestments were in use previous to this date.[1]

VIII CENTURY

During the eighth century the alb, as previously, fell to the feet and was girded, but in shape it was 'full and flowing,' and was alluded to as 'alba larga.' The side seams were cut more at an angle from armpit to hem, which resulted in the folds being more pronounced, and consequently more beautiful. The sleeves also became very wide at the wrists (known to-day as angel sleeves, see p. 168 under Surplice), the length varying according to the offices being performed: for baptisms the sleeves were quite normal, and the same applies to the rest of the garment.

THE GIRDLE (*continued from page 14*)

The girdle in this century was now recognized as an ecclesiastical vestment. It was then ornamented in various ways and often coloured. Golden girdles are mentioned, and there is no doubt that they were embellished with embroidery and precious stones. The length of an ecclesiastical girdle is said to be about 4 yards, but it is much more likely to have been only three. Being covered by the folds of the alb it was nearly always unseen, hence one of its names—subcingulum. One end or both would be visible, unless the over vestments were of unusual length.

[1] One or two authorities are of the opinion that this point is not clearly brought out in the Toletan canon.

XI CENTURY

Ornamental borders all round the hem and at the wrists were added, in the eleventh century, to the otherwise entirely plain alb, known as 'alba pura': the ornamented kind was referred to as 'alba parata.'

The pieces of embroidery which decorated the alb and amice were known as APPARELS, while the narrow strips and rectangular pieces of embroidery which embellished all other vestments were called ORPHREYS.[1]

Fig. 7. Segmentum

Segmenta

They may be said to have descended from the segmenta, which were embroidered ornaments, rectangular or circular, woven or worked into or sewn on to the linen tunicae of smartly dressed people of imperial Rome. Fig. 7 shows a circular segmentum of the third and fourth centuries with the design worked on to the linen in purple wool. The tunica, Fig. 6, shows five varieties of segmenta, four circular and one rectangular, each of a different design; but it was usual to use the same pattern for the whole of one garment.

The more elaborate design, Fig. 8, of vine leaves and grapes, is embroidered with purple wool as clavi on a natural-coloured linen dalmatic of the fourth century, and measures 3 inches in width.

Fig. 8. Embroidery on Clavus

It is obvious that this type of pattern is the prototype of the more intricate patterns used for ornamental bands during the following centuries.

Fig. 9 is part of an oblong panel of the fourth and fifth centuries. This segmentum has a linen foundation with a border filled with a succession of overlapping heart-shaped motifs in pale coloured wools and undyed threads. The centre contains a series of black octagons set with ornamental star-forms, also in pale colours. The whole design is relieved with black.

Fig. 10 shows a segmentum of a square or lozenge shape. It has a black foundation with a border and central motif, worked in orange wool, and is of the fifth century.

Fig. 11 is a drawing made direct from an actual segmentum of the same period. Oblong in shape, it is sewn on to the linen of natural colour. The oblong is linen

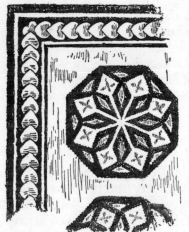

Fig. 9. Portion of Segmentum

---

[1] There seems to be no reason for this difference in name, there being no design which is peculiar to either, but the shape might vary.

dyed a dark purple, and the pattern is worked in natural coloured linen thread. As in most of these embroidered segmenta the worker is not too particular that the design should be absolutely symmetrical, nor are the lines always straight.

Apparels and orphreys are described on p. 64.

Fig. 10. Segmentum, V Century

Fig. 11. Segmentum

XII CENTURY

Before the twelfth century, or some time at the beginning of it, the alb underwent a great change in shape, following the pattern of the tunics worn by Anglo-Saxon nobles and civilians, and those of the Angevin period.[1]

If we may judge by the alb reputed to have been worn by Thomas à Becket, the ecclesiastical garment was fuller in the skirt, Fig. 12, which shows that to attain this effect the sides were pleated into small folds fixed to triangular gussets a little below hip level. These were sometimes embroidered. The arm-holes are cut large at elbow level, and the sleeves on the forearm are narrow and close fitting. At the wrists the seam is left open to allow the hands to pass through, and is fastened with a small button and loop. In diagram this alb follows almost exactly the shape of the contemporary fashionable tunic worn in Richard I's reign. A slit or opening made on one shoulder (see at A) or in front at the throat was fastened with a button and loop.

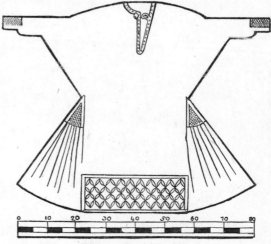

Fig. 12. Becket's Alb

This alb is made of very fine linen, with apparels of purple silk embroidered with a centrifugal design in gold at the hem front and back, and miniature apparels to match at the wrists.

[1] See diagrams, *Costume and Fashion*, vol. i, p. 259, and vol. ii, p. 96.

XIII CENTURY

According to Figs. 63, 64, and 65, the alb of the thirteenth century has returned to its original shape, and in these examples is without any decoration whatsoever.

XIV CENTURY

The alb worn by the cleric in Fig. 66 is a trifle longer than those worn by the three mentioned under the last century, and touches the ground; the sleeves are wider on the forearm, and its only decoration is the apparel back and front. The illuminated MS. from which it is taken dates about 1320.

XV CENTURY

Representations of clerics wearing an alb without the usual covering of dalmatic or chasuble are somewhat rare. Fortunately there is one at Sudborough, Northants. Fig. 115 is a drawing of the effigy on the monumental brass of the Rev. John West, a chaplain, and dates about 1415. In it we get a full view of the alb girded round the waist, which is obscured by the material of the vestment falling over it. The decoration consists of apparels on the wrists and at the hem, both front and back, see Fig. 14. The amice, stole, and maniple are worn and the chaplain's hair, although tonsured, is dressed in the style of the period.

2. THE PALLIUM

THE HIMATION

VI TO I CENTURY B.C.

DURING this period a garment, distinct in itself, came into general use among the Greeks, both men and women, and so remained until the end of the classic period. This was the HIMATION, which resembled a shawl. It was an oblong piece of material in its natural colouring, and of linen or wool, woven with a border, and in dimensions approximately 18 feet by 6. During the sixth century B.C. it was often the sole garment worn. It was draped over the left shoulder and arm, with one end hanging in front, the rest of the material being drawn across the back, round the body on the right side, and over the left shoulder again, the end hanging down the back: the man in Fig. 13 has allowed his himation to slip down over the upper (left) arm.

As time progressed it was deemed necessary by *ordinary* men to add an undergarment, either the chiton or the kolobus. Philosophers, sages, and learned men generally, who could not be considered as ordinary men, advertised the simplicity of their lives by wearing the himation without an undergarment. The statues of Sophocles (495–405 B.C.) and Demosthenes (385–322 B.C.) and others show it worn in this manner.

The arrangement of the himation was the subject of much care and consideration, as the wearer's character and culture was

Fig. 13. The Himation

judged by the way it was put on. As no pins or fastenings were used in fixing this garment, it required no little dexterity to keep the drapery steady and in its right folds, and success demanded considerable practice, and some assistance. However, it accorded with the mode of the day to throw it off or on at will, or to readjust it from time to time. To envelop the left arm, and even the hand also, was considered a mark of good breeding. To reverse this method, that is, to envelop the right arm, was distinctly bad form.

Fig. 14. Apparel

A.D. I CENTURY

The himation remained the characteristic dress throughout the civilized world of Greeks and peoples affected by Greek culture, and at the beginning of the Christian era it had become universal among intellectual people. As a garment associated with philosophers the himation, or as it was now called by the Romans, the PALLIUM, came to be regarded as the special monopoly of all learned men, including the orator. There was no deviation from the original method of draping it.

Clothes worn by our Lord

It is supposed that Christ and His apostles wore the himation over the colobium, because they were teachers. Plate I (frontispiece) is an attempt by the author to represent our Lord wearing the colobium woven in one piece (see p. 12), and therefore 'without seam.' The himation or pallium draped over it is the Greco-Roman equivalent of the professor's or teacher's university gown. The face is taken from the earliest known portrait-head of Christ.

The pallium thus became later invested with much sanctity, and was recognized amongst Christians as a garment of great honour and dignity.

Some readers may wonder how our Lord during His ministry came to possess raiment of such good quality. St. Luke's note (viii. 2, 3) on the devoted band of women who ministered to the needs of Jesus and His followers shows that there were then, as there have been ever since, enthusiastic people who as a labour of love use their means and skill over beautiful garments and accessories for the glory of God.

There is no reason to suppose that our Lord wore other than the ordinary garments of the Jewish teachers of Galilee:[1] two of which exactly correspond with those shown and described in Plate I. These consist, first, of the CHALUK, a tunic reaching to the calf or feet and girded at the waist, a facsimile of the kolobus of the Greeks. Over this came the TALLITH, an oblong, sometimes square, piece of white linen, the counterpart of the Greek himation. This garment had a border of light blue (hyacinth colour), and tassels at the four corners made of long white threads of the warp and woof knotted with threads of the same shade of blue. These tassels were often exaggerated, and therefore very conspicuous: such ostentatious tassels would, of course, be omitted from the pallium of our Lord.

The Jews wore as a head-covering a rectangular piece of white linen fastened round the head in the same manner as shown in Fig. 109. This was but a napkin known as the SUDAR, also a Jewish characteristic: it was familiar to the Romans as the sudarium. The MAAPHORETH was much the same in shape, but worn twisted like a turban round the head.

A.D. II CENTURY

As early as the second century A.D. the pallium, no longer called the himation, was a garment worn by church officers or teachers by reason only of its being the distinctive

[1] The student will find in Tissot's *Life of Our Saviour Jesus Christ* a wealth of illustration of Jewish costume.

dress of learned men.   In shape it was still three times as long as its width, that is 18
by 6 feet; in the manner of draping, as well as in dimensions, it remained in use during
this century and the next.

A.D. III CENTURY

The philosopher or scholar, Fig. 15, is wearing the tunica talaris with long close sleeves.
Over it is the pallium, with its coloured border—it might be plain white.   It was during
this century that the pallium began to be associated with ecclesiastical dignity, because
the teachers wore the pallium when engaged in their religious occupations.

Fig. 15. Philosopher   Fig. 16. Folded Pallium

IV CENTURY

Not until the middle of the fourth century did the pallium cease to be used for ordinary
dress, remaining only as an official garment of certain high officers of the empire.

For the sake of convenience it was then worn folded lengthways, 'contabulatum,'
two or three times, and most likely more, reducing its width to about 12 or 9 inches: it
was carried on the person according to its original arrangement, Fig. 16.   The result
was that it presented a great similarity to the turnover of the toga-umbo (see *Costume and
Fashion*, vol. i, Fig. 42, p. 94), such as is seen worn by the courtiers on the Arch of
Constantine (315) at Rome, and on the ivory diptych of the Consul Felix (428) and of
several other consuls; consequently it came to be regarded secularly as a very honourable
attribute.

The earliest method of wearing the pallium is described on page 21, and this fashion
still continued; but, when it was worn over the paenula (see p. 55), it was first placed
as usual over the left shoulder, one end hanging down in front.   It returned, however,

*B

to the front, having crossed the back of the neck, over the right shoulder instead of under the right arm for obvious reasons, then across the breast to the left shoulder again, and down the back as previously, Fig. 17.

Fig. 17. Pallium over Paenula

Some time during the fourth century the pallium ceased to be the usual width when folded. This means that the superfluous material of the folds underneath the top one were removed, the top panel only remaining, forming a long scarf of white woollen material about 8 inches wide or even less, by 12 or perhaps 14 feet in length, the method contabulatum being retained; and it became more and more a distinct mark of honour and dignity during this and the following centuries. Thus it ceased to be a garment and became merely an ornament. It was worn more or less in the same manner as described under Fig. 15, but its width was soon reduced to 4 inches. In order to maintain the pallium in its right position in the centre front and back, it was secured by three pins, one at the back, one in front, and one where it crossed the left shoulder, as in Fig. 18.

Probably the earliest occasion on which this latest type of pallium was used for an ecclesiastical purpose was when Marcus, Bishop of Rome (336–7), bestowed it upon a bishop: therefore henceforward the pallium became a vestment, or, as it is more properly called, an ornament, of ministers.

As mentioned earlier, St. Anastasius, Bishop of Rome (398–401) was the first to take the title of archbishop. He wore a pallium like other bishops, but unlike them it was His Holiness's exclusive prerogative to wear it on *all* occasions.

The pallium was a symbol of jurisdiction, and also an ornament of great honour, which indicated the highest dignity in the wearer, and the custom arose for the Supreme Pontiff to confer it upon archbishops and a few bishops as a token that the recipient participated in the plenitude of the papal authority. Some few bishops received it purely as an honour, devoid of all ecclesiastical power.

In due course the western Church conceived the idea of arranging the pallium, Fig. 18, in a more convenient way. Instead of using pins to bring the front panel to the centre of the

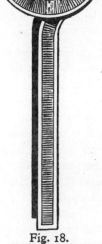

Fig. 18.
Pallium pinned

figure, this scarf or band was made up as a circle which surrounded the shoulders, with the long pendent ends attached front and back as shown in Fig. 19. This was a much more practical method than the one previously in use, and by this time all trace of its original form had disappeared. Also it should be noticed that the width of the band had been further reduced to three inches.

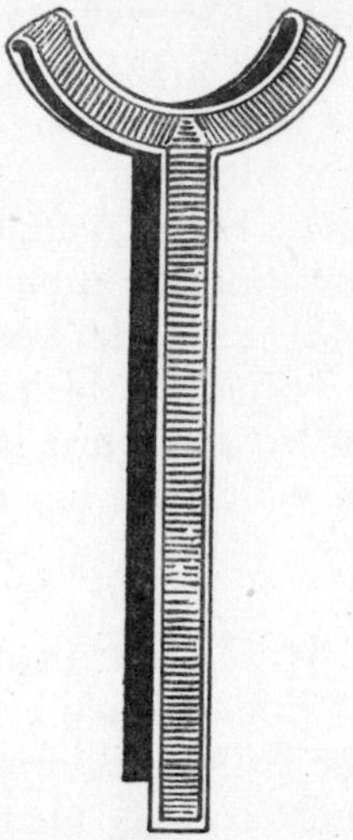

St. Isidore of Pelusium (*ob.* 449, a monk from his youth) wrote remarkable letters on the subject of doctrine. With regard to this latest arrangement of the pallium he explains that in its lines across the shoulders it symbolizes the authority of archbishops and bishops, in imitation of the Good Shepherd carrying the lost sheep in this manner (see Fig. 20). He also states that the bishop removes this 'vestment of imitation' when the gospel is read, because our Lord there speaks in person. Sentiments of this kind greatly impressed the people at this time, and developed more strongly during the following centuries.

The pallium still remained, however, an article of Roman official dress.[1]

Fig. 19.
Circular Pallium

The wool from which the pallium was made received very careful treatment and much ceremonial. It was furnished by the lambs reared in the Convent of St. Agnes, Rome, and two were specially chosen each year on her feast day (21st January) for their quality and whiteness. When they were ready for shearing the lambs were placed in panniers on a pack-horse and taken to the palace [2] of the pontiff who, from a window, made the sign of the Cross over these immaculate animals, which were then conducted to the Church of St. Agnes-without-the-Walls. Having been adorned with flowers and streamers the lambs were brought on Low Sunday to the Basilica of St. Peter (doubtless of the Vatican), and were led round the high altar while the 'Agnus Dei' was sung. During mass the celebrant blessed them, and handed them over to the canons of St. John Lateran. They were then taken back to the Holy Father, who passed them on to the dean and his sub-deacons, who delivered them up to the Convent of St. Agnes, where they were kept and fed. The wool was woven into cloth by the nuns.

When the pallium was about to be conferred many formalities were necessary.

On the eve of St. Peter and St. Paul (29th–30th June)

Fig. 20. The Good Shepherd

[1] See *Costume and Fashion*, vol. i, p. 162.
[2] The Lateran palace, the residence of the bishops of Rome, was originally the palace of the Laterani family. Adjoining this was the church of St. John Lateran, which the Emperor Constantine (306–37) had fitted up as a church, and presented to the Holy See, about 314. Although the palace was destroyed and rebuilt from time to time, the popes continued to occupy it until they migrated to Avignon in 1309.

the particular pallium was taken to the Basilica of St. Peter, and laid upon the tomb of that apostle to rest above his body for the night: from whom it was supposed to have contracted a share of apostolic authority. The next day it was deposited upon the high altar and, during a special blessing after vespers, was placed upon the shoulders of His Holiness. At the finish of these ceremonies this sacred pallium was enclosed in a silver box and conducted to a place of safety in the confessio (where the relics were kept), awaiting the time for its delivery by the papal embassy to the recipient.

If 'the Chief Pontiff, that is, the Bishop of Bishops,'[1] gave the pallium, he also took it back. 'Should a bishop or an archbishop prove unworthy of such an honour he was compelled to return it.' Mention is made in medieval writings of many such cases, some of which are not without a great deal of humour.

V CENTURY

H. O. Wakeman in his *History of the Church of England* says: 'Ever since the Church of England had existed it has been an invariable custom for its Metropolitans to receive the Pall [2] [pallium] from the pope.' The want of a pall had been considered one of the most serious blemishes in the canonical character of Stigand. It was true that the grant of the pall was in itself only a mark of honour, was unknown in the first four centuries of the history of the English Church, and had in reality no doctrinal or constitutional significance whatever.

Unfortunately we find in writings, both ancient and modern, the word pallium, like many other names of vestments, used as a general term for numerous other garments, for instance the toga,[3] paludamentum,[3] lacerna,[3] praetexta, paenula, and lorum.[3] This state of affairs is very misleading to the student.

It was at the beginning of the fifth century that the pallium branched off into two distinct garments: one, the secular or civil, known as the lorum; the other, the sacred or ecclesiastical, the pallium. It is the latter which became the distinguishing mark of the pope and archbishops.

VI CENTURY

By this time it was sometimes the privilege of the emperor to sanction the pope's decision before granting the honour of the pallium, especially if the recipient was not one of his own subjects.

Perhaps the earliest record of its being given to an archbishop was the case of Theodore, Archbishop and Metropolitan of Laureacus in Pannonia, who was granted it by Pope Symmachus (498–514), but without the imperial authority.

Pope Vigilius in 543 deferred granting this honourable ornament to Auxanus, Archbishop of Arles, until such time as it pleased the emperor to confirm it. It was not until two years afterwards that the imperial sanction was granted, and the honour conferred.

It appears that on some occasions Pope Gregory the Great (590–604) went so far as to *demand* the consent of the Greek emperor to the sending of this badge of honour to certain bishops who were not his subjects. This pontiff granted the pallium to several metropolitans in the West, the equivalent of archbishops. These included St. Augustine, the first Archbishop of Canterbury, on the occasion of his consecration in 600 at Arles,

---

[1] Quotation from Tertullian (*nat. c.* 150 or 160).
[2] In the West, especially in England, the pallium is sometimes referred to as the pall.
[3] For a description of these garments see *Costume and Fashion*, vol. i.

whose archbishop was at that time the metropolitan of the English nation. This was done, no doubt, to mark the striking success of his mission to England in 597.

Before an archbishop was enthroned and consecrated it was essential that he should have previously received the pallium. It was the mark of rank; and it was the rule that it should be worn particularly when officiating at mass up to the reading of the gospel; only the pope kept it on all the service. However, it is recorded that the Bishop of Ravenna at this time (sixth or seventh century) 'fell into the sin of pride,' and insisted on wearing his pallium the whole time, as well as when giving audience to the laity. The dispute on this matter with Pope Gregory the Great (590–604) continued after his death.

The pallium worn in the Eastern Church, known as the OMOPHORION, which corresponds to the Roman pallium, was about 9 feet long and 6 inches or more wide.[1] From the way in which it is seen hanging in illustrations it is obvious that pins are used. One end, which descends to a little below hip level, is placed on the left shoulder,

Fig. 21. Eastern Pallium

passes round the back of the neck, over the right shoulder to the middle of the breast where it is turned over; it is then taken over the left shoulder again and under the first end, with the other end hanging down the back on the left side the same distance as in front. This turnover necessitates the scarf being finished off completely on both surfaces, or perhaps only half way on each side.

Fig. 21 illustrates this arrangement, and is a drawing from a sixth-century mosaic in

Fig. 22. Cross on Pallium

Fig. 23. Byzantine Rose Motif

the Basilica of St. Apollinaris at Ravenna. It represents the first bishop of that place, St. Apollinaris, who suffered martyrdom in A.D. 79.

The single cross of unusual shape, appearing in Fig. 21, and enlarged in Fig. 22, is the 'Crux Decussata,' and is the white ground of the pallium,[2] flanked by black

[1] It varied in length and width at different times and in different places. A modern Russian omophorion measures 13 feet 5 inches long, and 10 inches wide.

[2] A square outline is faintly perceptible in the original mosaic, which suggests that the black is worked on to a separate piece of white cloth and sewn on to the pallium, in the same manner as badges, etc., are sewn on to modern uniforms. Whether or not a cross is embroidered on the other end is difficult to tell, as back views of archbishops are not easy to find. The odds are—both ends.

embroidery; the design is influenced by the Byzantine rose, Fig. 23. The heart-shaped petals of this type of rose were of any colour, but usually red and white, and the barbs green.

Even as late as the sixth century we meet the old-fashioned pallium, worn in the old-

Fig. 24.
A Prophet, VI Century

fashioned way. The mosaics in the Basilica of St. Apollinare Nuovo, Ravenna, show panels of prophets each wearing a tunica with close sleeves, a dalmatica with clavi, and the original shaped pallium draped over them, Fig. 24, in the same manner as Fig. 13. This, no doubt, is artistic licence, intended to distinguish them from other churchmen.

It was about this time that a conventional method was adopted by artists when depicting the early saints, who are represented in the costume of a still earlier period, irrespective of their own.

These representations show some knowledge of the original shape and manner of draping the pallium as worn in bygone centuries. This method is often met with.

Notice that the prophet is holding a book of the gospels or a book of the law in his left hand, covered with a part of the pallium in the orthodox fashion. Sometimes it is steadied by the bare right hand.

Another example is in the same basilica, where there is a long sixth-century mosaic, showing the original pallium worn by all the martyrs in procession offering their crowns to Christ, who is seated on a Byzantine throne, between four angels. The latter are all robed in white albs and pallia, and have brown wings and nimbi of blue. Fig. 25 is a drawing of one of them. A 3-inch fringe finishes the two ends, a mode of decoration now coming into use. This is also to be seen in the mosaic of Bishop Maximian, Plate IV.

Minor Orders

Towards the end of the second century the minor orders of clerics were introduced into the Western Church (see p. 3), and here is the opportunity of describing their vesture and office.

An illustration in the Autun Sacramentary of uncertain date, though probably of the tenth century or somewhat earlier, shows a subdeacon and four members of the minor orders of the clergy, each holding the symbol of his grade, presented to him on his ordination. The drawings, Figs. 26–30, reproduce them.

With regard to their vestments, all four appear to be robed in the alb, each with different-shaped sleeves, and over it the old-fashioned pallium, draped in various ways, the whole effect being similar to that in Fig. 24 and in Fig. 38.

The subdeacon, Fig. 26, vested in a tunicle over an alb, stands elevated in the centre, holding a chalice in his right hand and an earthenware pitcher in the other.

Coming now to the lowest grade, Fig. 27 is the ostiarius or doorkeeper, carrying the symbol of his office—two keys looped together with a cord and ring. Among other duties he stood during service at the door of that part of the church occupied by the men. The office dates back to the fourth century.

Fig. 25. Byzantine Angel, VI Century

Fig. 26. Subdeacon

Fig. 27. Porter

Fig. 28. Exorcist

Fig. 29. Lector

Fig. 30. Acolyte

Subdeacon and Minor Orders of Clerics, *c.* X Century

The next above him in rank is the exorcist, Fig. 28, who holds with veiled hands the 'Book of Exorcisms,' usually a 'Pontificale' or 'Rituale.' His business was to cast out evil spirits, but his office has been obsolete for some time.

On the left of the subdeacon is the lector, Fig. 29, with his open lectionary, whose chief duties were to intone the lessons and to sing the epistle.

The acolyte, Fig. 30, ranking the highest, holds his candlestick and lighted candle: he was usually a youth or young man, the office dating from the second century. His chief duties were: to light all candles and act as taper-bearer to light the officiating cleric; to take charge of the earthenware pitcher used to hold the communion wine; and to be in general attendance at the altar. At his ordination the acolyte received a candlestick and a pitcher from the bishop.

The functioning of some of these clerics is now obsolete, and those that remained were vested in more elaborate garments. An illuminated MS., *The Pontifical of the Three Bishops*, of the late fourteenth century, in Corpus Christi College, Cambridge, shows an ordination of a doorkeeper in which the bishop is presenting him with two gilded keys: the reader in search of further details should consult this MS.

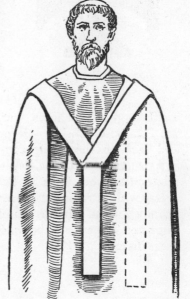

Fig. 32. Pallium, IX century

The observant student will notice in some works of art representations of saints and clerics having a large letter or monogram embroidered or woven on the left-hand portion of an outer garment about knee level. These letters, Fig. 31, are usually of the Greek alphabet, and it is stated by early Christian archaeologists that the T and X represent the 'Cross Tau' and 'Crux Decussata,' or saltire. IH stood for Jesus, and T for an apostle. An example of the latter letter is shown in Fig. 50, but there it is partly hidden by the drapery of the pallium. To-day no satisfactory explanation of it has been arrived at by authorities.

T IH Γ X Υ

Fig. 31. Monograms

VII CENTURY

During the seventh century the pallium, as a garment for general use among the laity, gradually became obsolete.

Fig. 32 is a drawing from an ivory, said to be of the ninth century, but much more likely to be of the seventh. It shows the western pallium adapted from the eastern, Fig. 21, and was either contemporary with it or came into use at some time later. It was put on as described under Fig. 21, except that the front end—which hitherto hung on the left as shown by the broken line—is dragged to the middle of the figure, and with the underfold pinned underneath the top band, thereby concealing it.

According to some illustrations there does not seem to be any hard and fast rule as to the *length* of the pallium. One example (there may be others) is met with in the seventh-century mosaic, in the baptistery of St. John Lateran, representing St. Maurus, the fourth-century Bishop of Verdun, who is robed as in Plate IV, except that the loop of the pallium comes well below hip level, and that the end reaches to half way below the knee.   There is only one cross on the front, and it may be presumed that there is one behind; and that is like Fig. 33.

The number of crosses embroidered on the pallium as used in the Western Church varied, in fact there does not seem to be any specific rule about them.   Sometimes there was only a single one front and back, but often five were used to symbolize the five wounds of our Saviour.   Later and in the Middle Ages one finds only four, and even as many as eight.   In shape they were usually the Greek cross, as seen in Fig. 34, or they had their ends splayed as in Fig. 35.

On the pallium worn by Pope Innocent III, Fig. 140, the crosses are less splayed, but the uprights are longer than the transoms.   Fig 37 shows the finished-off terminals: this style was very generally adopted throughout the ages.

Honorius of Autun, writing at a much later date, described the special insignia of an

Fig. 33.
Cross on Pallium

Fig. 34.
Greek Cross on Pallium

Fig. 35.
Cross on Pallium

archbishop as a pallium, with purple crosses on it in order to manifest to the people the Passion of Christ.   He points out that the two hanging ends of the pallium, front and back, are the purple signs of the holy cross.

As an example of the grip which the Greek emperors had over pontifical affairs, it is related that when Pope St. Benedict II was elected in 684 his enthronement was delayed a year while awaiting the Greek emperor's confirmation, which up to that time had been usually sought.   It was mainly on account of this delay, and of the death of both the pope and emperor in the following year, that the imperial sanction was dispensed with thereafter.[1]

VIII CENTURY

The acceptance of the pallium came to imply, by the eighth century, the acknowledgment by the recipient of the supremacy of the apostolic see.   Therefore it was specially stipulated that the pallium should under no circumstances be lent.

In a letter from St. Boniface (*nat. c.* 680, *ob.* 755), 'the apostle of Germany,' Papal Legate (738), and Archbishop of Mainz in 745, St. Cuthbert, Archbishop of Canterbury (740–60), is requested to declare his willingness to obey the see of Rome.   It seems

[1] Further incidents connected with the relations of pope and emperor, concerning the papal prerogative, will be found on pp. 100 et seq.

that St. Boniface had already applied to Pope Zacharias (741–52) for 'pallia' for several metropolitans under him.

IX CENTURY

About this time, the early part of the ninth century, a slight innovation was made in the Roman pallium. Its shape was now a double Y, as shown in Fig. 36, which very strongly emphasizes the symbolical allusion to the Good Shepherd.

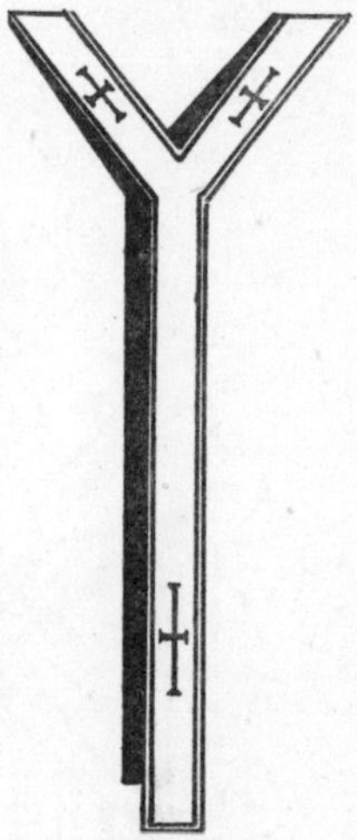

Made of the conventional white woollen cloth, it is seen in some illustrations with a narrow edging of gold, and in this example it is embroidered with six black crosses with uprights longer than the transoms and the terminals splayed as in Fig. 35 (see p. 32).

To keep the Y over the shoulders in its correct position it was sometimes, especially at a later date, customary to use an ornament of gold, perhaps jewelled, with a pin behind it, as in Fig. 37, to secure it to the chasuble.

This episcopal pallium, Fig. 36, is worn by archbishops of the Catholic Church during the following centuries and down to our own day.

The circular form, Fig. 19, however, seems to have remained in favour in the Roman Church, and to have existed simultaneously with the former. Paintings and sculpture of the ensuing centuries to the fifteenth show indifferently the one or the other. For example, St. Clement at the altar, Fig. 96, is in eleventh-century vestments and wears the Y

Fig. 36.
Pallium, IX Century

pallium, whereas the circular pallium, Fig. 19, is worn by Paschal II, the first of the twelfth-century popes (see Plate V).

Even in the ninth century an emperor of the West had to obtain the consent of the Eastern emperor before the pallium could be bestowed.

X CENTURY

In its rectangular shape and unfolded form, but of smaller dimensions, the early secular pallium (not the lorum or imperial pallium) was revived about the end of the tenth century by nobles of the Byzantine imperial court as a fashionable drapery or mantle. It was not, however, worn in the old-fashioned manner, but as shown in Fig. 38. One of the ends was fixed under the left armhole by a corner, or was taken round the arm and pinned to itself in front, so that the other corner hung over the left leg: the material then passed in front over the right hip, enveloped the lower part of the loins, came back under the left armpit, and was thrown over the right shoulder, sometimes covering the upper arm, the remainder hanging down the back. The left arm was

Fig. 37. Pallium with One Pin

thus free, while the right might project under the folds as shown in Fig. 38. The whole of this arrangement could be reversed.

This type of modified pallium, which might measure 12 feet by 5 feet, continued in vogue for less than one hundred years.

The drawing is made from a bas-relief on the principal porch of Vézelay Abbey, Yonne Department, France, and dates from the last years of the eleventh century.

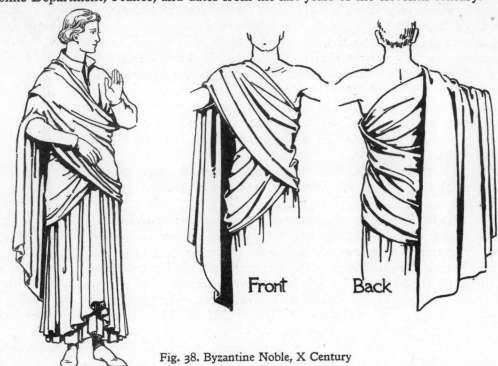

Fig. 38. Byzantine Noble, X Century

XI CENTURY

Early in the eleventh century English and French nobles adopted from the East the fashionable secular pallium. This noble, Fig. 39, comes from an illuminated MS. of the time of William Rufus. He has probably served in the First Crusade, and has brought back with him a pallium which he wears in the latest modish manner.

The prevailing custom, which lasted for many centuries, of dressing saints and scriptural personages in more or less old-fashioned attire, now revived by the nobility, and seen in works of art, is well represented in Fig. 39. This style corresponds exactly with that worn by the saintly trio in the three remaining choir clerestory windows [1] in Canterbury Cathedral.

The pallium is draped by fastening one corner to the girdle of the undergarment in the middle of the back. The length of the material then passes in front of the body over the right hip to the left shoulder and across the back, the other end resting on the right shoulder—a simpler arrangement than in Fig. 38.

In an Anglo-Saxon eleventh-century illuminated MS., the three angels visiting

[1] These windows were not put up until the twelfth century; in design they were influenced by the style of costume worn in William II's reign. They were removed in 1792 to the south transept.

Fig. 39. Norman Noble, XI Century

Abraham are garbed in almost the same robes as shown in Fig. 25, but treated in a typically Anglo-Saxon manner, especially as regards the drapery.

XII CENTURY

Three representations of the sacred pallium are described, belonging to this and the following centuries.　The first, Fig. 140, dates at the end of this century.　It is from the fresco at Subiaco of Pope Innocent III, which shows that the artist who painted it favours the Greek manner of wearing the pallium.　It has a narrow border, and is decorated on both sides of the fabric to allow for its turn-over, with six black crosses like Fig. 35.

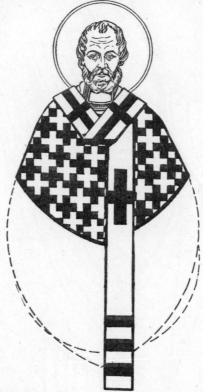

Fig. 40. St. Nicholas, XIV Century

XIII CENTURY

In the north porch of Chartres Cathedral there is a thirteenth-century statue of a pope in full Roman vestments.　He wears the circular pallium, which descends rather low on the shoulders, and is quite plain except that it has six Greek crosses embroidered upon it of the same type as Fig. 34.

XIV CENTURY

The Omophorion

The Greek pallium or omophorion, Fig. 40, is taken from a Russian ikon, dating between the twelfth and fourteenth centuries, in the Monastery of the Holy Ghost,

Novgorod, and painted by an artist on traditional lines in the style of the earlier national Byzantine school. It represents St. Nicholas (*ob.* 326), Bishop of Myra, the patron saint of children and better known as 'Santa Klaus.' He is dressed in the orthodox vestments of the Greek Church, but the head and shoulders only are shown. His omophorion is worn more or less as in Fig. 21: the width is 6 inches or more, and it is 12 feet long. The six red crosses are large and cover the width of the band, and three red bars finish off the ends which descend to just below the knee. The top portion of the Greek chasuble is the only part shown on this ikon. The manner in which it is worn is shown in Fig. 96, and its shape in diagram Fig. 97. It is made of silk or woollen material, and the pattern of black and white Greek crosses is probably woven, not embroidered.

Fig. 41 comes from another ikon representing the same saint, in the Museum of Russian Art at Novgorod, and painted about the same time and of the same school. This four-pointed white star is embroidered on the red cross, such as is shown on Fig. 40, at the place where the upright and transoms meet.

Fig. 41, Cross on Pallium

3. FOOTGEAR

VI–I CENTURY B.C.

In the pre-Christian era the sandal of leather was in general use; Fig. 42 shows one form. Boots were worn by certain important people.

During the period of republican Rome the CALCEUS or boot was the recognized footgear of the official class. It was the distinguishing mark of senators and higher magistrates,

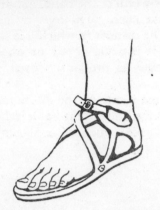

Fig. 42. Sandal, V Century B.C.

Fig. 43. Calceus

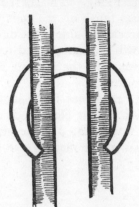

Fig. 44. Lunula

In the early days of Christianity, when the sandal (Fig. 42) was in general use, homage to the Bishop of Rome was paid by kissing the foot of His Holiness. Later, when shoes were worn, it became the custom to kiss the front part of the footgear.

and was called 'calceus patricius.' [1] This boot had a sole following the shape of the foot, with an upper part of red leather sewn to the sole, and covering the foot in the same manner as a nineteenth-century elastic-side boot without the elastic. A pair of straps was fastened to the back part of the uppers. These straps were wound round the ankle two or three times, to a distance of about half-way below the calf, and tied in front with a

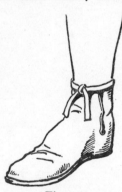

Fig. 45.
Calceus worn by Senators

knot and ends. A second pair of straps was attached on each side of the sole, at the widest part of the foot, and crossed over the instep, fastened round the ankle on top of the first pair of straps, and tied in a knot in front below the first one, Fig. 43. Hooks fixed on the top of the uppers may have been brought into use to keep the second tie of straps in their position. It was usual to have the long ends of the second pair trailing quite one inch on the ground on each side.

On the outer side of the ankle there was often an ivory crescent or lunula, which was popularly supposed to refer to the original hundred senators chosen by Romulus, the crescent being suggested by the Roman numeral C = 100. It may have been kept in place on the ankle by two straps, each passing over and under it, as indicated in Fig. 44: though, of course, the actual boot straps might serve, see Fig. 43.

Boots, 'calcei senatorii,' were those worn by ordinary senators, and were shaped

[1] The Emperor Caius Germanicus (37–41) is known as Caligula, a nickname given to him as a small boy by the soldiers because he was wearing *little boots* ('calceus patricius') at the time his father presented him, dressed in miniature Roman armour, to the army.

as in Fig. 45: they were made of red leather, with only one pair of straps fixed to the back and tied round the ankle. The straps may sometimes have been of black.

Patricians in general wore the same kind, but of tanned leather and with black straps. Ordinary well-to-do people had boots of similar make with tongues; these finished lower at the ankle, where they were fastened over the instep with a buckle. When worn by a centurion the calceus had a sole of more substance, shod with iron hobnails. Footgear treated in this manner were known as 'clavi caligarii.'

Another kind of footgear, called UDO, was a low shoe, in shape rather like a modern one, but frequently made to reach higher up the ankle, thus assuming the shape of a sock. They were of felt or goatskin, worn for comfort, and were much used by the peasantry, Fig. 73. A stout boot, used generally by shepherds and labourers, and known as PERO,[1] was of untanned leather, and had a similar appearance to the udo except that it was heavier.

A.D. I CENTURY

Under the empire footgear was practically the same as already described.

The Romans, like their prototypes the Greeks, were very particular about their footgear, and bestowed much care upon this important detail of self-respect.

Though the lower classes generally wore sandals, the udo or the pero, they often went barefooted.

In St. Mark vi. 9 we read that Christ commanded that His disciples 'should be shod with sandals.' In a 1608 Bible there is an explanatory note stating 'which were a kind of light shoes tied to the feet with strings.'

Fig. 46. Military Boot, III to V Century

Fig. 47. Shoe, VI Century

III TO V CENTURY

Under the later empire in the West and the Byzantine Empire footgear became more elaborate in design and decoration, especially when worn by the nobility and wealthy.

A boot, CAMPAGUS, worn by military officials, Fig. 46, is of scarlet leather, the front

[1] 'Pero' must not be confounded with 'pera,' a wallet.

cut in straps edged with gold. These are buckled on the outside of the ankle, the foot being slipped into loops, and are worn over short PEDULES or socks of fine white linen, although sometimes the feet were un-socked. The wearer was then described as 'discalced.'

VI CENTURY

The sixth century marks the general use of the shoe in preference to the sandal. An attractive and well-shaped shoe is shown in Fig. 47. It is made of soft red leather,

Fig. 48   Fig. 49   Fig. 50

General Types of Shoe, VI Century

sewn to a substantial sole, and ornamented on the toe part with gold and pearls; golden jewelled clasps fasten it at the ankle.

Another similar shoe, Fig. 48, fastens on the outside by two straps and buckles in gold. Red leather is used for the heel and toe parts, with a band of gold over the toe joints, and a pointed piece over the toe. This latter decoration of the toe part is seen in Plate IV; it may be the origin of the cross-motif often seen on the footgear of clerics.

Fig. 49 is quite plain, of black or brown leather: the toe part is shaped like a heart, and is tied round the ankles with latchets. Fig. 50 is of simple make, and one much in general use.

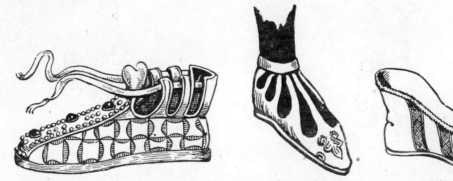

Fig. 51. Campagus, IX Century   Fig. 52. Shoe, XI Century   Fig. 53. Shoe, XII Century

IX CENTURY

The campagus, Fig. 51, is a shoe of the time of the Emperor Charlemagne, and is similar to those worn by him at his coronation in 800. It is of scarlet leather embroidered in gold: the gold band developing into a tongue over the instep is ornamented with three large cabochon emeralds and many pearls. The back part of the shoe is cut into straps, forming loops, through which the strings for tying in front are passed.

XI CENTURY

A shoe worn by the Emperor Henry II (1002–24), Fig. 52, shows much the same treatment of the uppers and back as Fig. 51; this was still in vogue except that the gold or coloured leather is cut into radiating straps, which meet and are fixed to the buckled ankle strap. These shoes are worn in this example over dark-coloured hosae.

XII CENTURY

Footgear does not appear to have been in liturgical use before the twelfth century when, it must be noted, all forms of footgear as a vestment are technically known as SANDALS.

A further development of the fashionable shoe, which was used by the wealthy laity and clergy alike, is given in Fig. 53. The band over the instep, often embroidered,

Fig. 54. Embroidered Shoe

and sometimes set with jewels, still prevails. Two bands of gold are sewn obliquely at the sides for the purpose of masking the seams. At the back the upper rises in a curve, and the edge is bound with some soft material or very short-haired fur.

XIII CENTURY

Shoes worn with state and full dress, ecclesiastical, royal, and laical, were very rich, made of coloured leather, cloth, or silk, and ornamented with bands of gold covering the seams. The foundation was often embroidered, chiefly in lozenges, squares, and circles, as shown in Fig. 54. Inset is a sole plan.

Fig. 55 is a shoe worn by important personages of the Church and State. It is

Fig. 55. Embroidered Shoe, XIII Century

Fig. 56. Banded Shoe, XIV Century

made of velvet, silk, cloth, or leather, and embroidered with gold. There is a cord or rib attached to the front which might cover a seam, and also give it extra strength. The join of the front with the back is concealed by a vertical band of decoration so that the foot may pass, or the shoe would be slit. The shoe fitted close to the ankle, and was secured by a button or buckle attached to the ankle strap.

XIV CENTURY

The dress-shoe of the fourteenth century was of normal shape, and but slightly pointed in the toe, contrary to the absurd contemporary fashion, when worn by the clergy. The ornamentation was altogether simpler than in the preceding centuries. Footgear were made of rich material and the bands, at first used for utility but now more for convention, were generally of gold passement.[1] Altogether there are eight bands covering the front, back, and side seams. Fig. 56 is one such shoe, fastened round the ankle with a button and loop.

XV CENTURY

The clergy in the fifteenth century did not indulge in the ridiculously long pointed fashionable shoe. Ecclesiastical footgear was pointed, but considerably modified, as will be seen in these drawings of this period.

The BUSKINS in Fig. 204 (from Matthew Paris) are part of the bishop's full dress: they are silk pedules or stockings, reaching to the knee, and cross-barred with gold thread, enclosing tiny ornaments of gold. The colour would match the vestments. Pedules were very common amongst laymen as well as clerics, and Ivo of Chartres (*ob.* 1115) is the first to call them buskins.

Pedules, or buskins, sometimes had leather soles: when they had not, shoes were worn over them as over modern socks. These might be made of some material; but the soles, at any rate, would be of leather.

[1] Passement is the name given to an ornamental braid in gold, silver, or coloured silk.

4. THE DALMATIC

(DALMATICA)

A.D. III CENTURY

A NEW-SHAPED garment, known as the DALMATICA, came into use during the third century, but its first appearance dates back to the year A.D. 190, when it became the custom among decadent young patricians of imperial Rome to introduce into the world of frivolity and fashion garments of foreign origin, in spite of the outrage against national sentiments. A storm of abuse was poured upon the eccentric Emperor Commodus (180–93) for his audacity in appearing publicly in a costume copied from the dress in general use in Dalmatia.

Long sleeves were peculiar to this garment, and hitherto much disliked by the Romans in general; so they attracted much attention and no little scorn. In the year 218 even greater dissatisfaction was expressed when the Emperor Heliogabalus (218–22) made his triumphal entry into Rome garbed in a loose-flowing robe with wide long sleeves of foreign make. This garment was merely the usual type of robe worn by orientals for generations, as also in the province whence it derives its name — the Dalmatica. This local item of costume was made of a material woven from the fine white wool of that province, already famous for its sheep farming.

Fig. 57. Roman Dalmatica, III Century

After this display by the emperor the dalmatica was adopted by the upper classes of imperial Rome, and in a simple form by the populace in general; Fig. 57 shows an ordinary Roman citizen wearing it.

Many writers of this and the following centuries give graphic details of the dalmatica, from which we learn that it was a *closed* garment, and had to be put on over the head, and that the wide sleeves [1] were its distinctive feature. When laid out flat, and before the side seams were joined up, the material—wool, silk, linen, or cotton—formed a Greek cross: 'in modum crucis facta' are the words used by Rabanus Maurus in his work *De Institutione Clericorum* (c. 850). A horizontal slit was cut or left unwoven in the centre for the head to pass through, and when folded in half and sewn together at the sides sleeves of moderate length and width were formed. Fig. 58 gives a diagram of a dalmatica of the following century, drawn and measured from one in the Victoria

[1] It is sometimes stated that the original dalmatica had no sleeves at all, or only short ones, and so was equivalent to the colobium. The author disagrees with this, since so many references stress the fact that when introduced into Rome it already had very large sleeves, as seen in Figs. 57, 58.

and Albert Museum. It is woven in one piece of natural-coloured linen, and has a blue-purple pattern worked in wool upon the clavi and sleeves, such as are shown in Fig. 81.

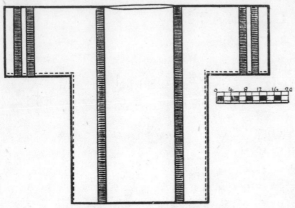

Fig. 58. Dalmatica, IV Century

The dalmatica was in natural colourings, and was always worn without a belt; it was often the only garment, but if necessary the tunica or colobium could be worn under it, usually showing beneath. The angusti clavi, which decorated the tunica and colobium, were now transferred to the dalmatica, and became its characteristic ornamentation. As previously, these two stripes of red, russet, or purple went up the front and down the back, with two rows on each sleeve set a little way from the hem. The dalmatica was worn by ordinary men and also by women, with or without the clavi; the skirt of the tunica talaris, and of the women's stola, covered the legs to the ankle or touched the ground.

St. Cyprian, a great authority on the Roman and other episcopal churches, was born at Carthage about A.D. 200, and became its bishop in 248. During the persecution which began under the Emperor Valerian (253–60) in 257, and because of the edict that all bishops, priests, and deacons should be put to death, he was executed at Carthage in the presence of an immense crowd, 258. It is recorded that when led out to martyrdom he divested himself first of his byrrus (cloak, see p. 157), and then of his dalmatica, both of which he handed to his deacons; and went to his death clad only in a linen undergarment.

According to the *Liber Pontificalis*, St. Eutychianus, a native of Tuscany, who succeeded to the papacy in 275, and was martyred in 283, had great veneration for the remains of the martyrs of both sexes, and is said to have interred several hundreds of them with his own hands. For their burial he ordered their bodies to be covered

Fig. 59. Dalmatica, III Century

with the colobium and dalmatica, adorned with purple clavi.

The dalmatica shown in Fig. 59 is of the third and following centuries, and presents the same appearance as that in Fig. 57, but the sleeves are not quite so large. Both Figs. 59 and 74 have their arms outstretched, which designates the attitude of prayer in the manner which was common to both Jews and Gentiles. In the previous century St. Justin the philosopher and martyr (*ob.* 167) explains in his inimitable *Apologies for the Christian Religion* that this attitude of outstretched arms represents Christ on the Cross. Portraits of the departed were usually represented in this manner in the frescoes painted on the walls of the catacombs. The epithet 'orans' is applied generally to these paintings, though they are often only the artistic symbol of the souls of the departed faithful.

The edict of the Emperor Diocletian (284–305) states that the dalmatica at the end of the third century was made of various materials, wool, silk, linen: sometimes the ornamented clavus was present. There were three different qualities for each sex, the price varying according to the quality and the place of manufacture: Scythopolis, Tarsus, Byblos, and Laodicea are mentioned.

It has been suggested by Father Braun (mid-nineteenth century) that the popes themselves were the first to wear the dalmatica, and that it was granted by them to their deacons to distinguish them from the other clergy, and to mark their special relation to the Holy See. Thus it remained a distinctive dress (though not yet a vestment) of the Bishop of Rome and his deacons, and could be worn by other clergy only by special concession.

IV CENTURY

No doubt the earliest description of an elaborate dalmatic to be worn when officiating at baptism, and therefore a vestment, is that of the robe of gold tissue given by Constantine the Great to Macarius,[1] Bishop of Jerusalem. This robe is mentioned by Theodore, Bishop of Cyrus, in Syria (420–57). The narrative is brief, and relates that on his return from the West the emperor stayed for a time in Constantinople.

While he was there, Acacius, Metropolitan Bishop of Caesarea and a rabid Arian,[2] brought many accusations to Constantine against the bishops assembled at Seleucia, abusing them as a pack of mischievous men got together for the ruin and destruction of the churches; and so prejudiced the emperor against them. What most excited the imperial indignation was the false charge devised by Acacius against St. Cyril,[3] Patriarch of Jerusalem. This was to the effect that St. Cyril, the original owner of this sacred robe, had sold it to a stage dancer who had worn it at a public entertainment. It was reckoned a judgment on the latter that he had fallen during his sacrilegious performance, and was fatally injured.

The chief point of this story is not so much the apostolic origin of this sacerdotal vestment, as the proof of the imperial and secular origin of the dalmatic.

This 'sacred robe' might be the colobium, but the fabric does not suggest this garment: most probably it was a dalmatic. Fine threads of pure gold were interwoven with a gold-coloured silk warp and weft to form a rather stiff dress material, which is

[1] Macarius was the thirty-ninth Patriarch of Jerusalem, and a strenuous defender of the orthodox faith against the Arians. Amongst other achievements he planned Constantine's magnificent Basilica of the Holy Sepulchre. He died about 353.

[2] The Arian Faith, so named after Arius, a pastor of Alexandria (*nat.* c. 256, *ob.* c. 336).

[3] St. Cyril of Jerusalem, born there in 315, ordained a priest in 345, and became patriarch in 350. Having been banished thrice he died in his native city 386. Much opposed to Arianism, his persistent and unscrupulous antagonist was Acacius of Caesarea. The writings of St. Cyril on religious subjects are most valuable, and he is numbered by Pope Leo XIII among the Doctors of the Church.

mentioned in the writings of the early years of the first century. The earliest illustration of a bishop wearing the dalmatic and paenula (chasuble, see p. 55) is in the mosaic of St. Ambrose in the church of St. Ambrogio, Milan, which was erected shortly after his death in 397. It has been damaged and restored to such an extent that details are by no means clear. Still the dalmatic and paenula are faintly visible.

Towards the end of the century Roman deacons began to wear the dalmatic in church, and it became their distinctive vestment when serving at holy communion.

By degrees the tunica talaris and dalmatic became acknowledged as garments appertaining to the clergy, for, according to tradition, they were ordered by Bishop Sylvester to be worn by deacons. His Holiness lengthened and widened the sleeves according to the priority of office, and retained the clavi. Black and sometimes brown appear to have been the original tones of these clavi, as shown on the dalmatics worn by the clergy of the Eastern Church. Later, the red or purple clavi became those generally worn in the West.

It is said that about the fourth century the dalmatic replaced the colobium (or alb), or was worn over it: in such illustrations as mosaics and frescoes it is not always easy to discover to which the sleeves belong.

V CENTURY

According to Walafrid Strabo, who wrote in the ninth century, priests [sacerdotes, that is doubtless bishops and priests both] wore dalmatics before chasubles were introduced. When, however, they began to use chasubles, they allowed their deacons to wear dalmatics. It was some time before the custom of wearing a dalmatic under a chasuble became general: we hear from time to time of the pope—who himself first began this habit early in this century—granting the use of them 'after the Roman fashion' to some bishops, and refusing it to others, and again of bestowing it as a special favour on the deacons of visiting bishops. At the end of this century Pope Symmachus (498–514), for example, granted the right of wearing the dalmatic to the deacons and subdeacons of Caesarius, Archbishop of Arles (480–542). In later centuries this privilege was widely extended.

Strabo further says that Sylvester, Bishop of Rome (314–35), had previously appointed that deacons should use dalmatics in church: by the end of the fifth century the dalmatic had become the recognized badge of all clergy, from the Pontiff downwards.

VI AND VII CENTURIES

During this time the dalmatic had become universally worn by all clergy, but it must be remembered that it was also worn by laymen, and that there was little difference in the cut of the two garments, whether lay or clerical.

During the seventh century the dalmatic became old-fashioned as a lay garment, and so fell out of general use: the clergy, however, retained it, making it one of their distinctive garments. Before long the dalmatic formed part of the coronation and full dress of emperors and kings, a custom which lasted from this time until 1937.

VIII CENTURY

Abbats, later abbots, appeared in the fourth century, and were the superiors of monasteries: for the next four hundred years they bore no other title. By this time abbats were recognized as prelates of the Church, and as such ranked the same as a bishop.

PLATE III (see page 6)   British Museum.   By kind permission of the Governors

Bishop   Archbishop   Abbot   Monks

It was during the eighth century that abbats, who wore the dalmatic with the chasuble, had to be restrained from wearing insignia to which they had no right. Thus the Council of Frankfort (794) forbad the wearing of mitre, ring, gloves, or sandals as being the prerogative of a bishop. But the practice grew in the West during the succeeding centuries, and was again condemned, unsuccessfully, by the Council of Poitiers (1100), as also by St. Bernard (1091–1153) and Peter of Blois[1] (1135–1212). At this same council, however, it was decided that an abbat might carry a pastoral staff of simple design: it was also settled that he was to be clean shaven and tonsured. Cases where the right to wear a mitre was granted are reported, nevertheless, from Theodorus I (642–9) to the Abbat of Bobbio, Pavia, and from Sylvester II (999–1003) to the Abbat of St. Savianus in 1000. A staff of distinctive form was the special insignia of an abbat in Anglo-Saxon England at this time, and was formally presented to him by a bishop at his benediction.

IX CENTURY

At first the dalmatic was made of plain white or natural coloured linen; a more luxurious age substituted white silk. Later, different colours were used according to the fancy of the wearer, these having no necessary connection with the liturgical colours.

The dalmatic was, of course, open on both sides from about waist level to hem: in the case of bishops the edges of both slits and of both sleeves, as well as the lower hem, were fringed, evidently introduced from the East, see Plate IV. A deacon's dalmatic, however, was fringed only on the left sleeve and on both sides of the left slit. This custom was often neglected in the Middle Ages, which is the reason why one finds illustrations of deacons whose dalmatics are devoid of any fringe: Fig. 64 is a case in point. Nor were they very particular as to which side the slit was fringed, see Fig. 229.

Possibly the earliest occasion on which the dalmatic was worn by a monarch was when Charlemagne received the crown of the Caesars from Pope Leo III at St. Peter's on Christmas Day, 800. It is said that he was robed, amongst other items of imperial insignia, in a dalmatic, worn as a garment symbolizing his protection of the Church. It was, so it is thought, of white silk or linen, with heavy borders in scarlet and gold embroidery;[2] the girdle was of gold, and jewelled, and from it was suspended the state sword.

The emperors of the Holy Roman Empire[3] continued to wear this vestment at their coronations as part of the imperial robes until 1790, when a portrait of Leopold II shows him wearing it.

IX, X, XI, AND XII CENTURIES

The ornamentation, as well as the shape of the dalmatic underwent certain changes during these four centuries, its decoration becoming much more varied and elaborate as time went on.

By the ninth century fringe had been introduced as a distinctive badge of the deacon: a little later small strips of coloured material were knotted and sewn on, either with some symbolical idea or as a mere whim.

One example of a decoration of this kind, and probably the earliest, is to be found in the Bible of Charles the Bald, a work of the middle (844–51) of the ninth century.

[1] Peter of Blois. His *Epistolae* are a valuable source for the history of the reign of Henry II (of England).
[2] See *Costume and Fashion*, vol. i, Fig. 115.
[3] The designation 'Holy Roman' did not come into use until the twelfth century, and lasted until Napoleon dissolved the empire in 1806.

C

In the vignette representing the canons of St. Martin of Tours offering the Bible to the emperor, their white dalmatics [1] have scarlet clavi flanked with rows of scarlet knots

and ends (see Fig. 60) set parallel with them, but to the left of the clavi, except on the right sleeve, where they are on the right. This arrangement may echo the earlier rule as shown in the diagram, Fig. 61, regarding fringe on the *left* side.

Fig. 60. Tassel on Dalmatic, XII Century

It may be of interest here that the remaining vestments of the canons in this vignette consisted of white alb, chasuble in different shades of red or purple trimmed with gold, green tunicle, red and gold stole, white maniple fringed with red, and purple shoes. All the canons are bare-headed and tonsured.

Later still tassels were sometimes arranged, but in a different way: they were attached to the dalmatic (front and back alike), near the hem between the clavi, in pyramid form, Fig. 62, which restricted their number to 3, 6, 10, 15, 21, or 28, this last having a base of seven.

The wearing of the dalmatic over the tunicle (see p. 170) by deacons and subdeacons, when serving at high mass and at solemn processions and benedictions, was firmly established by the eleventh century.

Fig. 62 shows a dalmatic of the eleventh century, which differs considerably in some details from the more ancient examples seen in Figs. 57, 58, and 59. It is not so long, and the particular cut at the arm-pits should be noted. The back and front are seamed together from a point A below the sleeve to B, and securely stitched, especially at the point A; thence the sides are left open, taking an oblique line downwards. The sleeves have become narrower, and the neck opening has taken a different line.

Before the twelfth century decoration had taken the form of vertical bands, like the clavi, or else horizontal bands across the front (and presumably the back) at various places between the shoulders and the hem, see Fig. 68. Further, it was not unusual for a band of embroidery to be sewn all round the bottom hem.

The episcopal dalmatic at this time was very elaborately embroidered with gold thread and beautifully coloured silks, and as already stated fringed on both sleeves and both sides.

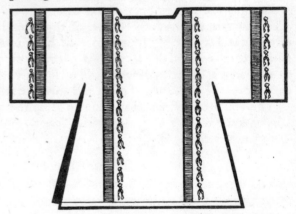

Fig. 61. Dalmatic, showing Position of Tassels

XII CENTURY

The effigy of Henry II of England (1154–89) at the Abbey of Fontevrault, which at any rate until recently preserved traces of its original colouring, shows the king wearing a garment with wide sleeves like a dalmatic. It is of crimson, woven or worked 'à pois'—

[1] The distinguishing dress of canons regular is the white linen rochet, but this vestment did not make its appearance until the twelfth century.

a diaper design of six gold spots round a single one—and bordered by a band of gold passement at the neck, on the edge of the sleeves, and at the hem.

Richard I's effigy at the same abbey wears a red dalmatic, bordered with gold and lined with white; and on the effigy of King John in Worcester Cathedral the dalmatic is obviously of more flexible material, and similar in shape to the diagram, Fig. 67; the sleeves fit close on the forearm, and apparently there are no slits at the sides.

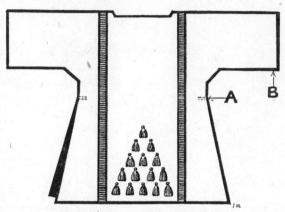

Fig. 62. Tassels in Pyramid Form

It is from the twelfth century that the shape of the ecclesiastical dalmatic is definitely altered for a time, the sleeves being replaced by shoulder pieces. The eastern Church has retained the earlier form, the dalmatic worn by deacons recalling very closely the primitive garment.

XIII CENTURY

Figs. 63, 64, and 65 come from an illumination in a thirteenth-century Latin missal dated 1250. They depict a subdeacon carrying a flabellum, a deacon holding a paten or large wafer in his veiled hand, and a priest consecrating the elements. The subdeacon is wearing an alb, but here we find much larger sleeves than usual, cut small at the arm-hole, and widening out towards the wrist. No girdle is worn. The deacon is in an alb, and over it the dalmatic: this is opened up the *right* side, perhaps an error of the artist, and is without fringe. The priest shows the front bottom portion of the dalmatic beneath the chasuble; this dalmatic, like that of the deacon, has an embroidered border at the hem only, and is without fringe. The altar is covered with a cloth having an embroidered or jewelled border and draped to form an inverted box-pleat. On it stands the veiled chalice and beside it a wafer stamped with a Greek cross.

The deacon carrying a flabellum, Fig. 229, is vested in a tunicle with an embroidered fringed border, and worn over an alb (unseen): above is the dalmatic with the slit on the *right* side of the wearer, and having the fringe on the back edge only: the left sleeve is surrounded with fringe, as is usual in the diaconal dalmatic. The decoration of the deacon's dalmatic, illustrated in Fig. 230, is interesting: it consists of bands of embroidery at the neck or on the amice, at the waist line, at the bottom hem, where apparently pearls are introduced, and at the edges of the sleeves. These last are moderately close and short, and the alb shows at the wrist and ankle. The large rectangle at the waist *may* be a jewel, though it is hardly likely there would be one or more on a deacon's dalmatic or in that position. The hairdressing of this deacon is very characteristic of the thirteenth century.

Abbots of the thirteenth century wore dalmatics with long sleeves: when albs had wider sleeves than usual (see p. 17) these sleeves protruded at the wrists below those of the dalmatic.

Fig. 63. Subdeacon, XIII Century   Fig. 64. Deacon, XIII Century   Fig. 65. Priest, XIII Century

XIV CENTURY

A dalmatic worn by a deacon in the early fourteenth century is shown in Fig. 66; it is taken from an illuminated MS. dating about 1320, in which this vestment is painted a lilac colour, and is quite plain. The sleeves, it should be noted, are smaller and the garment fuller in the skirt, reaching to the calf: it would be cut as shown in Fig. 67. An amice surrounds the neck, and the alb is decorated with an apparel. This cleric is tonsured, his hair being dressed in the fashionable manner, and he wears a beard. The

Fig. 66. Deacon, XIV Century

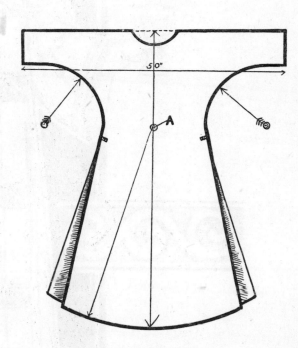

Fig. 67. Diagram of Dalmatic

dimensions of the diagram, Fig. 67, are: from neck at the back to hem about 50 inches, and the width from sleeve to sleeve is also 50 inches: the centre for the circumference of the skirt is shown at A, and the curves of the arm-holes are indicated by the arrows.

The deacon holding a chalice, Fig. 68, is of the fourteenth century, and probably earlier. He is arrayed in a dalmatic, shaped like Fig. 67, but the skirt part is not quite so wide: the sleeves are wider but cut off just below elbow level, thus exposing more of the sleeves of the alb. The decoration of the horizontal bands is in colour, and possibly of silk, embroidered with a scroll design in coloured silks, perhaps mixed with gold thread: they are of the same pattern throughout, including the amice. It should be noticed that a fringe finishes off the hem of the left sleeve, and at the hem only, not up the sides of the slits, and that the right sleeve has two narrow bands of colour. This young

Fig. 68. Deacon with Chalice, XIV Century

man's hairdressing is that in vogue except that he is tonsured. The slightly pointed toes of the shoes are a modified form of the prevailing fashion.

A mitred abbot of the fourteenth century wore the same vestments as a bishop: they are shown in the famous brass of Thomas Delamere, 1360, in St. Alban's Abbey. In this he is clad in amice, alb, stole, maniple, tunicle, dalmatic, and chasuble, these being enumerated in the order of vesting. A mitre is worn; he carries a pastoral staff, enclosing in its crook an Agnus Dei. He is gloved, and on his feet are embroidered sandals.

The coronation of Edward II of England took place on 23rd February 1308, and the illuminated MS. No. 20 in the library of Corpus Christi College, Cambridge, entitled *The Order of Crowning*,[1] illustrates the king in full robes. These consist of the alb (Colobium Sidonis), a red tunicle, and the dalmatic of rayed cloth of gold and silver, the gold embroidered with a scroll pattern in orange. The dalmatic hangs midway down the leg, and the sleeves are not more than 18 inches round the wrists. The waist is girded, and from it hangs a sword.

XV CENTURY

Dalmatics of the fifteenth and later centuries were of very rich material, and of elaborate workmanship. They were often made of one of the beautiful Italian brocades of the period. These might be in monochrome, or the pattern in one colour and the ground of another, or the foundation of cloth of gold or silver with the pattern of velvet or silk, and vice versa; sometimes both of some rich colour. They were frequently embroidered in addition.

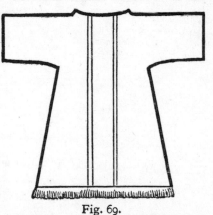

Fig. 69.
Diagram of Dalmatic, XV Century

One extant example of a dalmatic, of which a photograph cannot be obtained for reproduction in this book, is shaped like Fig. 69. It is made of a gorgeous silk brocade of an intricate floral design in three colours, and has two gold bands at least 4 inches wide down the front and back, after the manner of clavi. These are connected across the chest with a horizontal band, and are embroidered on each side, front and back, in coloured silks and gold, with a series of saints in tabernacles. A narrow gold fringe finishes the edges of the sleeves and side openings, with a wider fringe at the bottom hem.

A diagram of the cut of a dalmatic dating the second half of the fifteenth century is given in Fig. 69. It measures 42 inches from shoulder to hem, and 46 inches from one end of the sleeve to the other, and 20 inches round the wrists. Sometimes it is left unsewn at the lower edge from arm-pit to wrist. In some of these dalmatics the pillar orphrey is as much as 6 or 7 inches wide.

The Early Perpendicular church at Ranworth, near Norwich, possesses a magnificent painted Rood-screen which is unsurpassed in the country. Taken as a whole it ranks first amongst painted screens in England. It contains twenty-two panels of saints,

[1] See *Costume and Fashion*, vol. ii, p. 208, Fig. 292.

which are thought to be the work of Flemish craftsmen in 1485. Each has a background, alternating red and green, and powdered diaperwise with gold floral designs.[1] They were daubed over with tar in Oliver Cromwell's time. Plate XV is a reproduction [2] of one of these panels, which represents the third-century St. Laurence in fifteenth-century vestments. He served as archdeacon to Pope St. Sixtus II, and as such is shown robed in a red episcopal dalmatic with fringe of gold, headed by a narrow band of pale green with gold spots. The pillar orphrey is of black-and-gold brocade, and the apparels on the amice and the alb are of the same rich material. The book and gridiron were originally in red and gold, the latter all gold.

[1] Similar designs are shown on Figs. 244 and 245.
[2] By kind permission of the Rev. E. D. Everard, vicar, who has been most helpful in supplying all details, and giving much valuable information. This applies also to Plate XVI. The author offers his very sincere thanks.

5. THE CHASUBLE

The Paenula
The Casula.   The Planeta.   The Phelonion

The chasuble descends from the paenula and casula, garments of the people, each of which is dealt with separately.

THE PAENULA

VI CENTURY B.C. TO A.D. I CENTURY

A USEFUL garment, worn by the lower classes of classic Greece, was a calf-length cloak of felt or coarse cloth, and sometimes of skins, often if not always with a hood attached.   It was adopted by the Romans of the republic, and was in common use amongst all classes, both men and women, as a comfortable travelling outfit, and was an important garment with the peasantry.

To all and sundry it was known as the PAENULA, Fig. 71.   In colour it was dark, usually a chestnut-brown, and in shape a semicircle with the straight edges generally

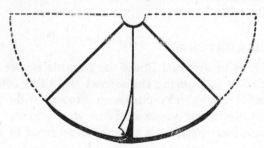

Fig. 70.
Diagram of Pre-Christian Paenula

Fig. 71. The Paenula, Pre-Christian

fastened down the centre front.   It might, however, be sewn up, thus converting it into a funnel-shaped garment, Fig. 70, or as Chaucer's friar expresses it: 'Round . . . as a bell out of press.'   In either case it hung in radiating folds, and entirely enveloped the figure.   To raise the arms and free the hands it was necessary to gather up the material into folds on the forearm.   A hole was left for the head, which was usually covered with a hood known as a CUCULLUS.

In the earliest years of the Church the paenula may very well have been cut as a complete circle of material, with a hole *near* the middle for the head to pass through.

55

Fig. 72. The Cucullus,
Pre-Christian

There seem to be few, if any, contemporary illustrations of such a voluminous garment worn by the early clergy.

The cloak which St. Paul had left behind at Troas (2 Timothy iv. 13) was the paenula. In the discomfort of his prison cell at Rome he must have felt the need for such a warm garment.

Civil headgear was almost unknown to the Romans, except the cucullus, which was used primarily for protection. It was worn by travellers and countrymen, also by people in general when wishing to remain unobserved or unrecognized. It was in use among the common soldiers when on service in cold climates. Fig. 72 shows the cucullus, and the man in Fig. 73 is wearing one attached to his paenula. It was made in substantial material, and square in shape. When a separate item it sometimes had long ends which could be wound round the neck to keep it in its place, and for further protection.

A.D. I CENTURY

Although the paenula in its original form and thick homely material was considered commonplace, the gentlefolk of imperial Rome used it on occasion, and even senators: the latter had to obtain a special grant from the emperor in order to do so. Because it was so commonplace it is said that Roman emperors *never* used it, but knowing their idiosyncrasies and consequent need of disguise, it is very doubtful!

A.D. II AND III CENTURIES

When worn by the nobility and upper classes of imperial Rome the paenula was of a larger size, considerably more than a semicircle; and during the second and third centuries the usual colour was of a dark tone of claret, inky-purple or brown, without decoration except that occasionally the two bands of the angustus clavus were added.

About this time the longer and more voluminous paenula is sometimes referred to as the AMPHIBALUS on account of its size.

St. Alban, the protomartyr of Britain, was converted to Christianity by a certain priest, whose name is now unknown. This saint suffered persecution under the Emperor Diocletian (284–305) and was executed at Verulamium, probably in 303. Previously he had disguised the priest in his own very ample paenula or amphibalus. In consequence of this the anonymous priest (who also suffered martyrdom, 304) is known to posterity as St. Amphibalus.

IV CENTURY

Fig. 74 shows the paenula as worn by better-class people toward the end of the third and during the fourth centuries. This is a *closed* garment, otherwise it is shaped as

Fig. 73. Peasant of Republican and Imperial Rome

Fig. 74. Paenula, IV Century

Fig. 75. St. Philip wearing Paenula, IV Century

Fig. 76. St. Romanus, Priest, IV Century

shown in Figs. 70 and 71; there is no hood attached, and the hole at the neck is sufficiently large for the head to pass through with ease.   It appears to be made of a white or light coloured woollen material, and decorated with the latus clavus.

The paenula was prescribed by Sylvester, Bishop of Rome (314–35), to be worn by the recently appointed overseers or bishops of the Church, as a comfortable outdoor garment for everyday use, but also as a garment when conducting Church ritual, and even while celebrating the eucharist.

St. Martin (316–97) was a tribune in the Roman Army stationed in Gaul before his conversion in 356, and was later known as the 'Apostle of Gaul.'   In 371 he became Bishop of Tours, when he strenuously resisted the persecution of heretics and was pre-eminent for his self-denial and works of charity.   'Martin of Tours' usually wore a tunica and paenula on ordinary occasions; but when on horseback the amphibalus completely covered himself and the back of his mount.[1]   At the altar he wore a clean tunica and a fresh paenula.

IV TO VI CENTURIES

Two interesting figures are shown: Fig. 75, a bishop, and Fig. 76, a priest.   They are taken from the mosaics in the cupola of the Basilica of St. George at Thessalonica.

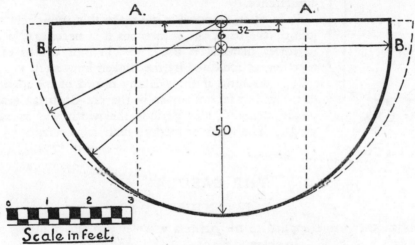

Fig. 77. Diagram of Later Paenula

Some authorities say the mosaics date from the fourth century, but as the Church was not built until St. Sophia at Constantinople was completed they must be definitely of the sixth century.

What makes them so valuable is that they represent several martyrs, all of whom were laymen, except two, a bishop and a priest, who are wearing everyday civil dress, such as these clerics wore in the streets.   Fig. 75 is a representation of St. Philip, Bishop of Heraclea, who suffered martyrdom by being burned at the stake, 22nd November 304. His attire consists of a white subucula without sleeves, with a tunica of dark green above it.   Over this is draped the paenula, in colour a lighter green.   His hair and beard are

[1] Without a helmet, but in his grey cloak on a wet day, St. Martin must have looked like one of the modern Royal Horse Guards.

characteristic of the second and third centuries, and are dark brown. White shoes are worn.

Fig. 78. The Casula

Fig. 76 is St. Romanus, said to be the bishop's deacon, but in the inscription he is styled a priest. He wears a white tunica with close sleeves, and round the neck a decoration in red: over this is a dark purple sleeveless tunica, and a paenula of the same colour, but paler. The hair and forked beard are white, and the shoes black. This saint suffered martyrdom in the same manner as the bishop, 24th November 304.

The paenula as worn by the commonalty was discarded by degrees from the end of the fourth and during the next century.

Fig. 77 is a diagram of a model paenula, which is, without doubt, prototype of the later chasuble. It shows two methods of cutting it: firstly, a semicircle as indicated by the solid line with an 8-inch addition at the top at B; this gives an extra 4 inches in length at the back. Alternatively the broken line gives a complete semicircle of 15 feet circumference.

It is often impossible to make this semicircle without a join up the back, and sometimes it is necessary, when a still narrower material is used, to join four widths of material together, as indicated by the broken lines at A.

It is doubtful if there is any record of the measurements of the widest fabrics woven in the pre-Christian era. In the medieval and Tudor periods the width was as much as 2 yards. The width of modern materials averages 54 inches.

Continued on page 63.

THE CASULA

IV CENTURY

This was another name applied to the paenula when it was closer fitting round the figure, and longer, Fig. 78. In shape it was similar to the paenula except that it was cut as two-thirds of a semicircle, see Fig. 79. The cut straight edges AB and AC were folded over AD and AE, so that B and C meet at F, and AF is sewn up, forming the front of the garment. This is clearly visible in Plate IV.

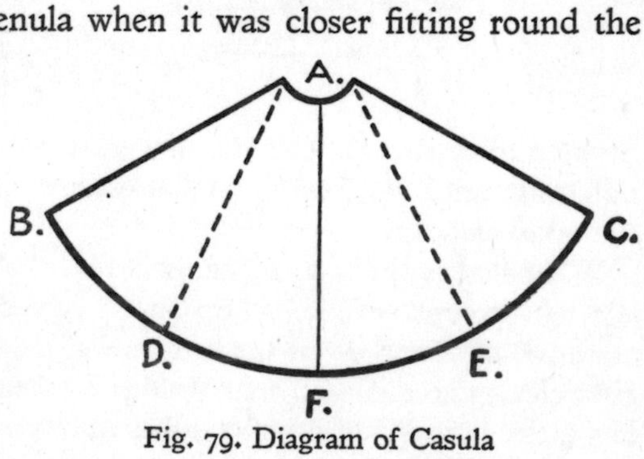

St. Augustine of Hippo (354–430), when writing of this garment, alludes to the paenula by the name of CASULA, which is possibly the

Fig. 79. Diagram of Casula

first instance of this name being mentioned in connection with clerical dress. He says it was for outdoor use by working men, and much worn by the populace. He also refers to it as a garment which any one of his congregation might be expected to possess, and one which every one would take care to have good of its kind.   These cloaks would be of reasonably good cloth.

VI CENTURY

Because the casula covered the wearer entirely it was likened to a 'little house' (*casa*, a cottage), and St. Isidore of Seville (560–636) writing about 600 is the first to mention this fact.   He says: 'The casula is a garment furnished with a hood; and is a diminutive of "casa," a cottage, seeing that, like a small cottage or hut, it covers the entire person.'

In its earlier stages the casula, according to the purpose required, was made of various materials, such as skins dressed with the hair worn inside or out: of felt, or of thick rough cloth, any of which made it a useful and comfortable covering in cold and wet weather.   To the neck opening was attached a hood, but there is no reason why the hood should not be detachable.

Philo Judaeus, writing about A.D. 39, states that this cloak provided the lower orders with a portable house, suitable for travellers, soldiers, peasants, monks, and others who were obliged to be in the open air.

An MS. dating about the ninth century, but referring back more or less to this period, gives a description of the shape of the casula.   It mentions that it is '*made in one piece throughout*,' but this does not technically mean without a seam, certainly not in the case of skins.   If the material was not wide enough before the garment was cut out, the selvedges of the cloth were joined together, thus converting it into 'one piece.'   Also it was 'without sleeves' and 'without slit or opening in front,' therefore the neck-hole was fairly large.

It is evident that the casula and paenula were to all intents and purposes the same garment.

Originally only worn by the commonalty, the casula became popular among the better-class owing to its usefulness, although it was still considered a garment of humble pretensions.   Wealthy persons, however, did not disdain the use of it on certain occasions; it became the characteristic dress for outdoor wear of the clergy, and also of monks of certain monasteries during the period from the fifth century to the eighth.

A particularly ascetic bishop of the beginning of the sixth century retained his monastic habit, even after being advanced to the episcopal dignity, and it is reported that 'he neither wore a costly casula himself, or one of bright colour, nor did he allow his monks to do so.'   Also it is recorded of an archbishop [1] of this time that he possessed two casulae, in one of which, a 'casula villosa,' or long napped cloak, he walked about the streets.   The other, a 'casula paschalia,' he used in processions, and as a vestment in church on Sundays and on high festivals.   This was altogether richer in colour, decoration, and material.   In fact, he had in his possession before his death, besides these garments just mentioned, a paschal alb; and he bequeathed all three to one who did not possess such vestments.   'These,' he says, 'were given me by my Holy Lord Archbishop, who worthily succeeded my unworthy self.'   Actually they divided his remaining clothing, except his favourite birrus, as well clerical as lay.   This archbishop also

---

[1] St. Caesarius of Arles, born 470, retired in 490 to the famous monastery of the Isle of Leros in the Mediterranean.   In 500 he became Archbishop of Arles, and presided over several councils.   He is best known for his liturgical reforms, and for his efforts to propagate and perfect monachism—the rules for which are still extant. He also took a somewhat prominent part in the politics of the period.   He died in 542.

possessed the pallium which had been granted to him by Pope Symmachus (498–514), when he visited Rome.

In view of what has just been stated, it is clear that the CHASUBLE, a word derived directly from 'casula,' became an item of Church vestments in the West approximately during the early years of the fifth century.

THE PLANETA

V CENTURY

The name planeta was given to a special kind of paenula, and is said by Isidore of Seville (560–636) to have been derived from the Greek 'planeta.' 'I may add,' he says, 'that the Greeks hold that one of their names for these robes originates from their free and flowing borders. Hence the term planetary stars; that is, roving stars; stars which roll here and there with wandering maze and motion of their own.' 'Wandering' alludes to the borders or edges of these semicircular garments which zigzag (a characteristic of Greek dress) and hang in radiating folds when draped over both forearms.

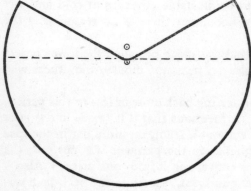

Fig. 80. Diagram of Planeta

The PLANETA was a rich article of costume, and as early as the fifth century, when its name first appears, it is referred to as being very costly, so that only wealthy persons of both sexes could afford it. In shape the planeta was obviously a semicircle, or perhaps [1] with a third of a semicircle added to it, and was open up the front, Fig. 80.

At this time the planeta was worn by nobles, and it is thought by officials in the entourage of the Holy Father, both cleric and laic, but whether these officials were exclusively clerical or not is uncertain. In the first case the wearing of the planeta 'was by virtue of their official rank, not their clerical profession, the privilege being shared by laymen.'

VI CENTURY

The first definite recognition of the clerical use of the planeta is in a letter of St. Germanus (496–576), Bishop of Paris, in 554, where it is called both amphibalus and casula.

VII CENTURY

By the time of the fourth Council of Toledo (633) the planeta has become part of the vestments of the clergy. One of the canons specifies certain vestments and ornaments appertaining to a bishop, who by now has the stole, ring, and pastoral staff; a priest the stole and planeta, and a deacon the stole and alb.

It has been the custom from early times until the present day for distinguished people to send gifts of rich garments to potentates, and it is recorded that Pope Boniface III (606–8) presented in the first year of his election a planeta to Pépin de Landen, a very virtuous magistrate who became palace-mayor (613–49) and ancestor of the Carlovingian

---

[1] Some authorities suggest that it takes the shape of a complete circle, with a hole in the centre for the head.

dynasty of Frankish kings, and who was later canonized. This planeta was made of a material combining silk and very fine goat's hair, probably of some gorgeous colour and beautifully decorated: no doubt it would be worn by him on special occasions, though, of course, without any ecclesiastical significance. During this century, and until the ninth, the words planeta and casula are precisely equivalent, denoting exactly the same garment.

VIII CENTURY

A late example of the use of the planeta occurs in the eighth century when Chrode-gang, Bishop of Metz (743–66), issued an order that canons living 'foris claustra' (outside the gates) must attend the chapter every Sunday in planeta or official vestments—including the chasuble.

The word 'planeta' disappears in the western Church about the end of the eighth century, the vestment being universally called a 'casula,' i.e. a chasuble.

VI CENTURY

By the sixth century the casula had developed into the sacerdotal vestment of cele-brants: the word became casubula in medieval Latin, chesible in middle English, and chasuble in modern times.

It has been previously stated that the garments of the clergy were made of good materials, linen and wool: to these must now be added silken fabrics.

Silk

Going back to the first century B.C., silk was little known in Europe, and was of a prohibitive price. In the first century A.D. it was becoming more generally known to the luxurious Roman patricians. Silk had, of course, reached Palestine much earlier, and in consequence is mentioned by the Hebrew prophets as a contemptible luxury, as, for example, by Amos (eighth century B.C.), who speaks witheringly of the effeminates who reclined 'on the silken cushions of a divan.'

At the end of the first century A.D. silk formed part of the luxurious merchandise of Rome, according to the author of Revelation xviii. 12, wherein he lists 'merchandise of gold, and silver, and precious stone, and pearls,[1] and fine linen, and purple, and silk, and scarlet.' Purple and scarlet, of course, refer to the rich fabrics dyed these costly colours.

During the sixth century silk became much more used, and mention is made of this rich fabric being employed for chasubles when worn by the higher clergy. Subserica is another material which was popular because it was less expensive. It is described on page 16.

THE CHASUBLE (continued from page 62)

Plate IV is copied from one of the well-known mosaics in the Basilica of St. Vitalis, Ravenna. It represents Maximian, Bishop of Ravenna, who stands on the left of the Emperor Justinian. He built this wonderful church, and consecrated it about 537 in the presence of the Emperor and the Empress Theodora.

It appears that this bishop of the Greek Church wears a white *dalmatic* with dark brown clavi over his white *alb*, of which only part of one sleeve is visible, surmounted by an unlined *chasuble* of golden-brown silk. The neck-opening is of white, and of the usual shape, see Fig. 100. Even in the mosaic work the seam up the front is clearly

[1] For purple of Tyre see *Costume and Fashion*, vol. i, p. 57.

D

defined.   Over the chasuble is the *pallium* (omophorion), arranged as shown in Fig. 31;
embroidered with a black cross, front and back, Fig. 33, and fringed with gold.   In his
right hand the bishop grasps a richly jewelled cross composed of precious stones and
pearls set in gold.   The left hand is enveloped in the chasuble.   His sandals are black
with white decoration, somewhat like Fig. 48, and worn over white hosae.   Altogether
these vestments are simple and dignified, contrary to what one would expect of an
important ecclesiastic of a luxurious era, officiating at a high festival such as is com-
memorated by these mosaics.   Bishop Maximian died about 556.

In the Eastern Church the vestments italicized above were known by their Greek names,
which are as follows: the dalmatic of the third century alone retained its original name,
but the alb in Greek became the STICHARION, and the pallium (as before mentioned) the
omophorion.   The chasuble was called the PHELONION; this was the only vestment of
these four which changed its shape.

The phelonion was originally shaped like the paenula, that is a semicircle: but by
degrees the front was rolled up to wrist or waist level, and kept in place with a button
and loop on each side.   This arrangement was made to ensure that the action of the
arms should not be impeded, but was soon found to be unduly bulky and somewhat
unsightly, besides making the elevation of the host unnecessarily difficult: so that the
superfluous material underneath was cut away, a process adopted from the West and
called contabulatum (see p. 23).   The front was thereby converted into a pointed cape,
leaving the remaining segmental portion hanging down the back in the usual perpendicular folds.   However, in some illustrations it appears that the back is treated in the
same manner as the front, but is longer, in which case the front and back portions would
probably be joined on the shoulders.   The front of the phelonion is well shown in
Fig. 40.   During a long period it was made of a plain dark coloured fabric, and usually
of silk.

A bishop of the sixth century in the Western Church is shown in Fig. 81.   He is
wearing first the tunica talaris, or alb, and secondly the dalmatic, with clavi in black or
purple.   Over this is the paenula or chasuble in dull red or brown cloth, having the
hood thrown back showing the tonsure of St. Peter.   Shoes are worn, called udones or
perones, and known in later times as sandals.

VIII CENTURY

One of the canons of the Council of Ratisbon, which sat in 742, was aimed at the
clergy, who when out of doors persistently appeared in the sagum (a short open cloak
worn by laymen) instead of the prescribed casula, originally the paenula (refer to Figs.
75, 76).   It sets forth that 'we have decreed that presbyters and deacons shall wear,
not the sagum, as do laymen, but the casula as becometh the servants of God.'

Continued on page 71.

A DIGRESSION ON EMBROIDERIES

During the eighth century embroideries began to be called apparels and orphreys,[1]
and were used to embellish vestments in the future.   They are, therefore, conveniently
introduced at this point, and their history continued from page 19.

[1] There is no real difference between these other than a slight variation in shape: the word depends on the
garment to which the ornamentation is applied.   See p. 18, footnote 2.

Fig. 81. Bishop in full Vestments, VI Century

The decoration of early chasubles was simple compared with other vestments: their beauty depended on the richness of the colour and of the fabric of which they were composed, as described under Plate IV. Those mentioned on page 68 come under this category, but are even richer, and were without doubt lined with a silk of contrasting colour to hide the back of the fabric. The wonderful brocade of a later date, shown in Fig. 102, deserves special admiration.

Fig. 82. Orphrey, VII to X Century

In the West during the Carlovingian period (700–986) embroideries were very rich in design, and Fig. 82 gives an example. It is a small portion taken from a larger piece in a private collection. Of Byzantine workmanship, it is typical of the decoration which embellished the full state costumes of the Byzantine and Carlovingian courts. The original is of a rich red-purple silk, much akin in texture to a substantial taffeta, with the scroll-leaf design worked in gold. Often the ground, shown black in Fig. 82, was thickly sewn with seed pearls, but leaving a narrow margin between them and the gold embroidery. The massed pearls, however, do not impair the flexibility of the material.

Fig. 83.
Celtic Orphrey, X and XI Century

Fig. 84.
Celtic Orphrey, X and XI Century

Figs. 83 and 84 are typically Celtic in character, and are of the tenth and eleventh centuries. The interlaced work persisted until the twelfth century, and by degrees leaf and flower motifs became incorporated with it as is shown in Fig. 85, a late twelfth-century design.

Fig. 86 is definitely an orphrey, a narrow band of woven gold—a braid [1] which was very much used for the embellishment of vestments as is seen on the chasuble, Figs. 100 and 101; and for full ceremonial dress in general.

Dating from the end of the eleventh century onwards many varieties of the orphrey appear, but the plain chasuble with an edging of gold braid was the most common, and used chiefly by priests.

[1] This type of braid was later known as passement.

The higher orders of the clergy ornamented their chasubles with richer embroideries. As mentioned under Fig. 102, the perpendicular band known as the 'pillar,' which

descended the whole length front and back, became considerably wider and often very elaborately decorated. To it was added later a short horizontal band at the top, thus converting it into a T-shaped cross, Figs. 87, 88. This kind of orphrey of varying widths survives until to-day.[1]

Another method of treating the orphrey was to add branches on the oblique; these passed over the shoulders and joined the corresponding branches on the back. Occasionally the top of the upright band was omitted, which arrangement resembled the Y pallium [2] as seen in Figs. 37 and 106. When this shape was used the space between

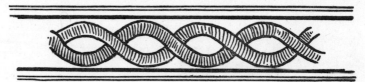

Fig. 85.
Orphrey, XII Century

Fig. 86. Narrow Orphrey

the upper members, the triangle, was usually filled with a scroll and leaf design in embroidery, see Figs. 100 and 101.

In the eleventh century the ornamentation of the alb was reduced to an oblong panel embroidered in gold or colours. This was placed low down the centre front and back, and measured approximately 12 to 18 inches long by 6 or 8 inches wide; pieces to match,

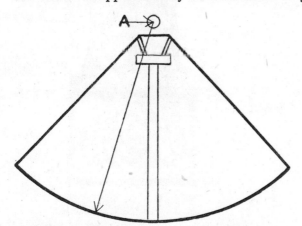

Fig. 87. Chasuble with Tau Cross Effect

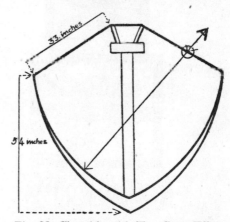

Fig. 88. Chasuble with Tau Cross Effect

about 2 inches wide, but with the design on a smaller scale, surround the sleeves at the wrists in accordance with the antique fashion as shown in Fig. 6. Later, about the

[1] For more details of this orphrey see *Roman Liturgical Vestments* by Raymond James, 1934
[2] The Y orphrey on the chasuble has often been supposed to be derived from the pallium proper to archbishops, and in consequence to have been worn only by them. Father Braun has shown definitely that this derivation is inaccurate.

middle of the thirteenth century, these sleeve apparels were reduced to a square or oblong of 2 or 3 inches.   These ornaments were sewn on, so that they could be easily removed when the alb was washed.   All other vestments (except the amice) were decorated with *orphreys* embroidered with a rich gold design, and sometimes set with precious stones.   The name is derived from the Latin *auri-frigium*, meaning gold embroidery, an art in which the Phrygians were expert craftsmen.

From the twelfth to the fourteenth century was the great period of English Church embroidery.

XIII CENTURY

From the thirteenth century onwards many brasses furnish us with designs for embroidery.   Fig. 89 is an example from the end of a thirteenth-century stole, com-

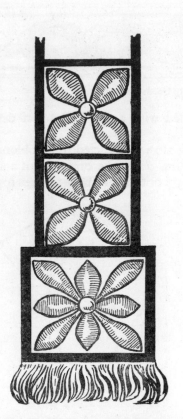
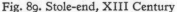

Fig. 89. Stole-end, XIII Century

Fig. 90. Stole-end, XIII Century

posed of white or coloured silk, with a dark tone edging.   The embroidered design is in gold, with the centre of each set with a pearl or jewel.   The handsome stole-end shown in Fig. 90 is of the late thirteenth century.   It is suggested that its fabric and colouring should be as follows: The band might be of white silk edged with red (shown black) silk or velvet, set inside with a line of raised gold or a cord: the trellis and the outline of the red cross motif also in raised gold.   Sometimes the base was wider than the band, as in Fig. 89, and often the band curved out to the width of the base as

seen in Fig. 90.   This might have a foundation of cloth of gold with the decoration in red, outlined with gold braid and finished with a fringe of gold bullion.

Fig. 91. Embroidery on Amice, XIV Century

A portion of embroidery on an amice from a brass dated 1320 is given in Fig. 91.   It appears to be composed of a dark-coloured velvet or silk, with trellis-work of gold enclosing quatrefoils of silver having petals of gold, the centres set with five pearls or jewels.

Fig. 92 shows an apparel which ornaments an amice.   It is taken from a brass of a priest dated 1337.   The five-petalled motif is probably worked in coloured silks, and is contained in circles of raised gold, which continue the whole length of the cloth of gold

Fig. 92. Apparel on Amice, XIV Century

Fig. 93. Apparel on Amice, XIV Century

ground.   The leaf motifs in the spandrels are treated in like manner, but possibly in a different colour.

Fig. 93 is a portion, one of a series, of a design on the band of an amice, taken from a brass dated 1370.   Each of these portions is about 3½ inches square.   The original

Fig. 94. Embroidery, see Fig. 115

would probably be of white or coloured silk, with the design embroidered in gold thread, and perhaps a pearl set in the middle of the central motif.

Pieces of brocade were sometimes used for apparels on an alb, if we may judge rightly from fourteenth- and fifteenth-century brasses.   Fig. 14 is a portion of one having a ground of cloth of gold, with a pattern of coloured velvet or silk woven upon it   The section of a stole, Fig. 94, comes from one of the same period, woven or embroidered in some colour on a gold, silver, or white foundation, edged with gold, and terminating with a gold or silk fringe.

Other apparels and orphreys are to be seen in Fig. 66, Plates VIII, XV, XVI.

Craftsmen

One may ask who were the craftsmen responsible for the creation and design of these marvellous ecclesiastical embroideries of English workmanship, known far and wide as 'Opus Anglicanum'—i.e. needlework in silk, wool, thread, etc., and 'Opus Phrygium,' which, of course, is gold work. The answer is that most abbeys contained within themselves craftsmen and artisans for every species of manufacture which necessities demanded. These workers consisted of weavers, tailors, tanners, cobblers, carpenters, smiths, master-masons, and embroiderers, both male and female.[1] Their reputation was extensive, and even reached Rome, so we are told.

Matthew Paris relates that, in 1246, Pope Innocent IV (1243–54) so greatly admired the handsome gold fringe on the vestments of some visiting English ecclesiastics, that he sent to all the Cistercian abbots in England for some choice gold fringe 'as though they could get them for nothing': for they had to buy them from the London merchants at their own price.

Liturgical use of Colour in the Roman Rite

During the first eight centuries of Christianity there was no special assignment of colours to the various seasons of the ecclesiastical year. By the time of Pope Innocent III (1198–1216), however, the Roman use in this matter had become fairly well defined: it was adopted in this country in the large cathedrals, but has only become standardized during the nineteenth century through the decay of other usages.[2]

According to Innocent III, who is said to have formulated them before his elevation to the papacy in 1198, the rules about colour are as follows:

> White [he says] is used on high festivals, such as Christmas and Easter, for feasts of confessors and virgins and the conversion of St. Paul; as also at consecrations of bishops and dedications of churches.
>
> Red is for apostles and martyrs, and also for Whitsuntide. It may be used on the Feast of the Exaltation or Finding of the Cross, but it is better to use white.
>
> Black is worn during Advent, Lent, days of affliction, and for the departed.
>
> Green [he states] remains for week-days which are not festivals.
>
> Violet. There is a dispute about the colours for Innocents' Day: some use black, some red. We now use violet, as on *Laetare* Sunday.

Abbots of the Order of St. Benedict, says St. Jerome (*ob.* 420), wore violet up to modern times (fifth century), when they adopted black. In ancient times virgins of recluse life wore violet veils.

In art angels are normally represented robed in white, though their wings are frequently coloured, commonly (as with seraphim) red: when accompanying our Lord during His Passion, or urging men to amendment of life, however, they wear violet.

---

[1] 'With the Cistercian Order, several communities of females were associated, but I must beg to decline all further notice of these ladies than merely to observe that the rules by which they bound themselves were analogous to those of the brotherhood, and as well observed.' So writes Thomas Alcock Beck in his *Annales Furnesienses*.

The three mitres and pair of sandals, presented to Pope Adrian IV (1154–9)—an Englishman born Nicholas Breakspear—by Robert, Abbot of St. Albans, had been embroidered in a wonderful manner by Christiana, Prioress of Markgate.

[2] For a more comprehensive study of this subject see *English Liturgical Colours*, by Sir William Hope and Mr. E. G. Cuthbert Atchley (S.P.C.K.)

PLATE IV *(see page 63)*
Maximian, Bishop of Ravenna, VI Century, in Contemporary Vestments

THE CHASUBLE (*continued from page* 64)

X CENTURY

Up to this time chasubles were made of plain materials, and in the West they continued to be made of fine cloth or subserica, in which threads of gold or silver were sometimes woven into the woof. On occasion rich silk was used, but this was only obtained at fabulous prices, an ounce of raw silk costing as much as six gold bezants.[1] However, the Venetians now began commercial relations with Constantinople, and for centuries continued to be the channel for supplying western Europe with silken fabrics of all kinds at more reasonable prices.

Anglo-Saxon prelates profited by this commercial undertaking, and among many was one whose fame survives to-day—St. Swithun. He was a monk who was consecrated Bishop of Winchester in 852, and became Chief Councillor to King Æthelwulf. He died in 862. The saint's relics were translated to Winchester, 15th July 964, amidst torrents of rain.[2] When the new church, the nucleus of the great cathedral, was dedicated on 8th April 1093, the saint's bones, which were found under the altar of the old church, were transferred to it. They eventually found their permanent resting-place in one of those feretra or chests which may be seen surmounting the platform in the chancel.

The *Benedictional of St. Æthelwold*, owned by his Grace the Duke of Devonshire, contains (folio 36) a miniature of St. Swithun, of which Fig. 95 is a drawing, but it must be realized that this is the work of one hundred years later than the period of the saint, having been written and illuminated between the years 963 and 984.

Vestments changed scarcely, if at all, in the meantime; therefore this miniature without doubt is a reliable authority for those in use during St. Swithun's episcopate, and also during the tenth century. He is shown vested in full pontificals. The alb is unseen except at the neck and wrists, which are banded with two rows of gold: the dalmatic, stole with curious terminals, maniple, and shoes are all of cloth of gold; and the chasuble above them is of light blue soft silk, which produces very small and numerous folds. Down the centre is a pillar-orphrey, and the neck-band is of gold tissue. The saint is giving the benediction with his right hand, and is holding in the left a Book of the Gospels, with gold covers ornamented with studs of gold. He is grey-haired and tonsured.

At the end of the manuscript, on the verso of the penultimate leaf, there is a bishop, presumably intended for St. Æthelwold himself, giving the benediction to a congregation who are all bare-headed except the women. He is auburn-haired, tonsured, and clean-shaven, and is vested in a white alb orphreyed with gold, and in stole, long maniple, and shoes, all of cloth of gold. The chasuble is of a rich deep blue, the high-lights denoting a soft substantially woven silk, possibly samit; it has a 2½-inch gold edging all round it, but no pillar-orphrey. The bishop stands in front of a golden altar draped with a purple altar-cloth, on which a gold chalice and paten are placed. The congregation, whether of clergy or lay-folk, is merely outlined in bistre, a brown pigment prepared from soot. The men's heads are uncovered, and the women wear veils in the Anglo-Saxon manner.

[1] 'Constantinople was first called Byzantium: which name is still preserved by the imperial money called besants.' Quoted from William of Malmesbury, 1087. This gold coin varies in value between the sovereign and half sovereign, or less. A silver bezant was worth from a shilling to a florin.
[2] This legend is 'purely wanton fabrication,' states Professor Skeat.

Fig. 95. St. Swithun in Contemporary Vestments, X Century

X CENTURY

Perhaps the most wonderful chasuble or royal mantle extant is that of St. Stephen, the first Christian king of Hungary (977–1038), who was so successful in bringing about the conversion of his subjects, that Pope Sylvester II (999–1003) conferred upon him the hereditary title of 'Apostolic King.' This chasuble is of the usual shape, of dark-coloured silk, and covered with a series of saints and kings: these are embroidered in gold, and separated by elaborately designed borders arranged in three rows parallel with the circumference. On the breast is an oval medallion of God the Father, and below it another medallion enclosing God the Son.

Several illustrations of this work of supreme eleventh-century art are to be found in the more comprehensive books on vestments.

Among other chasubles in existence are those preserved (at any rate until recently) in Augsburg Cathedral. Two belonged to the bishop, St. Ulric (*ob.* 973), and two to St. Willigis, Archbishop of Mainz (*ob.* 1011). They are made of a Byzantine glossy satin-like silk in monochromes, yellow (orange-yellow-saffron), green, red, and violet respectively, and woven in such a manner that the linear designs appear as though they were engraved. No golden ornamentation is used upon them.

Of slightly later date is an original chasuble at Brixen in the Tyrol. This is composed of purple silk, having a design of large golden eagles displayed; these measure at least 18 to 20 inches in length, and are arranged in rows between circular motifs in gold. These, and the eagles, are closely woven with an elaborate pattern very like thick embroidery and of Byzantine manufacture.

XI CENTURY

There was a deviation in the shape of the chasuble as seen in illustrations of the eleventh century. This has already been alluded to on page 64 as having been in use in the Eastern Church since the sixth century. Chasubles, short and pointed in front, and very long and wide behind, are characteristic in the West during the eleventh century.

As an example, there is a fresco in the lower Church of St. Clement [1] at Rome which depicts this saint vested in the Greek manner.

Fig. 96 is taken from this fresco, and we see St. Clement, Bishop of Rome (89–97), standing on the left of the altar, and wearing a chasuble of this shape. Fig. 97 is a diagram of it. It is in two parts: taking the back first, this is less than a semicircle, as shown by the broken line. The radius from the centre A is 4 feet $6\frac{1}{2}$ inches. The front is a separate piece, the top points of which are fixed to the back at the points B and D, $7\frac{1}{2}$ inches from the centre A. The two upper sides of the front are sewn to the back along BC and DE. The dimensions of the diagram are suitable for a bishop six feet in height. The material of which this vestment was made would probably be silk of some rich colour, embroidered or woven with a diaper pattern of gold quatrefoils. It is bordered at the neck with gold tissue, and has a narrow band of gold ornamental braid all round the hem. The lining would be of silk in a light tone of colour.[2] It is surmounted by the pallium, and the maniple to match is borne in the left hand in the regular manner. Under the chasuble is the dalmatic, having wide sleeves and a border at the hem; and under it is the alb, the sleeves at the wrists being the only part visible.

[1] St. Clement was martyred by being cast into the Black Sea with an anchor fastened round his neck.
[2] Archbishop Stigand, represented in the Bayeux tapestry, wears a chasuble of this shape.

Fig. 96. St. Clement at the Altar, XI Century

On the altar stand a chalice, a paten, and an open missal; on the pages of the last are abbreviated inscriptions: 'Dominus vobiscum' and 'Pax Domini sit semper vobiscum.'[1]

The altar is covered with a cloth, and over it is another narrow one, known as a corporal, with a border of embroidery at the bottom edge.

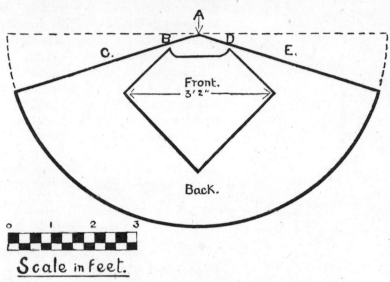

Fig. 97. Diagram of Chasuble, XI Century

The Corona

Above the altar hangs a 'corona lucis,' a circular band of precious metal having seven oil lamps attached to it.[2] These appear to be shaped like the bowl of a modern wine-glass, with a top in which there was a small hole for the wick to pass through to the oil.

There were also in use flat open-work bronze or silver discs with a series of circular holes all round the circumference, in which lamps of metal or glass could be placed. One of these lamp-holders can be seen in the British Museum Catalogue of Early Christian Antiquities, No. 529.

Fig. 98 shows a corona, the imperial Byzantine crown, dating the sixth century. It is a gold band about 3 or 4 inches wide, sloping outward to its upper edge, and decorated with jewels and rows of pearls on its top and bottom rims. From the fifth century it was the custom for sovereigns and other royal personages, prompted by pious motives, to dedicate their crowns to the Church as votive offerings. These were usually hung by three

Fig. 98. Imperial Byzantine Crown, VI Century

[1] 'The Lord be with you,' and 'The Peace of the Lord be always with you.'
[2] Some items in this illustration, especially the altar and corona, show curious inaccuracies in perspective: a common occurrence in early mosaics and frescoes.

golden chains above or near the altar. Plain or jewelled ornaments were sometimes added to the lower rim. Often other chains, or a single one, supported a lamp,
from the centre of which hung a jewelled
cross. Again, seven [1] lamps or candles set in
holders or on prickets were fixed to the corona,
as shown in Fig. 99. This drawing is made to
enable the reader to visualize the actual appearance of a corona when properly hung.

Eventually another arrangement of lamps or
candles was in use simultaneously; the corona
was attached to the top of an upright stand, thus
transforming it into a candelabrum, in some
cases 10 feet over all in height.

On the left of Fig. 96 hangs one of seven
sanctuary lamps, which were suspended only
in the neighbourhood of the altar.

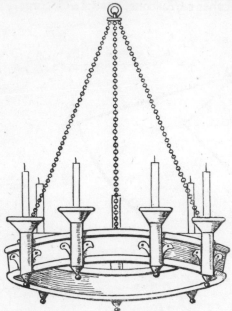

Fig. 99. The Corona

XII CENTURY

Figs. 100 and 101 are drawings of a chasuble,
traditionally assigned to Thomas à Becket, and
kept in the Treasury of Sens Cathedral. If
genuine it dates between 1162 and 1170. It is
made of a dull purple rich silk, and is shaped on the plan of the ancient paenula, except
that the lower edge comes to a point back and front. This is produced by taking two centres
(A, A), see Fig. 100, from which to describe the necessary arcs on opposite sides of the

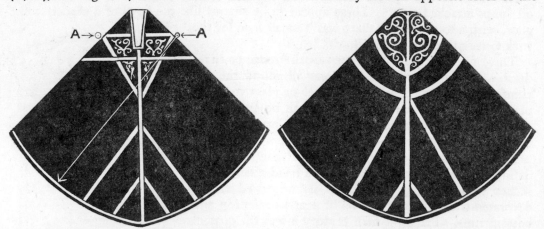

Fig. 100. Chasuble of St. Thomas à Becket, Front　　　Fig. 101. Chasuble of St. Thomas, Back

vertical. The shape of the neck-opening is well defined. The seam in front is masked
by a narrow band, an orphrey, a woven gold braid, with oblique bands meeting it. The
triangle on the breast encloses a scroll design, and seraphim in gold embroidery. The

[1] It is probable that the use of *seven* lights is inspired by the description in Rev. iv. 5: 'There were seven
lamps of fire burning before the throne, which are the seven Spirits of God.'

two horizontal bands at the top surmount the shoulders and descend in curves at the back, where the top one displays scrolls embroidered in gold. The gold passements on this chasuble are not the original ones. The lining was probably of a contrasting colour in silk, or possibly gold tissue. As an example of a chasuble of this and following centuries it furnishes us with an excellent authentic pattern. Also it is particularly valuable as there are monuments and illustrations executed between the tenth and eleventh centuries which represent the chasuble cut to hang short in front and long behind. This may be the result of the personal taste of the wearer influenced by the East, or the 'artistic licence' on the part of the artist.

The form shown in Figs. 71 and 100 was that worn in the Western Church for two centuries.

In the Eastern Church it became the custom about this time for the patriarchal phelonion to be decorated with a number of Greek crosses, usually in black and white. These crosses were placed so close together all over the surface that it suggests the pattern is woven in the material, see Fig. 40. On account of the large number of crosses decorating the patriarchal phelonion this vestment became known, after the eleventh century, as the POLYSTAURION.

Another very beautiful chasuble is still preserved (we hope) in the Treasury of the Church of St. Sernin, otherwise St. Saturninus, at Toulouse. It is said to have been worn by St. Dominic (b. 1170, d. 1221), and would accordingly date at the end of the twelfth

Fig. 102. Byzantine Brocade, XII Century

century. Some authorities suggest the middle of the thirteenth. The brocade, Fig. 102, is most probably of Byzantine manufacture. The design suggests its origin; the ground-work is of a rich red-purple silk, with mauvish-pink trails and leaves meandering between alternating rows of pelicans 'in their piety' applied symbolically to Christ,[1] and peacocks with spreading tails, in a raised weaving of jade-green silk and gold thread. Spiritually these peacocks represent immortality, suggested by the annual moulting and renewal of the tail feathers: or possibly because, owing to its extreme toughness, the flesh was believed to be incorruptible. On each wing of the pelicans is woven in gold the word 'Helice,' and between the peacocks appears 'Paone' in Byzantine lettering. 'Helice' evidently stands for Pelice.[2] On the perpendicular gold band, or pillar, about $3\frac{1}{2}$ inches wide, which covers the front seam, are saints with nimbi worked

---

[1] The pelican is the symbol applied to the Saviour, who so readily gave His own blood for mankind.
[2] The H is a mistake in the weaving. It should be a P. Possibly the craftsman got mixed between the Roman H and the Greek Π.

in coloured silks and set in architectural niches or tabernacles of gold. Around the neck-opening there is a scroll pattern in gold on a ground of alternating squares of soft shades of red and green.

This chasuble is altogether a wonderful example of rare beauty, such as reached its high-water mark in the thirteenth century.

There is an interesting point in the making of this chasuble. When worn these rows of birds are out of equipoise. They should be horizontal, not perpendicular. This is accounted for by the fabric not being properly cut and seamed up.

If the fabric of which a chasuble is to be made has a large pattern, and especially if it

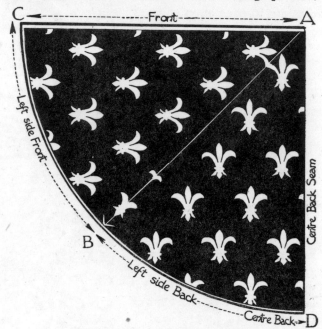

Fig. 103. Half Diagram of Chasuble

has an up-and-down design, the cutting out often presents a considerable problem, since the pattern must appear upright on the two fronts and backs when worn.

It is worth while taking some trouble to achieve this with a semicircular garment, such as a mantle, chasuble, or cope: Fig. 103 and its description have been worked out with this end in view. This half-diagram shows a semicircular cloak of deep blue silk, woven with a diaper design of fourteenth-century silver fleurs-de-lys. The whole garment is made up of four sectors (two being shown), of which A is the centre and AB the radius: AC will be the centre front, and AD the centre back, of the completed garment. The seams are at AB and AD: and at AC also in the case of a chasuble. When a double-width material is used that has no up-and-down design, this method of construction is not necessary.

Two variations in the shape of the chasuble are given in diagrams Figs. 87 and 88. The former is an amplification of the original or 'Gothic' form, wherein the centre of the circumference, indicated at A, is beyond the limits of the material. This construction produces heavier folds, which would require expert management in wear.

PLATE V (*see page* 99)

Pope Paschal II, XI Century, in Contemporary Vestments

Fig. 88 is a much modified chasuble that can be more easily manipulated. It is made in two pieces joined on the shoulders: the straight sides are much shorter than in Fig. 87. The curved portions come to a slight point in the middle—the end of the central join—their centres being on the shoulders at A. The back is a few inches longer than the front. Of the two Fig. 87 ranks first in point of beauty when correctly worn.

XIII CENTURY

There are some chasubles in the Victoria and Albert Museum, and nine of them are illustrated in the catalogue; which gives (Plate III) the front and back view of a chasuble dated the second half of the thirteenth century, which is probably the earliest of a new

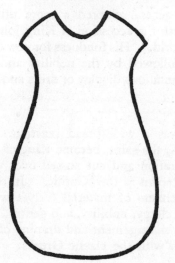

Fig. 104.
Fiddle-back Chasuble, VIII Century, Front

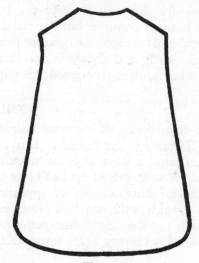

Fig. 105.
Fiddle-back Chasuble, Back View

shape, and shown in diagram, Figs. 104 and 105. One does not presume to doubt the authorities, but it appears to be slightly antedated. However, that is a trivial detail.

The ugly shape, which came about possibly at this time, is caused by the obvious inconvenience of the amplitude of the original form of the chasuble known in modern times as the Gothic.

A DISSERTATION ON THE WEARING OF CLOTHES

During the classic Greek period nearly every one, men as well as women, when they wore any clothes at all, wore them to perfection. The Romans inherited this art to a great extent, as so many statues of patricians wearing the toga exemplify. The Romans of the empire who wore the garments which eventually became the immediate ancestors of vestments were not in the least troubled how to manipulate them. This is not surprising when one realizes that generation after generation had had to deal with voluminous attire; it came naturally to them, so they wore it with ease and grace. Towards the end of the period a certain slackness became apparent.

The Anglo-Saxons were not far behind the Romans in wearing draperies gracefully,

E

as proved by the early illuminated MSS., see Fig. 95.   The costume of the masses it is said 'was modest and well fitted to the proportions of their bodies.'

At the end of the eleventh century long robes and mantles came again into fashion: these necessitated slow and dignified movements.   Short steps were essential if the wearer wished to avoid catching the legs and feet in the drapery.   The crusades, especially the first, were the means of introducing the prevailing extravagant modes of Byzantium; and these, in due course, transformed the fashions of the nobility in the West.

Ample garments are difficult to carry gracefully and require a complete education— habits learnt from infancy.

XII CENTURY

During the Angevin dynasty the nobility and gentry adopted a more utilitarian attitude towards costume, but the mode changed with the accession of King John, who was considered 'the most extravagant prince in the world.'   His fondness for new clothes, and these costly and showy in the extreme, was followed by the nobility and upper classes, who indulged throughout his reign in an ostentatious display of dress and jewels.

XIII CENTURY

After these years of sartorial vulgarity there was a widespread reaction.   When Henry III came to the throne in 1216 and Louis IX, the saint, became King of France ten years later, a wave of acute simplicity in decoration and cut passed over western Europe.   A new style of art had come into being, known as the 'Gothic.'   In costume sober magnificence, dignity of appearance, and richness of material (velvet was first used in 1250) was the standard most desired by the clergy, nobility, and gentry.

In the art of wearing clothes *perfectly*, and in the management and draping of ample garments, this century bears favourable comparison with the classic Greeks.

NEW MATERIALS

Attention is called here to the fact that until after the middle of the thirteenth century a certain rich silken fabric was entirely unknown.

This was invented by the silk-weavers of Italy and is first mentioned in 1277.   At this time it is said to have had the name 'villosa,' because its surface was covered with very fine short hairs forming a thick close-set pile.

Later it was known as velvet, and made chiefly at Lucca and Genoa.   Obviously this material, dyed in various colours, was very expensive, and only the wealthy could afford it; Henry III was the first English sovereign to wear it, but it did not come into more general use until the fifteenth century.   Existing specimens of earlier date are extremely rare.

As time went on the craft of weaving velvet greatly developed, and different kinds were invented.

Velvet upon velvet was of two piles, that of the pattern being raised above the pile of the background.   The richest and most costly was of three piles, and was stiffish in texture.

Some velvets had either a gold pattern on a velvet ground or a velvet pattern on a gold ground.   Shot velvets were in use as early as 1353.

A flourishing manufacture of brocade was carried on in Lucca in the thirteenth century, and later in Venice. Brocade is a fabric, generally of silk, with a pattern woven in it, often of a different colour from the groundwork, and frequently raised. It is in this last characteristic that it differs from damask.

Camacas brocade, manufactured chiefly in Cyprus, had a raised design in gold, usually of birds, a very favourite subject.

In the fourteenth and fifteenth centuries this type of fabric was much used by the courtiers and the wealthy, including the potentates of the Church.

Baudekyn was a rich fabric of Byzantine manufacture used for making some of the best vestments. It was woven with a silk weft and a gold woof, which had the effect of a coloured silk shot with gold or silver.

XIV CENTURY

The tenor of the foregoing dissertation leads us to conjecture that the alteration which took place in the shape of the chasuble, as shown in diagram, Figs. 104 and 105, must have been in the fourteenth century, and was caused without doubt by the impatience and awkwardness of certain ungainly clerics who could not be bothered to control their vestments carefully. In the exercise of their official duties—duties performed by their predecessors for centuries past—their arms became impeded by the ampleness of their chasubles. Therefore the sides were cut away, thus converting the semicircular form into the unlovely shape (irreverently likened to a gigantic flannel chest-protector) shown in these two diagrams. This chasuble most certainly deserves the name contemptuously flung at it of 'the Fiddle-Back.'

That the 'Gothic' was still worn simultaneously with the newer-shaped chasuble is proved by many illustrations, illuminated MSS., and brasses of the clergy of this and the following centuries.

Fig. 106 is a case in point. The drawing is made from a brass at North Mimms (Herts.) to the memory of a vicar (a bishop's deputy), Thomas de Horton by name, 1360, who is represented in full mass vestments, such as were usual at the beginning of the fourteenth century and onwards. These consist of an apparelled alb, and over it a dark silk (or *perhaps* velvet) chasuble cut like the diagram, Fig. 77, and lined with a lighter colour edged with gold or silk embroidery. The Y-shaped orphrey passes over the shoulders and down the front; its line, described on page 71, must not be mistaken for the pallium. Apparels are seen at the wrists and hem of the alb, and on the maniple hanging from the left wrist. The tonsure, an amice, and slightly pointed shoes of the period are worn: the stole-ends appear below the chasuble. This ecclesiastic or (more probably) his church,[1] must have been very wealthy and popular to possess vestments so rich and so elaborately ornamented. The apparels and orphreys are all of one design (it should be noted) but on different scales, and on this account they are definitely embroidered, not woven bands sewn on. One motif is inset.

Plate XIII represents William of Wykeham, Bishop of Winchester (1367–1404): it is based upon the effigy on the tomb in his chantry in the nave of the cathedral. He is in full vestments, the chasuble being exceptionally rich in material: it is of crimson

[1] It was a frequent medieval practice for grateful or conscience-stricken parishioners to present rich 'suits' of vestments to their parish churches.

Fig. 106. A Vicar in full Vestments, XIV Century

silk, either embroidered or woven in a trellis-work pattern enclosing a Gothic leaf motif in gold. The border is of gold set with alternate rubies and emeralds, and embellished with numerous pearls. The tunicle is visible beneath the dalmatic, and both these vestments are of the same deep peacock-blue silk edged with gold fringe. The white garment reaching to the ground is, of course, the alb: the shoes are gold. The stole and maniple are entirely of gold, as are also the tassels at the ends of the sudarium attached to the crozier. Part of the bishop's mitre ('Mitra Pretiosa,' see Figs. 136 and 137) is preserved at New College, Oxford. It is more or less like that on the effigy, which is entirely of gold; the jewels are rubies, and crockets of gold outline the gable. For the crozier see p. 126 and Plate XII.

For greater effect Plate XIII shows the bishop wearing white gloves with a monial on the back.

In the days to come the chasuble reached an even higher standard of beauty and splendour.

6. THE AMICE

SUPERHUMERALE

III CENTURY B.C.

AN accessory to men's dress appeared in republican Rome some time in the third century B.C. It was a linen cloth or kerchief, oblong (about 12 by 30 inches) in shape, and was worn by people in general during the following centuries. An example is shown around the neck of Fig. 107.

A.D. I CENTURY

During the period of imperial Rome the dimensions of this white linen kerchief increased to about 42 inches long by 22 or 24 inches wide. It was put round the neck

Fig. 107.
The Superhumerale, Pre-Christian

Fig. 108. The Superhumerale as worn

and shoulders in the manner of a small shawl. Two cords attached to the two ends of one of the long sides were passed under the opposite arms, crossed at the back, and tied in front, giving the folds as shown in Fig. 108. The outer garment was put on over this, its neck taking the broken line seen in the drawing. This kerchief was worn for comfort, and to fill in the space above the wide neck-opening of the body-garment; and as the centuries progressed it often served as an ornament as well.

84

VIII CENTURY

By the year 755, according to *Ordo Romanus*, this neck cloth had been adopted by the clergy, and so became a vestment of ritual, known as the AMICE. This word derives from the Latin *amictus*, used by classical writers for any outer garment: here we seem to have another case of a garment shrunk to a mere fraction of its original self. (Compare stole, p. 88, and pallium, p. 23.)

X CENTURY

The first reference to the use of this vestment *in England*, is in an Anglo-Saxon pontifical of the tenth century, wherein it is called a SUPERHUMERALE.

XI CENTURY

Occasionally, however, one sees in late eleventh-century effigies an amice which is simply a plain disc of white linen, with a round hole in the middle for the head to pass

Fig. 109. Amice
worn on Head, XII Century

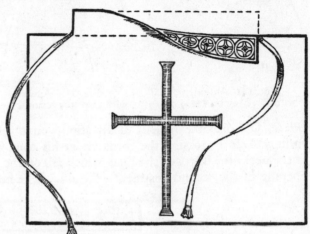

Fig. 110. Diagram of Amice, XII Century

through. It falls in folds around the neck over the chasuble, Fig. 128. This type is somewhat rare: the amice in its original form, as shown diagramatically in Fig. 110, is that most generally used.

XII CENTURY

Honorius of Autun (*c.* 1130) is the first person to mention the amice being placed on the head.

It still retained its shape as a rectangular piece of linen; but it was slightly increased in size to 22 by 27 inches, and was tied on the head in a similar manner to the head-covering worn by a modern nurse. At first, when worn in this way, it had no additions, it was just plain white linen; but later a band of the same material was added, which gave place eventually to a fillet of gold as shown in Fig. 109.

Not until about the middle of the twelfth century were any additions made to the rectangular amice. Then to the band of gold, plain, or figured tissue, placed along the shorter edge, was added a large gold cross at the back. Fig. 110 shows an amice of this period laid out flat; it measures 30 inches long by 24 wide: the band, known as the apparel or PARURA, is 26 inches long by 3½ wide, and is turned down at the right-hand corner to show the embroidery mounted on the other side.

The amice was the first vestment to be put on. When the priest veiled, he kissed the cross; then taking the amice by the two cords he placed it on his head with a prayer:

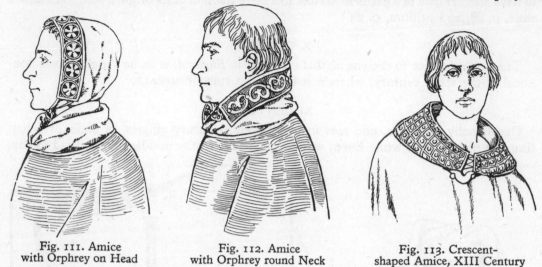

Fig. 111. Amice
with Orphrey on Head

Fig. 112. Amice
with Orphrey round Neck

Fig. 113. Crescent-
shaped Amice, XIII Century

'Place, O Lord, the helmet of salvation [1] on my head to the defeat of diabolical invasions' before crossing the cords under his chin, and again crossing them in the nape of the neck: the edges of the linen which fell on the shoulders were covered by the neck-opening of the second vestment—the alb. The head so covered is shown in Fig. 111.

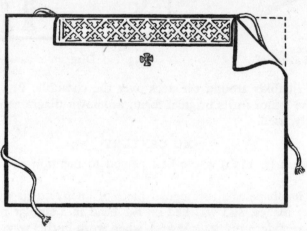

Fig. 114. Diagram of Amice

The priest, having arranged his other vestments in correct order, then unveiled; he undid the cords, and pushed the linen back off his head on to his shoulders. The apparel, or decorated band, being tied in front, surrounded the neck like a collar, Fig. 112.

[1] From Ephesians vi. 17.

The cords were then passed under the arms, crossed at the back, and tied in front over the alb.

Although the priest's head was normally bare when officiating, there seems some evidence at a later date that the amice was sometimes worn on the head—perhaps as a protection from draughts or when out of doors in processions. 'The peple pull the priest from the aulter, and the amice from his head,' states Sir Thomas More in 1537.

XIII CENTURY

Quite an unusual amice is shown in Fig. 113. It is seen on a statue in the south porch of Chartres Cathedral, and dates the thirteenth or fourteenth century. It differs very considerably in shape from the preceding examples, and is very like a hood. In cut it resembles a crescent, except that the points are cut off square where it is laced up the front. The material could be embroidered silk, a brocade or figured cloth of gold, bordered with a different stuff or ornamented in various ways.

XIV AND XV CENTURIES

During these two centuries one notices in illustrations that sometimes the bottom corners of the apparel meet, leaving the top open. Referring to only one example, St. Laurence, Plate XV, has his amice fastened in this way. Although no clue is forthcoming as to how it was tied, one may surmise that the same method of passing the cords under the arms was adopted.

In spite of Fig. 113, however, the amice worn generally in the West is that shown in Figs. 111 and 112.

Fig. 115.
The Rev. John West

The shape and dimensions of the amice were slightly altered during the course of the following centuries down to modern times. It took the form generally as shown in Fig. 114. The measurements are 36 by 24 inches: the apparel, shown folded forward over the amice, is 26 by 4 inches, and usually sewn along part of the longer edge. To put it on, the apparel is folded forward on to the linen, and the whole vestment put on the head. The Rev. John West, a chaplain (1415), Fig. 115, is wearing the amice, stole, and maniple in the approved manner of this period.

To-day the amice is tied in the same way, and so arranged passes under the alb as formerly, and in the Roman Church it is worn during mass by all orders of the clergy.

7. THE STOLE

SUDARIUM, ORARIUM, STOLA

I CENTURY B.C.

LATIN authors allude to an article for personal use which is the equivalent of the hand-kerchief of the Renaissance period and of modern times, under the name SUDARIUM: this was for the purpose of wiping the face and nose. It was a rectangular piece of fine white linen, often embroidered with silk and gold. It came into fashion about the first century B.C., but did not become very general as an item of the toilet until the period of imperial Rome.

A.D. I CENTURY

The sudarium was carried round the neck, in the hand, or in the sinus (fold) of the obsolescent toga, which served as a pocket.   ORARIUM is another name for the same article, and one more widely used, especially in the East: it was a larger napkin than those in earlier use, and it is thought that the name is derived from an Egyptian word meaning 'a linen cloth for wiping the face,' and we may take it that the nose did not escape the same treatment. The carrying of this napkin or sudarium was a common occurrence among all classes of Romans, and was also part of the usual dress of servants and slaves. They all wore it at first round the neck, and later over the left shoulder or forearm; and it was used by servants for cleaning vessels and culinary utensils of various kinds.

III CENTURY

Oraria are first mentioned as being given by the Emperor Aurelian (270–5) to the audiences at the public games, so that they could show their approval of the competitors by waving them instead of the ends of their togas, as had been the previous custom.

From the time when the Eucharist was first celebrated, a servant or some other person would be at hand to wipe the vessels which had contained the bread and wine, using an orarium of linen for the purpose.

IV CENTURY

We look to the Eastern Church of the fourth century for the liturgical use of the orarium. It is mentioned in the canons of the Council of Laodicea, 363; and Isidore of Pelusium (*ob.* 449) states that it was worn by the servants, i.e. deacons.

It was still in the nature of a large linen napkin, and must have been about the size of a towel, say 50 by 30 inches; it was carried by being draped over the left shoulder.

This napkin was first folded lengthways—contabulatum—probably about the end of the fourth century, or even later. By this means its width was reduced to about 4 or 3 inches, and its length increased to anything from 8 to 10 feet, its edges being parallel throughout. Through this change into a long band, it lost its utility, but retained its significance, and so became an ornament distinctive of the deacon. When deprived of its use it was replaced by a smaller napkin, known as the MAPPULA, and used chiefly by subdeacons.

The orarium of the Eastern Church was adopted for the use of deacons of the Churches of the West some time later; it served the same purpose and was worn in the same manner.

By the fourth century the two names sudarium and orarium became henceforth synonymous, as stated by St. Ambrose, and confirmed by St. Augustine of Hippo and St. Jerome, both in the following century.

VII CENTURY

A more detailed description of the manner in which the orarium was worn by a deacon is prescribed by the Fourth Council of Braga, 675; at a later date, under Pope Innocent III (1198–1216), the same order was in vogue, and has continued until our own time.

The orarium is placed on the left shoulder only, so that—the right arm being free—the deacon may be able to perform his duties more conveniently; it is tied with a cord under the right arm with the ends hanging loose. His orarium must be plain, not ornamented with colours or gold. A priest when celebrating the eucharist is to wear his orarium round the neck over both shoulders, forming the cross-over on the breast; it is confined by the waist-girdle at the sides, with the ends descending the sides of the front to about the level of the ankles. When the orarium end was finished off with fringe the bottom of the fringe terminated at the same level. This arrangement is shown in Fig. 115, a priest who lived at a later date (fifteenth century) whose STOLE is adjusted in the orthodox fashion.

An archbishop and a bishop wear the stole round the neck and hanging free, thereby showing the pectoral cross.

As the symbol of his universal jurisdiction, the pope wears the stole always and everywhere.

VIII CENTURY

It was in the eighth century that the ends of the stole were finished off with a 2- or 3-inch fringe. Sometimes it was decorated with crosses, although this ornamentation was not much used in England; but it was more generally embroidered, as may be seen in several of the illustrations.

By the end of this century the serving work of deacons had so increased that it was largely taken over by subdeacons, who in consequence used a napkin like the early orarium of the deacons: this was now called a MANUTERGIUM.

IX CENTURY

During the ninth century the Latin word *stola*, from the Greek *stole*, began to be used for what had hitherto been called an orarium. In classic Greek this word denotes a long flowing robe, such as was worn by the scribes in the Gospels: the corresponding Latin word meant much the same kind of garment, only it was worn by women. How such a garment came to be identified with an ornament so widely different from it in appearance has been a matter of much speculation, and there is no generally accepted explanation. It would seem that the narrow stole represents merely the hem or border of the robe from which it takes its name.

By the Council of Mayence (813) priests are to wear their stoles at all times, even when travelling, in order to distinguish them and their vocation.

X CENTURY

As an example of the high standard attained in Anglo-Saxon needlecraft we may take the celebrated stole and maniple, over a thousand years old, found in the coffin of St. Cuthbert at Durham in 1827.

St. Cuthbert died in 687, and was buried at Lindisfarne, which was plundered by the Danes in 793, the remains of the saint being carried from one insecure refuge to another, until after seven years' wandering the monks found a secure resting place at Chester-le-Street.

When Ealdhun, Bishop of Chester-le-Street (995–1018), built his new cathedral on the rock at Durham, St. Cuthbert's remains were brought into it; and at the end of the eleventh century were still found incorrupt. When the coffin was again opened, in 1827, the stole and maniple were discovered almost intact: hence they are generally known as St. Cuthbert's.[1]

As a matter of fact, however, Ælflæd, second wife of Edward the Elder (899–925) ordered, before 916, that they should be worked as a gift to St. Frithestan, Bishop of Winchester (909–31), who, on his resignation, is said to have returned the vestments to the queen's stepson, Athelstan.

It is known that when King Athelstan was at Chester-le-Street in 934 he gave rich gifts to St. Cuthbert's shrine, including a stole and maniple: these are almost certainly those found in the coffin as mentioned above, where they were no doubt placed when the saint's relics were moved to Durham during Ealdhun's episcopate.

Parts of the stole have disintegrated; but when entire it must have been 10 feet long, and the maniple 2 feet 8¼ inches: the breadth of both was 2⅜ inches. The embroidery was done on linen with coloured silks on a gold ground. The design of the stole represents numerous figures of prophets (and on the maniple, saints) in their natural colouring standing in panels on rainbow-tinted clouds. The backgrounds of gold are patterned with abbreviated names and conventional foliage, suggesting the Carlovingian acanthus. The fringed ends of both contain the words: 'For the pious Bishop Frithestan' and 'Ælflæd caused [this] to be made.' Lady Alford in her book on *Needlework*, 1886, rightly describes these vestments as 'in the most perfect style of Anglo-Saxon design,' and the stitchery of the silk embroidery as 'an exquisite example of the needle-craftsman's art.'

A full description, by G. Baldwin Brown and Mrs. Archibald Christie, will be found in the *Burlington Magazine*, vol. 23, April to September, 1913.

It was in this century that tassels and little bells and the like, as well as fringes, began to ornament the ends of stoles, at any rate when worn by archbishops, bishops, and priests. A further development, between the ninth and thirteenth, was to add to the

---

[1] The chronology of St. Cuthbert's life presents many difficulties, and the only fixed points seem to be his entry into the monastery of Melrose in 651, his migration to Lindisfarne in 664, his election as bishop late in 684, followed by his consecration on 26th March 685, and his death on 20th March 687. See F. M. Stenton, *Anglo-Saxon England* (Oxford University Press, 1943).

ends rectangular or triangular pieces of embroidery with a motif matching those on the stole, or else one of quite a different design.

As for fringes, from the thirteenth century onwards, they became very beautiful, the gold or silk strands being knotted or woven in patterns or criss-cross—'fretty-wise.'

During the Middle Ages stoles were worn at almost all liturgical functions, and nearly always crosses were incorporated in the pattern.

When the stole is used by a priest of the Byzantine rite it is called an EPITRACHELION.

This is a silken band about 5 inches wide, worn round the neck and shoulders, fastened in front, with its two long ends almost reaching the ankles. A priest wears it when fulfilling his liturgical duties.

The resemblance of this orthodox vestment to the pallium or orarium is so close as to make them easily mistaken one for the other in illustrations and descriptions.

XII CENTURY

From about the middle of the twelfth century the deacon wore his stole unfastened at the hip, the two ends being looped so that they hung down under the dalmatic on the left side.

As an epilogue it should be stated that the stole has changed very little, if at all except, of course, in its decoration—from this period to the present day.

The stole is shown worn by the following figures: 95, X century; 106, XIV century; 115, XV century. Figs. 89 and 90 are stole-ends of the XIII century, and Plate XIII of the XIV century.

8. THE MANIPLE

Mappa. Mappula

THE origin of the MANIPLE is much the same as that of the stole and amice. In fact, they were in the nature of handkerchiefs. The smaller version of the sudarium was a plain linen napkin called a MAPPA, and used by the Greeks and Romans at meals for wiping the mouth and hands. Serving-men in pairs were in attendance on the guests, both before and after dinner; one of them served each guest with a basin of scented water, and the other wiped the guests' hands with a mappa which he carried on his left forearm.

A.D. I CENTURY

The mappa, or the more diminutive mappula, was also an official badge of the Roman empire and a magisterial decoration of importance. It was used by the consul or praetor to give the sign for the chariots to start their race in the circus: when not in use it was wrapped round the left forearm.

From the earliest times of the Church's history such a piece of white linen was used by the priest to wipe the communion vessels and hands at celebrations: it was attached to the left wrist.

IV CENTURY

The first reference to the mappa is in the order of Sylvester, Bishop of Rome (314–35), that the left hand of a deacon should be covered with a cloth of linen warp.

At first it was hung over the wrist from the centre, but later (by the ninth century) it was carried between the first finger and the thumb, as shown in Fig. 96.

VI CENTURY

By this time, if not earlier, the maniple had definitely become a Church vestment. For details of St. Cuthbert's maniple (so called) see p. 90.

VIII CENTURY

The first definite occurrence in writing, however—'quinque manipuli'—of the maniple as a sacred vestment, and the distinctive badge with which a subdeacon was invested at ordination, is in a deed of 781.

An ancient missal of this century gives the following prayer when putting on the maniple, no doubt indicating its symbolical meaning: 'Encircle me, O Lord, with goodness, and ordain my life spotless.'

IX CENTURY

The dedicatory illumination of Charles the Bald's Bible, a work dated 844–51, shows the canons of St. Martin of Tours carrying maniples over their *right*-hand fingers: they are formed of folded white stuff, linen or silk, ornamented with red-and-gold fringe at each end.

St. Swithun (852–62), Fig. 95, carries his maniple over his left wrist, which is partly covered by his chasuble. Its conversion from a rectangle to a strip (contabulatum) evidently took place during this century. Its measurements would be anything from 2 to 4 feet long and from 3 to 4 inches in width. It was usually made of white linen. St. Swithun's is of cloth of gold with terminals of a particular shape characteristic of this period. At this time the maniple, like other vestments, was made of richer materials, and more elaborately decorated, as the wealth and power of the Church increased.

X CENTURY

Like other vestments, again, the maniple was embellished with embroidery and even with peculiar appendages. Fringe had been used to finish off the ends of the stole from early times (see Plate IV), likewise the maniple, and beads of gold or colour were sometimes incorporated in it. Jewels were also introduced. There were also some maniples which had 'sonorous metallic appendages' (i.e. bells). In 915 Bishop Riculfus of Helena in his will left to his successors six maniples embroidered with gold, one of which had little bells suspended from it.

XI CENTURY

St. Clement, in the eleventh-century fresco, Fig. 96, carries a maniple of the usual simple kind. It is decorated with two crosses only, and finished off with an ordinary silk fringe. He holds it between the thumb and first finger, as usual, of his left hand. By this time the maniple evidently lost its utility value, and became a mere ornament, with purely ceremonial significance: except in the case of the subdeacon, whose maniple, it would appear, continued to be a napkin for practical use.

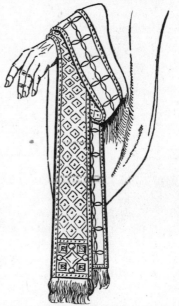

XII AND XIII CENTURIES

Maniples of this period are usually widened at their extremities, forming two slightly pronounced flaps resembling the stole ends.

Statues in Chartres Cathedral, south porch, show many embroidered maniples. The ends are ornamented with precious stones or fringes, and are attached to the sleeve of the undergarment at the left wrist, Fig. 116. It should be noticed that both sides are embroidered, but with a different pattern; the maniple is about 6 feet long and 4 inches wide.

The Eastern Church does not use the maniple, though deacons used to wear something similar attached to the girdle, to represent the napkin with which our Lord girded himself when washing the apostles' feet. The EPIMANIKION is quite different, a bishop's embroidered over-sleeves.

Fig. 116. Maniple,
XII and XIII Centuries

Note on Confusion of Terms

It is a fruitful source of confusion to the student that works of reference use so many different terms, according to the period or country or use, for the same garment: at the same time the confusion is increased by the use of the same name for a number of different garments. Thus the French word *fanon* means (1) a maniple when the eucharistic bread is wrapped in it, (2) a napkin when it covers the chalice, (3) a head-covering worn by the pope under the tiara, and (4) the infulae hanging from the episcopal mitre.

In the next section, 'Mitre,' p. 105, the same thing will be found to be true of the word 'infula' which, besides its application to the mitre, is used for the narrow bands for tying the cope, and as a synonym for the casula or planeta. Similarly the sudarium may be a napkin for wiping the vessels, a stole or maniple, or an ornament for a crozier. Other cases of diverse meanings for the same word are chimere, p. 177, and mappula, a small napkin.

The maniple is shown in the following figures: 95, X century; 96, Plate V, XI century; 204, XIII century; 106, Plate XIII, XIV century; Plate XVI, XV century. Patterns of embroidery on the stole and maniple are seen in Figs. 89 and 90, all of which are of the XIV century.

British Museum. By kind permission of the Governors
PLATE VI (*see page* 101)
Pope Gregory the Great enthroned, XI Century

9. THE MITRE

THE origin of the mitre is to be found in a head-covering of pre-Christian times.

Headgear in a decorative sense was almost entirely absent among the Greeks. For utility there were two head-coverings—the PILOS and the PETASOS.

The pilos, Fig. 117, was a skull-cap made of felt, fur, or skin, and worn by the lower

Fig. 117. Greek wearing the Pilos   Fig. 118. Greek Fez   Fig. 119. Conical Pilos

classes, such as soldiers, sailors, and artisans. A variation of this cap was conical in shape, with a top like the small end of an egg, resembling a truncated cone or fez, Fig. 118.

A band (Greek *mitra*) sometimes surrounded it to make it fit more tightly to the head, Fig. 119. Another type of the same cap had below the band a piece of the edge left, free all round, so forming a brim often of considerable width. It was not always circular,

Fig. 120. The Petasos   Fig. 121. Greek Headband

but cut into various shapes convenient for practical purposes, so that parts of it could be turned up, down, or sideways as protection against sun or rain.

To guard against wind a strap or cord could be fastened under the chin or at the nape of the neck. A hat of this kind was known as the petasos, Fig. 120.

F

95

The Greek word *mitra* was utilized for any kind of band, including one for binding the head worn by both men, Fig. 121, and women: to it lappets were sometimes attached which hung in front of the ears, possibly a fashion borrowed from the Egyptians. Cicero (106–43 B.C.) speaks indignantly of the *mitella*, a headband or fillet, being worn by effeminate young men. It was a very usual head ornament of men of Greece; Cicero was referring to the decadent young Neapolitan nobles.

According to Herodotus (c. 480–425 B.C.) the Persians wore a soft felt fez-shaped pilos, which was known as a tiara. The name was also applied to a kind of turban.

Amongst the people of Phrygia there was in use a head-covering similar in many features to the fez-shaped pilos. Fig 122 shows this headgear drawn from a Greek vase. The top was often rounded, and when worn, flopped forward. The whole cap was cut so that the part which came over the forehead might be turned back to form a front

Fig. 122. Phrygian Cap

Fig. 123. Greco-Roman Phrygian Cap

brim or coronet effect, the corners on each side being tucked under the lappets. Fig. 117 shows a later development of this cap: it is made of stiffened linen, and retains the early conical shape, like an extinguisher, as seen in Fig. 119.

The Romans of the republic adopted both the ordinary pilos, Fig. 117, which they named the PILEUS, or pileum, and the conical pilos, Fig. 119. These were worn by the commonalty of both sexes except slaves; who, however, when they had attained their enfranchisement, were permitted to wear this headgear to cover their shaven heads. On that account the pilos has been known as the 'Cap of Liberty.'

Before many centuries had passed both the Phrygian headgear and the Roman pileus had developed into a head-covering known as the Phrygian cap (Phrygius pileus), later called a phrygium or FRIGIUM. 'But,' says Isidore of Seville, writing at a later period, 'the pileus of men is, in fact, the mitre [i.e. turban] of the women.'

To describe this Phrygian headgear the word 'tiara' is frequently used: and in Greco-Roman art it generally decorates the head of Paris. and of Mithras when performing the rite of the Taurobolium, in which case the mitra was of gold.

Fig. 123 is a reproduction of a seventeenth-century engraving, which is most probably a Renaissance attempt after the antique, incorporating different Roman ideas: the crescent is a favourite adjunct to portraits of the third century A.D. The shape of this headgear is like that shown in Fig. 122, but the wearer has bound his lappets round the head on top of the 'coronet,' and knotted them in the nape of the neck over the back of the cap.

VIII CENTURY

By the eighth century the pope, being normally an elderly man, whose head needed protection from the cold, had adopted for outdoor processions and other purposes the common headgear of men of the period, which in his case was made of linen and served as a conical or skull cap.

The first mention of this headgear as worn by a pope is to be found in *Liber Pontificalis*, wherein it is stated that Pope Constantine (708–15) wore this kind of cap when making his solemn entry into Constantinople. It is there described as a CAMELAUCUM, i.e. imperial crown, because though really a frigium it is being worn by the pope.

The camelaucum dates back to classic Greek times, and was originally a skull-shaped cap or pilos, Fig. 117, made of camel-hair cloth with ear coverings like the flanges one sees attached to the helmets of the warriors by whom this cap was often worn.

During the period of imperial Rome royal and noble persons wore a similar cap, but of richer material and encircled with a golden band set with gems and jewels.

The early eastern emperors dispensed with the cap, but retained the jewelled circlet or fillet (mitra), see Fig. 124. At a later period this gold circlet became wider, from 2 to 3 or more inches, and was set with gems, jewels, and pearls, with ropes of pearls hanging on each side over the ears.[1]

A silver coin of Offa, King of Mercia (757–96), distinctly shows him wearing a camelaucum, consisting of a band of gold with a row of pearls top and bottom.

There is a story, resting on insufficient foundation, that Pope Sylvester (314–35), while refusing the imperial crown, accepted at the Emperor Constantine's hands a white frigium for use in processions. However that may be, by the eighth century the frigium was made of white linen, and though usually shaped like an extinguisher, later reverted to the hemispherical pilos 'like a helmet,' see Fig. 117, Plate V.

The example set by the pope was followed by the higher clergy, but English bishops, at any rate, did not as yet wear this headgear in church. Though Egbert, Archbishop of York (734–66), is said to be so represented on one of his coins, such illustrations as are available are too indistinct for the shape of the frigium, whether pointed or round, to be distinguished, and, in fact, no English archbishop or bishop is represented in either illuminations or effigies wearing any sort of head-covering until later. By the time of the Norman Conquest, however, prelates frequently wore their headgear, not only out of doors but also in their palaces, and especially when giving audiences or at councils. The uncovered head was, nevertheless, still the rule during divine service.

IX AND X CENTURIES

Up to the end of the ninth century there is no mention of the word 'mitre' to describe the papal or episcopal head-covering.

In the tenth century this head-covering was definitely almost a skull-cap of white,

[1] See Byzantine section, *Costume and Fashion*, vol. i.

surrounded by a *band* of gold—in fact, a combination of frigium and mitra; though there is an alternative theory that this round cap developed out of the *amictus*, the term used for that portion of the toga which could be pulled up over the head to form a covering.[1] It was during the tenth century that the pope first wore a distinctive headdress by virtue of his office.

Referring back to the Greek headband or fillet known as the 'mitra,' Fig. 121, it is interesting to compare this with that worn by the ecclesiastic in Fig. 124. This is taken from a miniature in an illuminated MS. of the tenth century, and one notices that these headbands have much in common despite the passing of 1,400 years. The band in Fig. 124 is also comparable with the royal crown known as the camelaucum; it is of gold, and between the groups of three bars of repoussé work are set alternately square jewels, and circular jewels in filigree mounts, with a ridge or rim top and bottom. It is

Fig. 124. The Camelaucum

Fig. 125. Bishop Henry of Blois

suggested that this gold circlet may indicate the cleric's royal rank, and is not an ecclesiastical head adornment in the strict sense.

Another interesting fact in connection with this headband or camelaucum is that when the small son of King Æthelwulf, Prince Alfred (*b.* 849, *d.* 899), was sent to Rome in 853 to receive the pontifical blessing, he so deeply impressed Pope Leo IV (847–55) that he adopted the young prince as his godson, and also hallowed him as a king [2] by placing the circlet of consecrated gold on his head, thus making him the first and only English king ever crowned in Rome. This Alfred afterwards became renowned as 'the Great.'

On one of his coins, Henry of Blois, brother of King Stephen and Bishop of Winchester (1129–71), wears by right of his royal descent (being grandson of King William) a camelaucum. This crown is set with ornaments very similar to fleurs-de-lys: the projection on the left presumably indicates a cap worn underneath as shown in Fig. 125. He is without mitre, but as a bishop carries a crozier.

[1] See *Costume and Fashion*, vol. i, p. 64, Fig. 32 at C. See ibid., p. 35, second line from top.
[2] Alfred did not succeed to the crown until 871.

XI CENTURY

It was during this century that the first reliable statement appears concerning the mitre, which now became a recognized item of episcopal insignia, though it was not common in England until well into the twelfth century. It is written that when Eberhard, Archbishop of Trèves (Trier) was in Rome in 1049, Pope Leo IX (1049–54) placed on his head, in St. Peter's on Passion Sunday, the Roman mitre. The pope's words in the charter are: 'We adorn your head with a Roman mitre, which both you and your successors will always use in the ecclesiastical office after the Roman manner, in order to remind you that you are a disciple of the Roman see.'

Even as late as the eleventh century the pope occasionally wore a frigium. Fig. 126 gives a diagram of one dating at this time. It is made in two pieces of white linen, stiffened with parchment, and joined up the sides. Its curved sides meet at a point, and the height varied, sometimes being the same as the half circumference of the band. The centres of the curves are shown at A and B.

Another shape in use at the same time, or even a little earlier, is the hemispherical form without the point at the top as shown in Fig. 127.

Plate V is a portion of a contemporary miniature in the Ekkehard MS. in Corpus

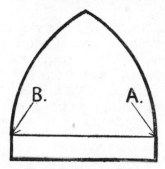

Fig. 126. Pointed Pilos

Fig. 127. Mitra Clericalis

Christi College, Cambridge. This miniature depicts Pope Paschal II (1099–1118) and the Emperor Henry V (1106–25), whose figure is here omitted. He forced the pope to crown him; and in the original miniature he carries a sceptre surmounted by a dove and wears a cap very like the pope's. Paschal is in the act of handing to the emperor an iron orb with a golden cross rising from it.

For this ceremony the pope dons his mitre, which at the period is a white, round linen cap: this is mounted on a stiffened foundation, encircled with a gold band, and finishes at the apex with a cone of gold. Unfortunately one cannot see if there are long ends hanging behind the encircling headband. Possibly there are, as these now become an appendage to the headband. Their source may be traced back to the 'mitra' worn by the Greek in Fig. 121. The Romans used them for ornament on festive and solemn occasions, and the name by which they were known was INFULA.

This kind of hemispherical mitre, Plate V, was worn by some bishops contemporaneously with the later triangular type, as is proved by Matthew Paris's drawings in his *Historia Maior*, finished in 1233. In this work, at least one (folio 52) shows a bishop in a mitre like Paschal's, standing between two bishops in mitres like Fig. 135.

Whether these personages in round caps are bishops is not quite certain, as this shaped cap was also worn by ordinary persons.

But to return to the pontifical vestments worn by Paschal II. These begin with an alb, which is as usual of white linen, but in this particular instance, Plate V, the shading in the MS. is painted a light green. The dalmatic is straw-colour, perhaps brocaded, but more likely embroidered with a design in light brown: it has a border round the sleeves of a soft tone of green, and a heavy border at the hem of the same shade embroidered with gold. Over this is worn a chasuble of scarlet and light green Byzantine shot-silk: the pallium and maniple are of white, having the crosses embroidered in pale blue-green silk. In his left hand His Holiness holds an ebony staff surmounted by a golden globe.

Henry was crowned by Pope Paschal II at Rome; but later when the pontiff resented the imperial claim to all rights over the Church, including that of episcopal investiture,[1] he and some of his court were thrust into prison and only released on Paschal's acceptance of the emperor's terms.

POPE AND EMPEROR

At this point it will be a convenience to the reader to summarize the various stages by which the popes reached the zenith of their power about 1200, of which struggle the quarrels between pope and emperor form but the concluding stage. For though in theory each supplied the complement of the other's power, in actual fact their spheres of action overlapped, and this in the case of two strong characters led to hostility.

Four stages of this rise to power can be distinguished, which, in order of their attainment, are as follows:

(1) Acknowledgment of the supremacy of the Roman See over other bishops, first claimed about the end of the fifth century, and complete by the eleventh.

(2) Freedom to elect popes. In the seventh century the Greek emperor's sanction was required, and in the tenth the Holy Roman Emperor appointed popes. Ultimately (1059), under Nicholas II, the right of election was vested in the cardinals.

(3) Papal investiture. As late as the ninth century the emperor's sanction was required for grants of the pallium, and the fight against lay investiture was not won until the Concordat of Worms, 1122.

(4) Claim of the pope to secular as well as spiritual authority. Gregory VII (1076) claimed the deposing power: his successors claimed—and often exercised—suzerainty over European states, including the right to appoint and depose sovereigns. This power reached its height under Innocent III.

Of these various stages we have already seen numerous examples, which may usefully be collected here. Thus the barbarian (and heretic) Emperor Theodoric besought John I (523-6) to crown him while on a visit to Constantinople; and the Empress Theodora,

---

[1] Overtures for peace were discussed between the Emperor Henry V and Pope Callistus II (1119-24). 'The pope for his part consented that episcopal installations could be graced by the imperial presence so long as there was no influence either by intimidation or simony. As a further gesture to temporal power it was agreed that the monarch should ceremoniously touch a bishop elect with his sceptre to show that the temporalities of the see were subject to him.'

PLATE VII (*see page* 103)

Archbishop, XII Century, in Contemporary Vestments

who had opposed the election of Pope Silverius (536–7) 'enjoyed the stimulating tonic of triumph' when her nominee Virgilius succeeded him.   Then the grant of a pallium to the Archbishop of Arles was delayed (543) for the emperor's confirmation, as was the enthronement of Benedict II (684).   The crowning of Charlemagne by Leo III (800) made it possible for later popes to claim the right to dispose of the crown as they pleased, but his successors still claimed (814) to elect the pope.

The crowning by Leo IV (853) of the young Alfred—afterwards 'the Great'—in Rome is not a case in point: but Henry II (1002–24) and his immediate successors did not assume the title of emperor till crowned at Rome.   Yet, being anxious to claim the empire of the German crown in perpetuity, they began to call themselves 'King of the Romans' before coronation, a habit which lasted until the pope gave Maximilian I (1459–1519) permission to use 'Emperor Elect.'

Hildebrand's (Gregory VII) views, and the dramatic penance of Henry IV at Canossa (1077) are detailed below: this emperor was excommunicated by Paschal II (1099–1118), and died unabsolved.   His son, Henry V, forced (1106) Paschal to crown him.   The concordat between Henry and Callistus II on investiture took place at this time, but there were further quarrels over supremacy between Adrian IV and Frederick I (Barbarossa) in 1154, continued in England between Henry II and Becket (1164): and Celestine III (1191), having crowned Henry VI, went so far as to kick the crown from the kneeling emperor's head to show his right of emperor-making and unmaking.

The papacy reached the pinnacle of temporal power under Innocent III (1198–1216), who excommunicated John of England, and put his kingdom under an interdict (1208). So the disputes continued: Gregory IX excommunicated Frederick II, who subsequently quarrelled with Innocent IV: yet so late as 1265 Charles I received the Kingdom of the Two Sicilies from Clement IV by Bull.

Of this autocracy the sole begetter was Hildebrand (1073–85), so the following extracts from his *Dictatus* are given:

'The pope is the only person whose feet are kissed by all princes': he may 'depose emperors and absolve subjects from allegiance to an unjust ruler': he warns the kings of France and England and the youthful German ruler, Henry IV, to forsake their evil ways: the papal power is obviously superior to the kingly, for it is responsible for it.

The matter soon came to a head, the pope was invited to come to Augsburg to consult with the princes whether Henry should be reinstated after his excommunication.   Henry anticipated the arrival of the pope.   He hastened across the Alps in mid-winter, and appeared as a humble suppliant before the Castle of Canossa, where the pope was.   For three days the German king appeared before the closed door, barefoot, in the coarse garments of a pilgrim, and penitent, and even then Gregory was induced only by the expostulations of his influential companions to admit the humiliated ruler.

XI CENTURY (*continued*)

During this century popes began the practice of granting the right to wear a mitre to those bishops to whom they desired to show special favour: Leo IX (1049–54) is said to have been the first to do this.

For a good example of a pope in eleventh-century vestments see Plate VI.   This, taken from an illumination in the Cotton MSS., was previously thought to represent

St. Dunstan, but it has since been discovered to be St. Gregory the Great (590–604) enthroned.[1]

The mitre is similar to that of Pope Paschal, Plate V, except for the addition of fanons or infulae: and is backed by a nimbus. It appears to be made of white linen stiffened with three rows of stitchery.

A dove, whose head is also framed in a nimbus, is no doubt symbolical of the Holy Spirit and whispers into His Holiness's ear.

The remaining vestments consist of the alb and stole, and over them the tunicle or dalmatic, open for a short distance up the sides, and ornamented with a band of embroidery in gold and colours. Above this is the chasuble, which appears to be arranged

Fig. 128.
Mitre, XII Century

Fig. 129.
Mitre embroidered with Cross, XII Century

in folds around the neck: though this may perhaps be the cowl of his monkish habit worn underneath. Surmounting the chasuble is the pallium.

It should be noted that these vestments differ but slightly in some details from those worn by an archbishop. The triangle on the left breast suggests an emblem, perhaps of the Trinity.

In the lower part of the picture an archbishop (left) and a monk in a white habit (right) are kissing the papal feet, and below a monk in a black habit is in an attitude of adoration. If these are intended for a Cistercian and a Dominican the artist has been guilty of an anachronism.

XII CENTURY

By the beginning of the twelfth century the round cap began to dip at the top, being bound by a band of gold passing from front to back, and attached to the surrounding

[1] Dr. Eric Millar, late keeper of manuscripts, British Museum, states in his book, *Early English Manuscripts*, that the central figure in the illumination represents St. Gregory, since he is shown inspired by the Holy Ghost in the form of the dove flying down and whispering in his ear. This is a well-known type for iconography of this pope.

As reproduced Plate VI has been cut in order to show the enlargement of the figures; but the complete illumination shows the ascription 'DUNSTA – – – NIAR – – – CHIE – – – PISCOPI' behind the top of the throne in what appears to be fifteenth-century calligraphy. This has created some doubt as to the identity of the saint. That it is St. Gregory seems certain on account of the presence of the dove and the mitre, and also from the fact that he is receiving the veneration of an archbishop and a monk in the manner always accorded to a pope. St. Dunstan was an archbishop, not a pope. It has recently been suggested that the archbishop kneeling on St. Gregory's right represents St. Dunstan, and the black-robed figure in the foreground is that of St. Benedict.

gold headband which ended in infulae behind. In consequence of this addition the cap bulged on either side of the band; and although slightly stiffened was probably padded to preserve its shape, Fig. 128. A similar mitre is shown in Fig. 129 taken from an illuminated MS. dating between 1121 and 1148. It is rather more lofty than the preceding, and, in addition, has four black crosses embroidered on it.

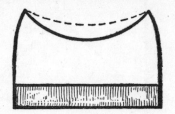

Fig. 130.
Diagram of Mitre, XII Century

A diagram of a mitre of the early years of the twelfth century is given in Fig. 130: a pronounced dip at the top has produced two points or horns at the sides. It is made of two pieces of white linen, shaped as shown, and sewn up the sides, possibly stiffened with parchment: the resulting gap on the crown of the head must have been filled in by a gore of material, as shown by the broken line. A mitre of this shape—a low cap with a crescent-shaped depression over the forehead—was, according to episcopal seals, worn by certain archbishops of Canterbury from about 1093 to 1190.

Fig. 131.
Mitre with Horn Effect, XII Century

St. Nicholas on the Norman font in Winchester Cathedral wears a similar mitre.

The enamelled figure of Bishop Ulger on his tomb in the Church of St. Maurice, Angers, presents a more pronounced horn-like effect, an amalgamation of the two types, Figs. 128 and 130. It is worn over a linen coif as seen in Fig. 131.

The mitre, Fig. 130, developed into the shape of a triangle at a later date, as seen in Fig. 132, and was at first worn as previously, that is, with the points over the ears: but by the middle of the century we find in illustrations that the position of the points is changed. The mitre was then placed on the head so that the points came centrally front and back.

An excerpt from an author of this time referring to the mitre reads: *Mitra ex bysso facta*, a cap made of linen.

Plate VII comes from an illuminated Bible by 'Magister Hugo' of St. Edmundsbury, in Corpus Christi College, Cambridge, and dates 1121–48. It is of an archbishop, said to be St. Dunstan (925–88). Here we see the mitre worn as just described. It is of white linen, with a band of gold encircling the brow, and a vertical band of the same front and back. His dalmatic is of a reddish-mauve silk, with a border of red dotted with pearls, so it would seem, and edged with gold. Notice that the openings at the sides do not extend to the hips as usual, and are rounded at the top—a fashionable touch introduced by the emperors of the West—and fringed at the lower edge. The

Fig. 132. First Triangular Mitre, XIII Century

chasuble is of a soft blue silk, without ornament and unlined. The dark green amice is spotted with white or pearls, the orphreys round the wrists of the alb match the amice, and the shoes are red.

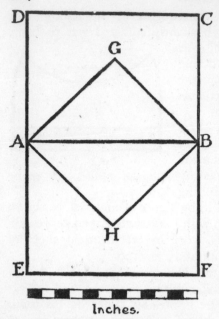

Inches.

Fig. 133. Diagram of Triangular Mitre

From this century must be dated the assumption of the mitre by all bishops of the western Church, with or without sanction: and the custom of investing the bishop with the mitre at his coronation.

With reference to the pope it is stated by Innocent III in the late twelfth century that the papal mitre was made partly of gold, and approximated to its later shape. The mitre, however, was only worn by His Holiness when pontificating like any other bishop.

When crowning the emperor the pope placed on his head first the *mitra clericalis*, probably a close-fitting cap like Fig. 127, and then above this the imperial crown. So states the fourteenth Roman *Ordo* (1241), and Charles IV (1347–78) is shown on a seal wearing both.

This seems to be the place for a note on ecclesiastical heraldry connected with the mitre. For this purpose the mitres of archbishops and bishops are the same; but only the Bishop of Durham is entitled to place a ducal coronet round his mitre when it surmounts the armorial bearings of the see. In pre-Reformation times the mitres of such abbots as were entitled to them usually lacked the infulae.

XIII CENTURY

A front view of an early thirteenth-century mitre is given in Fig. 132; this would be cut as in Fig. 133, but is not so high at the front BF and back AE as that shown in Fig. 134. The 'horns' now come at the front and back instead of at the sides: though mitres with them on either side continued to be worn far into the century.

A drawing by Matthew Paris (*Historia Maior*, folio 182) shows the Bishop of Paris earnestly ministering to the sick Louis IX, Fig. 135. The bishop wears a mitre as described above; there are many more drawings in the same work which prove how popular this type was.

The mitre when worn by the pope was made like that of any other bishop, of cloth of gold, and like it became more and more richly ornamented as the centuries progressed.

St. Donatus, Bishop of Arezzo in Tuscany (*ob.* 361), famous for his miracles, is represented in an early fourteenth-century illuminated psalter, which once belonged to Queen Mary I, and is

Fig. 134. The Mitre more fully Developed

PLATE VIII (*see page* 105)

St. Donatus restoring the Chalice. XIII-Century Contemporary Vestments

now in the British Museum, MSS. Royal 2, B.W. 1. The illumination, folio 259*b*, is reproduced in Plate VIII, in which the bishop is seen standing on the left. He wears vestments of this period, which include a white linen mitre made a little higher than that seen in diagram, Fig. 132, and banded with gold round the base and up the front. His other vestments consist of an apparelled alb, chasuble, and amice, and dalmatic or tunicle; he holds a crozier in his left hand. These garments appear to be almost free from ornamentation, which may be accounted for by the simplicity of the draughtsmanship.

Fig. 135. The Bishop of Paris, XIII Century

Houseling Cloth

The most prominent subject in this illumination is the method of administering the Holy Sacrament, and the use of the houseling cloth.[1] Although this is not considered a vestment in the true sense the insertion of the following particulars is justified, as so few references to it are to be met with.

The houseling cloth [2] was of fair white linen, sometimes of 'irys cloth,' about 3 or 4 feet wide, and of various lengths, according to the number of communicants. It was held in front of them by two clerics, obviously to catch any fragments which might fall from the host, in front of and close up under the chins of the communicants, who are kneeling with clasped hands.

In Plate IX the officiating priest in alb is shown standing on the same side, presenting a circular wafer with his right hand and holding the paten in his left. In the illumination, Plate VIII, it would seem that the four communicants have received the host, and are waiting for the chalice,[3] to which an accident has occurred, for St. Donatus is represented in the act of miraculously restoring the chalice of crystal which had been dashed to pieces by the pagans.

Soon after the beginning of the thirteenth century the mitre evolved into the familiar shape as shown in Fig. 134. It is formed from a piece of material shaped as a rectangle, about 12 by 18½ inches (not allowing for seams), Fig. 133, and folded in half at AB; the two seams are sewn together at EAD and FBC. It was again folded into a diamond, AGBH—a square set diamond-wise. The complete mitre was put on the head with the seams front and back: over these a band of gold embroidery, often jewelled, was set to mask the seam. Another band of the same material surrounded the head, and the two ends hung behind for about 18 inches or so, these being usually undecorated except for a fringe at the end. These ends are the infulae, sometimes referred to as FANONS.

The finished article is shown in Fig. 134, from a statue of a bishop on the west front of Chartres Cathedral. Compared with later mitres it is of moderate height: it is probably,

---

[1] Communion is given exactly as shown in the accompanying illustrations in churches of the Latin Rite in South America and possibly in southern Europe. At least one instance, among several no doubt, is to be found in the Home Counties to-day. In this case the long edge of the houseling cloth is fastened on the altar side of the communion rails, and the bulk is brought over the top and hangs down in front of the rails. The communicants hold the opposite edge in front of them while receiving.

[2] In 1929 an instruction directs that a plate of silver gilt may replace the houseling cloth. This is held by the communicant under the chin with both hands, and passed from one to another, the priest taking it from the last person and conveying it to the first of the next set. The term still remains very much in use.

[3] The practice of communion in one kind was introduced by the Council of Constance, 1415.

as usual, of linen, but might be of cloth of gold, as expensive material was more indulged in, along with more elaborate decoration. In this case the gold band is embroidered with raised gold: up the gold band front and back are set jewels in gold mounts.

The two sides between the vertical bands and the fillet became covered with rich embroideries, with pearls and jewels as shown in Fig. 136, and even with saints in niches.

The 'precious' mitre, or 'mitra pretiosa,' worn by the archbishop, Fig. 204, is reproduced on a larger scale in Fig. 136. Its shape is a further development of that shown in Fig. 134, and consists of two triangular sections joined at the lower sides, in fact, a made-up affair, resembling a modern tea-cosy, but open at the top, which has been in more or less general use ever since.

The foundation would be of cloth of gold or silver, or coloured or white silk. The bands are of gold set with jewels and pearls, and enclose triangles embroidered with a Gothic leaf design in gold and coloured silks. As the original drawing by Matthew Paris has been cut off at the top it is not known if there was a cross at the apex: such a

Fig. 136. The Mitra Pretiosa

Fig. 137. Mitre of St. Thomas, Plate XVI

finish was usual, so it has been added to Fig. 136. There is a cross to be seen in this position in Plate XVI. Such a mitre, adorned with gold and precious stones, and worn only by high ecclesiastics, was technically known as 'precious.' Less ornate mitres were called 'golden' if made of plain cloth of gold, or 'simple' if the material was plain white silk or linen.

The more ornate mitres cost large sums. Thus in the thirteenth century John Peckham, Archbishop of Canterbury—and he a Franciscan!—paid £173 4s. 1d. for a mitre in 1288, which must have been of exceptional magnificence. A bishop of Bath and Wells (John Drokensford, 1309-29), paid £23 6s. 8d. for two mitres, and a bishop of Hereford (Adam de Orleton, 1317-27) acquired one from his predecessor which had cost £40.

XIV CENTURY

By the fourteenth century the mitre had increased in height, as is seen in the brass to the memory of Abbot Thomas Delamere (c. 1360) in St. Alban's Abbey. In character, design, and form it is much the same as the mitre shown in Fig. 136, but it is considerably higher, and consequently the sides are steeper.

XV CENTURY

A reasonable example of a fifteenth-century mitre of more satisfactory proportions is worn by St. Thomas, Plate XVI, and Fig. 137 is an enlarged drawing of it.   The foundation is of blue silk, lined with scarlet: in place of embroidery on the triangles large jewelled ornaments are set.   Smaller ornaments are mounted on the gold bands, and those at the sides have, in addition, crockets of gold placed at intervals all the way up, finishing with a cross at the top.   Crockets were to become much more used in the future, and some were of beautiful design.

William of Wykeham's mitre on his effigy is of the 'precious' variety, set with rubies and emeralds: the crockets are formed of golden spheres, see Plate XIII.

Both height and decoration became enormously exaggerated during the coming years. Already at the Renaissance the mitre had grown out of all proportion to the human body, but the climax was not reached until the seventeenth century, when the effect must have been grotesque in the extreme.

10. THE TIARA

THE head-covering known as the TIARA (see pp. 95 and 97), the papal diadem or crown apostolic, obviously has its origin in the conical cap or frigium mentioned on p. 96 and

Fig. 138. The Tiara, VIII Century

shown in diagram, Fig. 126. The word is often used in medieval writings for mitre, hood, or cowl, and for a regal crown.

VIII CENTURY A.D.

The tiara is referred to as CAMELAUCUM in the *Life of Pope Constantine* (708–15), and is later mentioned as being used at the consecration of at least one of the pontiffs who reigned during this and the succeeding centuries.

The tiara is seen in Fig. 138,[1] which, although a work of art of the thirteenth century, conforms precisely to the description of a white linen conical cap shaped like an extinguisher: in fact, between the earliest forms of the papal tiara and those of the mitre there was no difference.

IX CENTURY

Further references to the tiara are met with in the ninth century, when it appears under the name of *pileus, phrygium,* or *pileum phrygium,* and is described as a helmet-shaped cap of white linen, Fig. 126.

The diagrammatic drawings of tiaras, Figs. 126, 141, 146, 147, and 149, may appear somewhat stunted. The cause of this is, that they are laid out flat as one could do with a modern tea-cosy; the straight line at the bottom therefore represents the half circumference rather than the diameter, so that when worn the tiara appears considerably narrower and in better proportion. In Fig. 126, if the *half* circumference AB (actually 12 inches or so) is taken as a unit, the height over all is a little more than this, and the plain headband is a trifle under one-fifth of this unit in width. The centres of the segments which form the sides are indicated at the points of the arrows A and B.

Fig. 139. Coin of Pope Benedict VII, X Century

X CENTURY

Some idea of the tiara of the tenth century can be gained from Fig. 139, a drawing made from a silver coin of Pope Benedict VII (974–83), whereon he wears a tiara. The details in these early coins are difficult to decipher, but the

---

[1] Fig. 138 exhibits one of the many pitfalls that await the unwary student. The original was the work of a thirteenth-century artist: the subject is a sixth-century pontiff in a tiara of the eighth century, holding a pastoral staff of the ninth, and wearing a pallium of the tenth century.

outline is sufficiently explicit. The cap appears to be worn over a coif which covers the cheeks, but the semicircles at the sides represent the ear flaps of the cap underneath. There is a suggestion of the pallium in the V line.

It is uncertain if the band, which at this time was ornamented in various ways, was intended to represent a coronet, or was simply a band of gold set with fleurons or jewels. See Figs. 140, 141, 142, and 143.

XI CENTURY

Already at the beginning of the eleventh century this conical head-covering was encircled at the base by a narrow band of white linen; a little later the linen band gave place to one of gold. This, like that on the mitre, was finished off at the back with infulae: according to a modern authority a single coronet appears at this time instead of a gold band. There is, however, a tradition that in 514 Pope St. Hormisdas was the first to add a coronet to his frigium.

There is a tradition that the first crown to be worn by a pope was one of gold adorned with gems, a gift from Clovis the Great, king of the Franks (481–511), on the suggestion of St. Remy (Remigius), Archbishop of Rheims (461–533) and apostle of the Franks: it was one which had been presented to Clovis by the Emperor Anastasius (491–518).

Fig. 140. Pope Innocent III

According to a late twelfth-century statement the pope wore his tiara, not only at his coronation, but also on all state occasions.

XII CENTURY

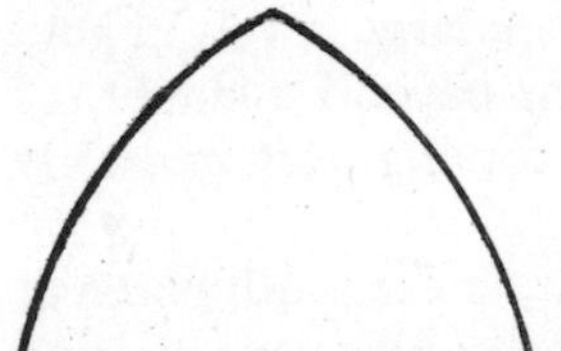

Whatever may be the truth about that, it is no easy matter to find an *illustration* of the earliest use of a single coronet. The thirteenth-century fresco, of which Fig. 140 is a drawing, shows Pope Innocent III (1198–1216)—a most punctilious personality—wearing a tiara with an engrailed ornamental headband which *might* be interpreted as a coronet. Born in 1161, Pope Innocent was before his election Cardinal Lotario di Conti. His life object was the elevation of the papal chair by the firm establishment of its temporal power. He had also written a book on the contempt of the world; and it is likely that his statement that there was no sacred character attached to the tiara, but that it was solely the symbol of sovereign power, is to be found in this work.

At the middle of this century it is definitely stated that a circlet was used to embellish the tiara. It would be of linen, or, as the custom now was, of cloth of gold. Fig. 141 shows such a circlet. Using the unit of AB in this figure

Fig. 141.
Tiara with Jewelled Head-
band, XII Century

the proportions are: the height overall is a little under six-fifths, and the centres of the arcs are at the points A, B, and the gold band set with jewels and pearls is one-fifth wide. (See Fig. 126 for comparison.)

XIII CENTURY

A tiara of a slightly different shape is shown in Fig. 142, which reverts to the description given earlier, p. 95, as that of a truncated cone with the top like the small end of an egg.

Fig. 142. St. Gregory the Great
in XIII Century Tiara

Fig. 143. Pope Innocent IV

Fig. 144.
The First Coronet on Tiara

Its ornamentation consists of the headband and a vertical band which ascends the front and back in the manner of contemporary mitres. These bands are of gold, and appear to be set with groups of large pearls: in the spaces between there are large jewels in gold mounts. The foundation of the tiara is, beyond a doubt, of cloth of gold, as this rich fabric was becoming very generally used.

The statue (1240) of Gregory the Great, in the south porch of Notre-Dame de Chartres, shows this sixth-century pope wearing a conical tiara with a jewelled band at its base: a flattened spherical ornament (fleuron) completes the top of the cone, Fig. 143. The tiara appears to be constructed of gold basket-work, most likely in metal: the horizontal ribs connect a series of vertical ones which diverge from the apex.

In Matthew Paris's (ob. 1259) drawing (folio 138b) Pope Innocent IV (1243–54) enthroned at the Council of Lyons in 1245 wears a tiara, which, although very simply drawn, appears to be identical with that in Fig. 143. The bishops wear mitres of the shape shown in Fig. 130.

Fig. 145. Pope Clement IV and Charles of Anjou

Pope Innocent, apparently Innocent IV (1243–54), is represented (looking very juvenile) in a highly decorated initial letter I in a bull granted to Furness Abbey, about 1250, Fig. 144. His tiara is of a colour (crimson) which is rather unusual; but what makes it particularly interesting is that it rises from a coronet, the earliest instance known to the author. The chasuble is of a golden-yellow coloured silk, for had it been cloth of gold metallic paint would have been used. The cross on the chest can scarcely be a pillar-orphrey: it is in all probability a pallium, although it is not shown continuing over the shoulders.

Fig. 146. Tiara with a more ornate Single Coronet

In an illumination (folio 294) in Queen Mary's early fourteenth-century psalter, a pope is shown wearing a tiara with a single coronet, similar to Fig. 144.

There was an interesting mural painting[1] in the tower of the town of Pernes, near Avignon, which existed until the Franco-Prussian War: Fig. 145 is a drawing of it made from a nineteenth-century reproduction. It depicts Pope Clement IV (1265–8) presenting, by papal bull, the crown of the Two Sicilies to Charles, Count of Anjou and Provence, 26th February 1265. The pontiff wears a gold tiara, cross-barred with gold, and a red band ornamented with roundels, which most likely are intended for jewels, or perhaps they are gold motifs called 'fleurons.' This band, however, cannot be termed a coronet, but represents no doubt a return to an earlier custom. His Holiness is dressed in a red under-robe, of which the hem and the wrist bands are visible; over this is seen the alb, then a red chasuble surmounted by the pallium embroidered front and back with six black crosses. In the left hand he bears the double keys of St. Peter, and on the left arm is a maniple in its earlier form—that of a small napkin. The sandals are red, with a white cross on each. The cathedra would be of ebony or porphyry.

King Charles Elect was the fourth son of Louis VIII of France. He conquered Naples and Sicily, and became king in 1266. The French were so hated by the Sicilians that a general massacre, known as the 'Sicilian Vespers,' took place in 1282. The king died in 1285.

Charles wears a cotte, the thirteenth-century term for a tunic with close sleeves, of blue diapered with golden fleurs-de-lys, and a gold collar and simple crown. His hairdressing is most characteristic of this century: even the clergy adopted the style.

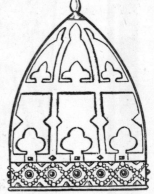

Fig. 147. Tiara with Two Coronets, XIII Century

During the middle of the century an undoubted coronet appears, and a tiara ornamented with a coronet very like that of a modern earl (but without the strawberry leaves) is shown in Fig. 146. Using the unit given on pp. 109–10 the height of the tiara is just under six-fifths of the half circumference; the width of the circlet is one-fifth, and the diameters of the six semicircles which support the balls are another one-fifth.

[1] In spite of the primitive style of this painting, thanks to the crude workmanship, it is none the less valuable as an authority in a period when contemporary subjects are rare.

PLATE IX *(see page* 105)

The Houseling Cloth, XIII-Century Contemporary Vestments

It is stated on good authority that Boniface VIII (1294-1303), who proclaimed that God had set him over kings and kingdoms, was the first to add a *second* crown to his tiara, significant of spiritual and temporal power combined.

Fig. 148. Pope John XXII,
XIV Century

Fig. 149.
The Triple-crowned Tiara,
XIV Century

This is substantiated by the three [1] existing statues which this pope erected in his lifetime.

Whether the tiara of Fig. 147 is a reproduction from one of these is uncertain; it certainly qualifies for that distinction. The uprights connecting what are obviously two crowns were probably of gold metal, a framework, so to speak, enclosing a frigium of cloth of gold or cloth of silver. As yet there was no elaborate decorative modelling in the treatment, or high relief of the motifs surmounting the circlet. That type of ornamentation is reserved for the next century.

XIV CENTURY

It was in the early part of the fourteenth century that the triple crown or TRIREGNUM appeared, and both Benedict XI (1303-4) and Clement V (1305-14) are credited with having introduced the *third* crown. In 1316 an inventory of the papal treasure was made, and it contains an entry of a tiara having three crowns.

In the cathedral of Notre-Dame des Doms, Avignon, in one of the chapels is a splendid canopied tomb of

Fig. 150. Pope Martin V

[1] There is one in the Lateran church, and two are in the crypt of St. Peter's, Rome.

John XXII (1316–34) by Jean Lavenier (1345), unfortunately mutilated during the revolution, and regrettably restored in 1840. The recumbent statue is that of a bishop, and not that of the pope, which is lost. The original head is said to be that in the Calvet Museum at Avignon, of which Fig. 148 is a drawing: in it the face has been restored, but the damage at the top of the tiara is shown. In consequence of this damage it is impossible to decide definitely if there had been a third crown: it seems doubtful, taking into consideration the height of the un-damaged portion, if there was room for it. Moreover, the addition of a third crown would make the tiara disproportionally tall. The spikes which surround the circlet and support the balls have already appeared in Fig. 146, and with the addition of alternate leaf motifs this crown suggests more than ever that the originator of the earl's coronet took this as its prototype. Tiaras of this elaborate nature must have been rather heavy and perchance wobbly, therefore a close-fitting coif was worn under the tiara and on the bald head for comfort's sake. We perceive that John XXII is wearing two.

Fig. 151. Pope Sixtus IV

The earliest monumental effigy of a pope whose tiara is certainly encircled by three crowns is that of Benedict XII (1334–42), of which the head is said to be preserved in the museum at Avignon.

The tiara, Fig. 149, is taken from the recumbent effigy of Pope Urban V (1362–70), also in the Avignon Museum, which gives perhaps a further example of the more elaborate ornamentation of the crowns on his triregnum. These are of solid goldsmith's work, and devoid of jewels. The cap itself, either of cloth of silver or cloth of gold, takes the same form as that shown in Fig. 142, but is not quite so high. The height is seven-fifths of the half circumference, according to the scale demonstrated on pp. 109–10.

XV CENTURY

Of Cardinal Otto Colonna, who was elected to the papal chair as Martin V (1417–31), there is an effigy on his monument in the Lateran which represents him wearing a triple crowned tiara of simple design, in which each crown has four fleurs-de-lys, Fig. 150.

This tiara, compared with the previous drawings, gives the impression of being much narrower and taller: the reason is that it is shown encircling the head. As a fact, it is of the same dimensions as the tiara, Fig. 147, which is drawn laid out flat.

The pope who succeeded Martin V was Eugenius IV (1431–47), but a few months after his election he was deposed by the Council of Basle, and fled disguised as a monk to Florence, where he remained nearly nine years in exile.

On his return to Rome 'in a spirit of rejoicing he set out lavishly to endow the city with those arts he had enjoyed at Florence. A host of painters and sculptors and architects received his commands, and while buildings grew and frescoes and canvassers progressed he commissioned the famous Lorenzo Ghiberti [ob. 1455] to produce, among other objects of beauty, a magnificent tiara, heavily encrusted with precious stones.' A reproduction of it is unfortunately unavailable.

' The famous tiara that Ghiberti had made for his uncle had cost thirty-eight thousand ducats,[1] but the one designed and made to meet [Paul II's] luxurious taste cost nearly four times as much.' [2]

Paul II (1464–71), like his uncle, was a devoted patron of the arts, and was resolved that Rome should be made the most beautiful and cultured city in the world.

His successor was Pope Sixtus IV (1471–84). He also was a great patron of the arts, and perhaps his greatest achievement was the building and decorating of the Sistine Chapel in the Vatican. His monument is a very beautiful piece of work, and he is represented wearing an elaborate bejewelled triregnum, Fig. 151. In all probability it was the one made for Paul II. The frigium itself would, as usual, be composed of cloth of gold or cloth of silver, mounted on a stiff foundation, and the three golden crowns, highly modelled in relief goldsmith's work, were set with numerous jewels and pearls. There is a glimpse of a white coif beneath, of necessity, and an infula hangs over what appears to be a neck-covering of fur: this is clearly the mozzetta, see p. 179. The pallium is also seen.

Henceforth this ensign of papal sovereign power, simplified or elaborated as regards its ornaments, was worn by all succeeding popes at coronation, council, and other occasions of non-liturgical solemnity.

For a hundred and fifty years past, nevertheless, artists in the West, both in painting and in sculpture, had sometimes represented the pontiff as wearing a tiara with only *one* crown: this is most likely due to imperfect knowledge on their part, though many medieval popes of conservative mind did continue to favour the single crown, which accounts for their being so represented on effigies of later times. In Rome the triple symbol of the Trinity, or, as John Guillim states in his *Display of Heraldry* (1610), 'the threefold jurisdiction that he [the pope] doth arrogate to himself as Christ's vicar general in heaven, in earth, and in his supposed purgatory' remained, and its usage was, and is, interminable.

By the fifteenth century the popes had definitely adopted the triregnum for all ceremonial occasions.

The six pontiffs painted by Pinturicchio in his frescoes in the library at Siena, 1503–8, wear tiaras all very much alike, coinciding exactly with the tiara shown in Fig. 151. The foundation is white or silver, and the three gold coronets are profusely set with gems.

[1] 38,000 ducats equals (say) £17,000. A gold ducat equals nine shillings or so.
[2] Quoted from John Farrow's *Pageant of the Popes*, 1943.

11. THE PASTORAL STAFF OR CROZIER

THE Latin word *ferula* stands for a cane, baton, staff, and walking-stick. When this word is used to describe the ecclesiastical staff it means a plain rod, the symbol of office, authority, correction,[1] and dignity.

To the top of this plain rod was added a hook or crook, 'crocea,' denoting pastoral ministration, thus forming a crozier or pastoral staff. It was also termed 'baculum,' a Latin name applied in addition to a sceptre and an augur's staff.

VIII CENTURY B.C.

There is good reason for the opinion that the crozier was a development of the 'lituus' of pagan times. Fig. 152 is one drawn from the frieze in the Temple of Jupiter the

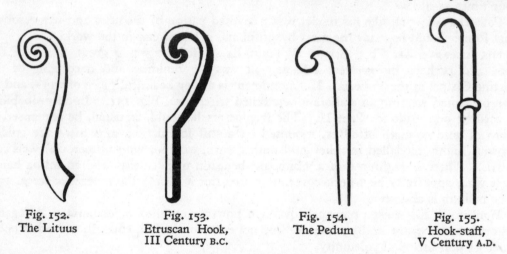

Fig. 152.
The Lituus

Fig. 153.
Etruscan Hook,
III Century B.C.

Fig. 154.
The Pedum

Fig. 155.
Hook-staff,
V Century A.D.

Thunderer at Rome, and said to represent the pastoral staff used by Romulus to mark out the different districts of the new city he founded in 753 B.C.! Later this became the badge of honour borne in the right hand by the augurs, who used it in the same manner to mark out the different regions of the heavens when drawing their prognostics. Its chief feature is that the curve at the top takes the form of a volute.

III CENTURY B.C.

Fig. 153 is taken from an Etruscan slab, which probably dates about the time of the conquest of Etruria, 266 B.C. The hook at the top is like a shepherd's crook, descending in a slight curve into a short perpendicular staff. It will be recognized in these two illustrations that the crozier of the Christian era embodies both these characteristics.

Among the different agricultural implements hung as offerings upon the boughs of trees at pagan rustic festivals would be a 'pedum,' or shepherd's crook, Fig. 154. Its stick tapers towards the base, and its total length might be anything from four times the diameter of the curve up to five feet.

[1] The word 'virga' is applied to a wand or rod for flogging.

116

It is recorded that bishops used a staff as early as the fourth century, but it is uncertain whether the reference is to the staff (ferula) or to the crooked staff (baculum), or whether the staff was the prerogative of the bishops alone.

V CENTURY

The earliest reference to the pastoral staff, the emblem of ministerial office, being carried in front of an archbishop by his chaplain, dates from the fifth century. The exact shape of this is not easy to define, but it is almost certain that the top took the curve of a hook like Figs. 155 or 156, the latter resembling the handle of a modern walking-stick.

It was a tradition, considered with favour at the present day, that the crozier is partly descended from the walking-stick (about 3 feet long), carried by aged and possibly

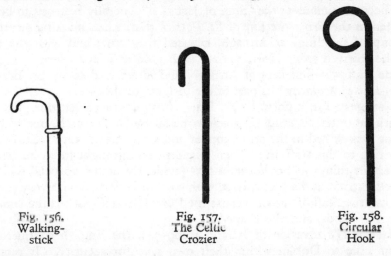

Fig. 156.
Walking-
stick

Fig. 157.
The Celtic
Crozier

Fig. 158.
Circular
Hook

decrepit bishops, who found its use very helpful in their perambulations in church, on the highways, and in the house.

It is conceivable that this tradition originated from the resemblance of the crozier, Fig. 155, to the handle of the walking-stick, Fig. 156, which is taken from an Anglo-Saxon illuminated MS. of the tenth century. Such a walking-staff was used by any middle-aged man in any sphere of life.

The crozier was carried by bishops on ceremonial occasions in Gaul at this time, although it was considered somewhat of an innovation.

A description of a crozier is given by a writer of a later period than that under consideration, but this refers retrospectively. He informs us that the top (crocea) is curved to indicate that the bishop should collect the sheep which have wandered from the fold: the middle part or staff (ferula) is straight, that he may rule the weak, obstinate, and disobedient; and the lower end has a sharp-pointed iron ferrule, to enable him to spur on the slothful of his flock. *Continued on page* 120.

THE CELTIC CROZIER

The earliest Celtic croziers originating from the staff—'ferula' and 'baculum'—had, for the most part, a hook-head, Fig. 157, a crook-head like Fig. 158, or one slightly curved without volute.

The word 'quigrich' is a Celtic name given to the Irish crozier, signifying 'The Stranger,' which alludes to the *unknown pilgrim*. Several early Celtic croziers are preserved in public and private collections.[1] These are mostly the staffs of early saints, and are of the plainest, as shown in Figs. 157 and 158. The veneration paid them during the course of at least four succeeding centuries caused some of them to be decorated by encasing them in precious metals, with gems and jewels, and with carvings of elaborate designs and workmanship.

Notable amongst these ancient croziers is that connected with St. Patrick.

The tradition that St. Patrick—the name 'Patricius,' given him by Pope Celestine when consecrating him Bishop of Armagh (422–32)—was given a staff originally belonging to an unknown pilgrim who announced himself as the Lord Jesus Christ, and which afterwards became famous as the 'Staff of Jesus,' is generally believed to be a myth.

It is related in the *Tripartite Life of St. Patrick* that, when marking out the enclosure for his group of buildings at Armagh, he used this staff; and with the pointed end scratched the thirteen stone idols overlaid with gold at Magh Slecht.

This same staff was first kept at Armagh, and is referred to by St. Bernard (1091–1153) in his *Life of Malachy* [2] as part of the insignia of this see.

It is also suggested in a poem by St. Fiacre (fifth century) that this pilgrim-staff was adorned with an outer covering of precious metal by St. Tassach, one of St. Patrick's braziers, who was skilled in the art of copper and goldsmith's work. St. Bernard's own words, referring to this staff are: 'Then Nigellus, seeing flight to be imminent, carried with him certain things of his house, a text [evidently of the gospels] which belonged to the blessed Patrick, and a staff *covered* with gold and adorned with very precious gems, which they call the Staff of Jesus, because the Lord Himself (such is the common belief) carried it in His hands, and also shaped it.'

During Henry II's invasion of Ireland (1169–71), the English conquerors removed this precious relic to Dublin within their own pale for security. It remained there until the Reformation, when it was burned by Henry VIII's soldiers in the public square.

VI CENTURY

By the commencement of the sixth century the form, that is of the spiral top, had become stabilized, although some other shaped heads appeared from time to time.

It was the recognized custom to present a bishop with a crozier at his consecration; and its significance on such an occasion is stated by St. Isidore of Seville (560–636) to be 'that he may rule, he may correct, or he may sustain the weaknesses of the weak'; but it is not made clear whether the staff is a plain rod or one with a curved top. The reference is possibly to the former.

A pastoral staff is mentioned in the will of St. Remigius, born in 439, who became

---

[1] See Plates X and XI.
[2] St. Malachy, born Armagh 1095, Archbishop of Armagh, 1132, appointed Papal Legate in Ireland by Pope Innocent II, died at Clairvaux 1148.

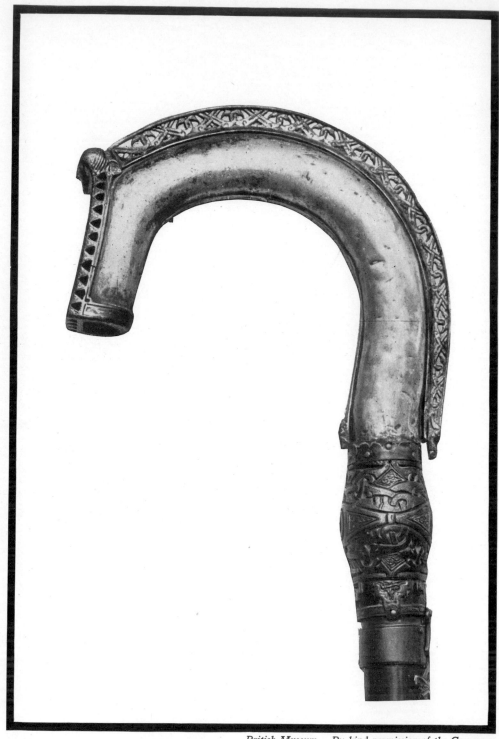

PLATE X (*see page* 119)

The Crozier of Kells, X Century

Archbishop of Rheims in 461: which office he held for seventy-two years, dying in 533. This crozier of the 'Apostle of the Franks' was of carved wood covered with gold plates, but the details of its ornamentation have not been preserved.

VII CENTURY

The pastoral staff or crozier was used by an archbishop as well as by a bishop: in his own primacy this was carried before him. At all other times he carried it himself, when the cross staff would be borne in front of him by his cross-bearer. This last was a special privilege of archbishops.

By the time of St. Isidore the crook-head to the crozier had become stereotyped.

One of the canons of the Council of Toledo (633) supplies the interesting information that the pastoral staff was positively the recognized distinctive mark of a bishop.

With regard to abbots carrying the pastoral staff (baculum), there is reliable authority, dating the first quarter of the seventh century, that it had been granted to them before this time. There is a widespread conviction nowadays that in the case of an abbot the head of the staff should turn inwards, that is towards him, and that the crozier of a bishop should turn outwards or rather away from him, but this is entirely without foundation. So is the belief that the general form of an abbot's pastoral staff is distinct from those used by archbishops and bishops.

Fig. 159. Crozier, VII Century

Abbesses were not granted the privilege of carrying the pastoral staff until a later date.

Fig. 159 shows a crozier in use at this period, taken from an illuminated MS. in the British Museum.

Its full length is about 6 feet, the diameter of the crook or volute being 11 inches (see scale). Decoration now appears, and in this example seems to be achieved with coloured enamels set in gold.

Fig. 160. An Irish Bishop, X Century

VIII CENTURY

Doubtless the above type of crozier continued in use more or less during the eighth and ninth centuries, though the author is not able to discover any examples dating from this period.

X CENTURY

It was during the tenth century that the pastoral staff makes its first appearance on monumental effigies. It is usually represented lying parallel with the figure on the left side: it rests on the bend of the arm and the palm of the hand.

Plate X is a photograph of a celebrated crozier of this century, the crozier of Kells, which is dated about 967. Describing this, Margaret Stokes (*Early Christian Art in Ireland*) says: 'This crozier is an old oak stick cased in silver, with an open-work formed of interlaced birds terminating at the upper end in a male head, and at the lower in that of an animal. Below this there is a knob decorated with trumpet pattern designs, and interlacings inlaid with silver and niello. The lower end appears to be a solid piece of brass with bands of inlaid silver. It terminates with three little feet. The crozier would seem to have been carried over the shoulder, consequently the central knob,[1] and not the upper one, is rubbed and worn by handling.'

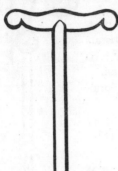

Fig. 161. Walking-stick, Anglo-Saxon

Irish croziers have their own special peculiarities. To quote Margaret Stokes again: 'This staff was not designed to represent the shepherd's crook, only to be carried as an emblem of episcopal functions, but it was the covering made to protect the old oak staff or walking-stick of the founder of the church in which it had been preserved. Thus the form differs from that of the ordinary medieval crozier, the top of which, imitating the shepherd's crook, takes the curve of an S reversed, a double curve, not the mere crook-handle of the Irish staff.'

The interesting effigy of an Irish bishop, Fig. 160, is drawn from a small panel of sculpture in the centre of the High Cross at Durrow, King's County, which was erected about 1010. This bears a double-headed crozier with two volutes resembling the classic Greek anchor, Fig. 182, and the Anchor Cross of the early Christian era, Fig. 183. In his left hand he holds a simple cross-staff, and appears to be wearing an alb, and there is the suggestion of an amice: he is tonsured in the Celtic manner. It must be borne in mind that owing to the isolation of the Irish people their clergy were, in point of time, far behind those of England and the West in the matter of vestments. In fact these were of the simplest nature. Fig. 81 is a very fair example.

THE PASTORAL STAFF (continued from page 117)

Until some time in the tenth century the pope, like other bishops, carried a staff surmounted by a crutch or a crook; but as the temporal power of the papacy increased less emphasis was placed upon its purely spiritual aspect, and the crozier gradually fell into disuse by future popes.

This crutch, of course, symbolized, like the crook, the pastoral care of the pope: it was specially popular amongst Anglo-Saxon bishops.

Fig. 161 is the head of a walking-stick or crutch, such as was in general use among ordinary folk during the Anglo-Saxon and Norman periods, and is to be found in many illuminated MSS. of these times. It is shaped on the lines of the cross tau or (as it is often called) a crutch-head.

The head of a tau-shaped crozier, Fig. 162, is of fine carved ivory, and a beautiful example, not of British

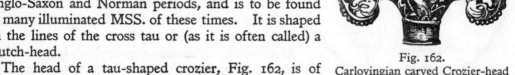

Fig. 162.
Carlovingian carved Crozier-head

workmanship, but late Carlovingian, although it was discovered at Alcester, Warwickshire, and most probably belonged to a British bishop. It much resembles Fig. 161 in outline, thus upholding the theory that some croziers had their prototype in the walking-staff.

[1] Not shown in the photograph.

The tau-cross crozier was also used in the eastern Church: evidently this design was widely diffused over Europe.

A staff surmounted by a globe is peculiar to some Anglo-Saxon bishops, though sometimes used by the pope as seen in Plate V.

Although there was a theory that the pastoral staff was used by the pope until the end of this century, Innocent III at a later date disclaims only the staff with crooked head, which was the special accessory of archbishops and bishops; but he admits that early bishops of Rome carried a short staff, baton, or sceptre, surmounted by a cross.

At any rate the pope, alone amongst bishops, has relinquished the use of the pastoral staff since the following century.

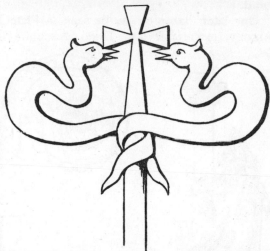

Fig. 163. Eastern Crozier, XI Century

XI CENTURY

In an eleventh-century fresco in Rome, showing St. Clement at the altar, there is a cleric standing in the background holding a crozier of a different type, which appears to be exactly like the twelfth century one as shown in Fig. 168. Such innovations in shape sometimes occur.

The Roman crozier shaped with the curved head and volute was adopted by all bishops of the Eastern Church, except the Byzantines. They used a shorter stalk, with the top formed of two serpents head to head with a cross between and their bodies bent outwards, symbolizing prudence. Fig. 163 is a drawing of one made from a description.

Another Eastern crozier is shown in Fig. 164. It is of the same type, but more elaborate; the serpents rather suggest dolphins.

XI CENTURY

Use of the Sudarium

During the eleventh century it had become usual, at least in certain dioceses, to knot a napkin to the episcopal staff, or to

Fig. 164. Eastern Crozier, more elaborate

attach it with fine cords: the purpose was apparently to absorb moisture from the hand.

One later example may be seen in Plate XIII, and another, Fig. 165, used by St. Antony, on a retable in the Dijon Museum.　In the latter case the sudarium (see p. 88) or

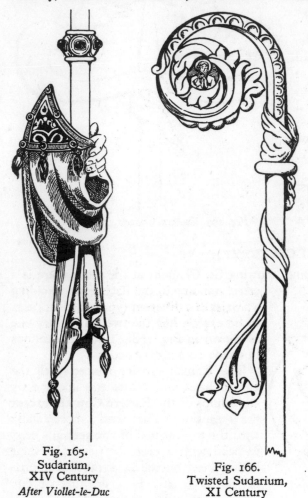

fanon is attached by an attractive triangular jewelled ornament, a method which may be peculiar to that diocese. Both are of the late fourteenth century.

The more usual method of arranging the sudarium is to knot the centre of this scarf-like napkin of white silk, linen, or chainsil (cambric), say 64 by 16 inches, round the base of the crook, tying it for security: the two lengths are then twisted below the socket. Thence the remainder of the fabric hangs freely, and is sometimes wound once or twice round the staff as shown in Fig. 166. Fringe or tassels of white or colour could be attached to the lower ends. There are instances where the napkin is plaited round the staff about 8 or 10 inches below the socket.

The sudarium attached to William of Wykeham's crozier as seen on his effigy is painted red, possibly an anachronism of the artist.

An illuminated MS. of a later date [1] has a miniature of St. Cuthbert showing him in full vestments of this century, and holding in his left hand a crozier equal in length to his height, Fig. 167.　The head of the crozier is a spiral ending in a volute, although not quite true in form, and is a little more advanced in design than that shown in Fig. 159.　Where the spiral straightens out into the socket, it is strengthened by a spiked upright.

Fig. 165.
Sudarium,
XIV Century
After Viollet-le-Duc

Fig. 166.
Twisted Sudarium,
XI Century

The archbishop, Plate VII, carries a crozier having a crook, obviously of ivory, almost the same shape as in Fig. 167.

At this time the staff of the crozier was often surmounted with a knob of crystal, above which the crook-head was attached.

[1] Bede's *Life of St. Cuthbert*, late twelfth century.　B.M., Add. MSS. 39943.

XII CENTURY

In the Galilee, Durham Cathedral, is a mural painting of an archbishop of the twelfth century, holding a crozier in his left hand while giving the benediction with his right.

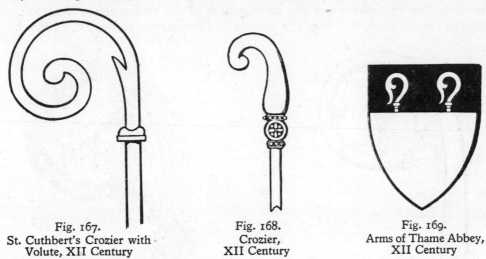

Fig. 167.
St. Cuthbert's Crozier with
Volute, XII Century

Fig. 168.
Crozier,
XII Century

Fig. 169.
Arms of Thame Abbey,
XII Century

The crook of the crozier is shaped like the pedum, Fig. 154, and appears to be of ivory; its base swells slightly, and there is a golden ornament encasing the socket, from which

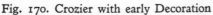

Fig. 170. Crozier with early Decoration

Fig. 171. Crozier with
Leaf Motif

descends the rod made of some precious wood: Fig. 168 illustrates this crozier-head. The painting is damaged, and the light is not very good for observation.

Another example of this period is to be seen in the arms of Thame Abbey, founded 1138: 'Argent, on a chief sable two crozier heads of the first,' Fig. 169. These are in the abbot's parlour at Thame Park, on a frieze decorated in the early sixteenth century with armorial shields of white plaster-work: in this case, however, the plasterer has erred by extending the crozier staffs to the base of the shield—no doubt because the heads apart from the black chief would appear to be floating in the air.

The following examples show the development of the decoration which took place during the twelfth century. Fig. 170 is from an illumination in the St. Edmundsbury

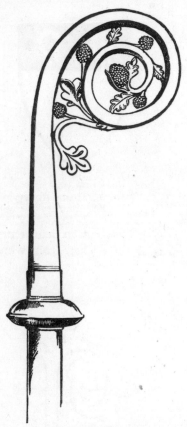

Fig. 172. The Hyde Abbey
Crozier, XII Century

*Victoria and Albert Museum. By kind
permission of the directors*

Fig. 173.
The Cluny Crozier, XIII Century

Bible (1125–50) by Master Hugo. The crozier may be of wood or of precious metal, and there is a suggestion of the later leaf motif about the head. As in other examples the ornament, which generally finishes off the crook, is a socket to contain the top of the staff, and is frequently of gold.

Fig. 171 is from a late twelfth-century illuminated MS.; in it for the first time the leaf motif is definitely introduced, and a tail-piece appears.

The leaf becomes more prominent in Plate VIII, where St. Donatus holds the crozier in which the trefoil is enclosed by the curve and the volute.

Fig. 172 is a drawing of a crozier-head in the Victoria and Albert Museum dating

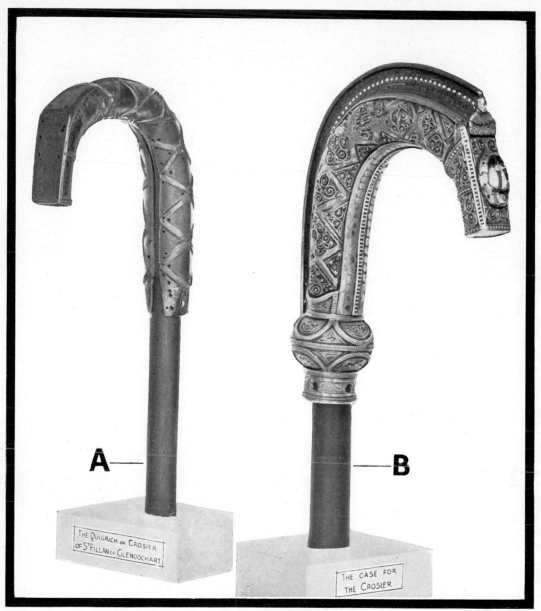

A — THE QUIGRICH OR CROSIER OF ST FILLAN OF GLENDOCHART

B — THE CASE FOR THE CROSIER

By kind permission of the National Museum of Antiquities, Edinburgh

PLATE XI (*see page* 125)

St. Fillan's Crozier, VIII, X, and XIV Centuries

early thirteenth century: it originally belonged to Hyde Abbey, Winchester. In gilt copper, it is an excellent specimen of metal-work. The curve of the volute extends further than previously, and from it spring alternately oak or other leaves and clusters of berries, all conventionally.

XIII CENTURY

There are some very lovely croziers of this and the following centuries scattered throughout Europe. One of the first decade of the thirteenth century is in the Louvre, and represents the annunciation: it is carried out in champlevé enamel.

Fig. 174. Crozier with Central Leaf Motif

Fig. 173 is a drawing of it from a photograph. The volute is formed as a serpent biting the stem of a lily, and encloses the figures of the Virgin and the Archangel. The socket is like the upper part, of gold scrolls on blue, and is flanked by three serpents with curled tails. The boss, surmounted by a crown of water leaves, is of open-work lilies in gold, and surrounded by a golden band. On the volute is the inscription in red enamel—AVE MARIA GRA. PLENA.

Wings were attached to the Archangel Gabriel at a much later date, so they are omitted in the drawing.

According to Doctor Anderson of the Scottish Society of Antiquaries, Scotland can boast of only two croziers: that of St. Fillan of Glendochart found at Killin at the head of Loch Tay, and a fragment of a second, both preserved in the National Museum of Antiquities, Edinburgh. He illustrates a third, which he says is of Irish origin, but which in any case is of extraordinary interest as exhibiting three periods in the history of Christian art in these islands. This statement applies also to St. Fillan, who was Irish-born, but migrated to Scotland, where he became a monk and laboured as a missionary to extreme old age. The place where he died was later called Strathfillan. His quigrich,[1] or crozier, Plate XI, consists of three distinct parts; first the original oaken hooked staff of the eighth century: secondly the encasing of copper with trellis-work bands of niello (apparently of the tenth century), through which the original staff is seen (A): thirdly the outer case (B), of silver gilt, ornamented with zigzag bands, enclosing triangles of fine wire filigree scrolls in true Celtic fashion, of the fourteenth century. The outer edge of the hook-head is raised into a ridge, and the front end is finished with a mask.

Fig. 175.
Crozier from XIV-Century Stained Glass

[1] This crozier, which has been in the possession of the family of Dewar, the hereditary keepers of the relic, since the time of Robert Bruce, had been removed to Canada some time in the 1860s, and was acquired by the Society of Antiquities of Scotland in 1877. The word 'dewar' is derived from 'deorad,' which means a stranger, pilgrim, exile.

Returning to the leaf motif of the last century and Fig. 173, a further development is seen in Fig. 174. The central leaf is deeply divided, and the crook is partly sheathed by another leaf. This crozier-head would almost certainly have been in one of the precious metals, and as the enameller's art was being revived such crozier-heads would be embellished with cloisonné or champlevé work.

Fig. 176. Crozier, XIII Century

Fig. 175 is taken from one of the windows on the south side of the chapel of New College, Oxford. Most of the fourteenth-century glass was destroyed by the Puritans, but, fortunately, a few small portions were spared. Some of these represent the heads of episcopal staffs, and have been incorporated in the mid eighteenth-century glass. Fig. 175 shows a crozier head of the late thirteenth century, having the crook shaped almost as a complete circle, and imitating that of Fig. 158: the volute, in addition, being entirely composed of a leaf, as also the end of the curve. The head joins the staff, most likely of ebony, with a simple design of tabernacles.

The crozier, Fig. 176, is a magnificent specimen of elaborate thirteenth-century workmanship, and is kept in the little church of St. Colomba of Sens: its preservation is the more fortunate in that the relics of this virgin saint (who was martyred in 273) were dispersed by the Huguenots in the sixteenth century.

The crook itself is of cloisonné enamel, the ground (hatched) being blue with a gold and vermilion scroll design. The outer edge of the curve has serrations in gold. The volute finishes in a grotesque reptile's head, holding in its mouth an elaborate floral motif (suggestive of an orchid) in vermilion, blue, gold, and a little black and white.

XIV CENTURY

It could not have been much earlier than the fourteenth century that niches or shrines with crocketed pinnacles containing figures of saints appeared beneath the crooks of elaborately decorated croziers.

One of the most lavishly ornamented croziers of this century is that of William of Wykeham, Bishop of Winchester (1367–1404), which is preserved in the chapel of New College, Oxford. Plate XII is a photograph of it, reproduced by kind permission of the college authorities.

There is an opinion that parts of this crozier belong to an earlier date than 1367, and that at least the staff was originally made for Wykeham's predecessor, William Edington (1346–66).

Wykeham's is made entirely of silver gilt overlaid on a foundation of iron, and its total length is 6 feet 9 inches.

The following is an abridged description of that given by W. H. St. John Hope.[1]

Starting from the bottom, at the blunted silver spike S, Plate XII.

The staff, circular in section, is decorated with panels formed of silver plates, each of which contains, stamped in relief, a group of five lily flowers growing on one stalk. The

[1] See *Archaeologia*, vol. lx, p. 465.

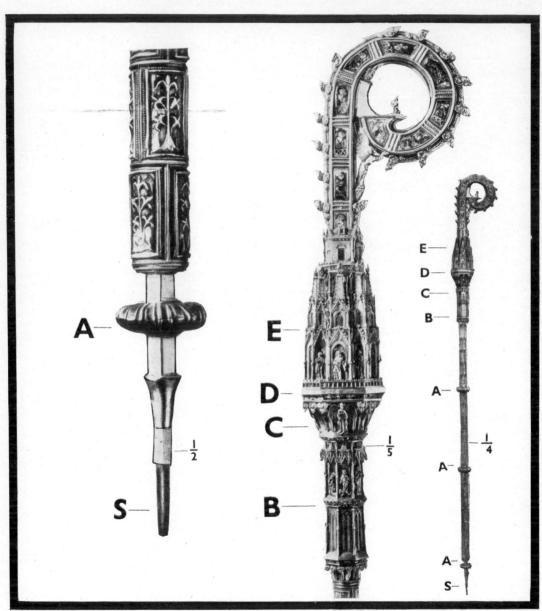

PLATE XII (*see page* 126)

William of Wykeham's Crozier, XIV Century

backgrounds are enamelled either green or blue, and are so arranged that each band contains alternately one blue and two green panels, and one green and two blue.   Three bosses, C, divide the staff into three sections.   From the capital at B rises an octagonal shaft, above which are figures of eight saints under canopies.   Above these is the main capital, C, containing four silver-gilt angels, sitting with wings outspread; their faces and hands are silver.   These support the octagonal enamelled platform, D, and from it rises the tower, E, the turret-shaped base of the crook, the first tier consisting of a series of richly canopied niches, the backgrounds filled alternately with green and blue translucent enamel.   These niches contain in all twelve figures—our Lord, our Lady, and ten saints.   Above these is another tier of niches, having similarly enamelled backgrounds, but no figures, and surmounted by tall elaborately crocketed pinnacles, each capped with a finial of blue enamel.   On top of the tower is set a little six-sided house. In each of the sides is a rectangular doorway, and above it a little dormer window: the angles of the house are masked with round pinnacled turrets.

Out of the roof of the house rises the crook proper.   The sides of it are flat, but the edges are ridged and ornamented.   On the outside of the curve are crockets of leaf-work (one is missing).   The incurved end of the crook is supported by an angel, who stands upon a corbel in the form of a bearded man's head.   The curve of the crook ends in an elongated six-sided platform, upon which is a small kneeling figure; there is a little bracket bearing another figure, and supported by a curved band of gold.   It is suggested that these two figures represent the annunciation.

The flat sides of the crook are bordered by simple fillets, and divided by double bands set with four-petalled flowers in ten compartments on each side.   The ground of each compartment is silver, engraved with an angel playing upon an instrument of music, and sitting or standing on a purple cloud in a deep blue sky.   The angels' wings are barred in two colours—blue and green.

The crozier with sudarium, which Wykeham carries in the Winchester effigy (see Plate XIII), differs in some details from that preserved in New College Chapel.

Cornelius O'Dea, Bishop of Limerick (1400–26) possessed an equally elaborate crozier of massive silver-gilt, being 7 feet long, and illustrated in *Archaeologia*, vol. xvii, p. 38. Both these croziers are truly magnificent masterpieces of gold craftsmanship and design.

The descriptions here given show the great variety and elaboration of design of croziers from the end of the thirteenth century onwards.

In sculpture, monumental brasses, illuminated MSS., and paintings of the period many other examples may be found.

H

12. THE CROSS

'Lift high the Cross, the Love of Christ proclaim.'—G. W. Kitchen and M. R.
Newbolt. (See Fig. 211.)

THE cross as an instrument of capital punishment was in use for some centuries before the Christian era.

It is said that the Carthaginians originated the custom of crucifixion, which penalty does not appear to have been much practised amongst the Greeks, although exceptional instances of its use are known.

Not until 184 B.C. was this method of execution introduced to the Romans, and then it was restricted to deserters and slaves. Later, crimes against the state or the person of the emperor were punished in this manner.

Three kinds of cross were in common use for executions:

The *crux commissa* or tau cross, Fig. 177. The upright post was known as 'stipes,' and

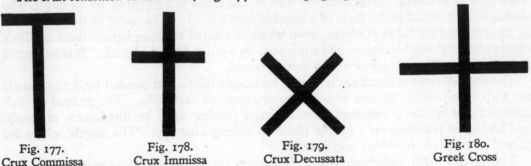

Fig. 177. Crux Commissa	Fig. 178. Crux Immissa	Fig. 179. Crux Decussata	Fig. 180. Greek Cross

its transverse beam 'patibulum'; it was this latter portion that the criminal carried to the place of execution, *not* the complete cross.

The *crux immissa* or Latin cross, Fig. 178, had the upright post extended. In the case of important criminals a second, shorter, transverse piece was fastened above the beam to take the inscription.

The *crux decussata* was in shape like an X, and is commonly known as St. Andrew's Cross, Fig. 179.

The Greek cross, Fig. 180, has all four members of the same length.

THE SIGN OF THE CROSS

A.D. I CENTURY

The custom of crossing oneself in honour of the Trinity, and in commemoration of Christ, was in use from early Christian times, and the first method in making the sign on the forehead or on sacred objects was with the thumb of the right hand.

II CENTURY

By the second century the custom had become so universal amongst Christians that Tertullian scoffingly comments: 'In all our travels and movements, in all our coming in and going out, in putting on our shoes, at the bath, at the table, in lighting our candles, in lying down, in sitting down, whatever employment occupieth us, we mark our foreheads with the Sign of the Cross.'

IV CENTURY

St. John Chrysostom, who became Bishop of Constantinople in 397, the antagonist of the Empress Eudoxia, one of the butts of his fiery sermons, mentions the use of this gesture upon sacred objects: 'Thrice he made the Sign of the Cross on the chalice with his finger'—apparently the right index finger.

VI CENTURY

By the sixth century a second method had already come into use.

The right hand was raised to the forehead, then drawn down to the heart, then to the left shoulder, and finally to the right; but in the Eastern Church first to the right and then to the left shoulder. Sometimes the thumb was laid crosswise over the index finger and kissed.[1]

A third method, usual in benedictions and consecrations, was to make the Sign of the Cross in the air over persons or objects.

A fourth method was to raise the hand to the forehead in the name of God, as the head of all, then to lower it to the mouth in the name of the Son, who is the word of the Father, then to the heart in the name of the Spirit, who is the bond of love. In all these cases some or all of the fingers might be employed with varying symbolical significations. Five fingers might represent the five wounds of Christ; three fingers the blessed Trinity; one finger the unity of the Godhead.

Fig. 181. Agnus Dei, V Century

THE USE OF CROSSES
A.D. I CENTURY

Although the cross as a sign or gesture was used by the early Christians, representations of our Lord nailed to a Latin cross—setting forth His humiliation and passion—are rare in Christian works of art before the fifth century: the reason being that there was a feeling of abhorrence amongst Christians for this object of grim association. Nevertheless it is a fact that crosses of the decussata type, Fig. 179, or representations of them, were used by most Christians in private, since they are mentioned in all the earliest records. They are also to be found in the catacombs. Here in addition are many

[1] In modern times all Catholics touch the forehead, breast, left and right shoulders with the tips of the fingers and thumb, with the words: 'In the name of the Father and of the Son and of the Holy Ghost.'

In the Eastern Church all, whether Catholics or not, make the sign from right to left, with the thumb and first two fingers held together. This is in accordance with primitive practice.

symbols of our Lord as the Lamb of God—the Agnus Dei—which consists simply of a lamb statant with one foreleg arched. This appears on the sarcophagus of Junius Bassus, dated 350, in the crypt of the Vatican. A little later a cross in the monogrammatic form appears on the head of the lamb. This is superseded by a crux immissa

Fig. 182. Greco-Roman Anchor

Fig. 183. The Christian Anchor

early in the fifth century. Shortly after, the lamb bears either a cross symbolizing the Blessed Sacrament as shown in Fig. 181,[1] or in place of it a pennon emblematic of the triumphant victim. Contemporaneously the lamb bearing the cross is seen 'lodged' upon a book, and sometimes lying 'as it were slain' at the foot of an altar above which is a cross.

Towards the end of the sixth century the wounds of the Cross are represented on the sides and hoofs of the lamb.

Mural paintings in the catacombs also depict our Saviour as a shepherd carrying the lost sheep over His shoulders, see Fig. 20.

Another method of disguising the Cross from unbelievers, found in the oldest parts

Fig. 184.
The Chi-rho, IV Century

Fig. 185.
The Chi-rho, another Form

Fig. 186.
The Chi-rho, a further Variation

of the catacombs, is the anchor, which appears to have its prototype in those used by the classic Greek and Roman navies, Fig. 182. The anchor adopted to represent this sacred object is shown in Fig. 183, and signifies Hope embodied in the Cross of Christ. This Christian anchor may also claim some affiliation with the Greek letter ψ (psi).

[1] This lamb is reproduced from the apsidal arch at St. Maria Maggiore at Rome, fifth century, and is haloed.

IV CENTURY

The Sacred Monogram

On his conversion to Christianity in 312 the Emperor Constantine the Great (306–37) adopted a combination of the crux decussata and the Greek initials XP (chi-rho),[1] the first two letters in the name of Christ (*ΧΡΙΣΤΟΣ*). Figs. 184, 185, and 186 show three variations, the first being the earliest and that most commonly used. Hereafter this type, Fig. 184, became official.

A contemporary explanation of this chi-rho cross is given by Lactantius, the preceptor of Constantine's eldest and unfortunate son Crispus (317–29), from which the following is an excerpt. 'With the letter X placed transversely, having one extremity bent round [Fig. 185], he marks their [the army's] shields of Christ.' And again, Eusebius (*ob.* 360) states: 'A monogram setting forth the holy name by its first two letters combined, the P in the middle of the X,' Fig. 184. This Christian symbol, commonly called the Chrisma, thus appeared on Constantine's standard or labarum: this is said to have been done in consequence of a vision seen by the emperor in the sky before his victory over Maxentius. In modern times the word 'labarum' is used as an alternative to 'chrisma.'

Fig. 187. A Chi-rho Symbol, V Century

Although the 'chrisma' (chi-rho cross), Figs. 184, 185, 186, dates from the fourth century, the Latin, Fig. 178, and the Greek, Fig. 179, were not used in decoration until the following century.

Constantine abolished crucifixion as a capital punishment; and from his time, first the monogram of Christ, and then the cross began publicly to be held in reverence.

V CENTURY

A variation of the chi-rho symbol (see Fig. 184) is given in Fig. 187, which is taken from the contemporary sarcophagus of Theodore, Bishop of Ravenna in the fifth century. This sarcophagus is elaborately decorated with symbols in slight variations of the chi-rho, enclosed in circles and probably carved in a special kind of stone reputed among the Greeks to have the property of consuming the flesh of the corpse. Fig. 187 is the principal motif. It should be noticed that the angles of the Cross are less than ninety degrees, and that the ends are splayed outwards; also that the P takes the form of a bishop's crook. Between the arms of the cross are inserted alpha and omega, the first and last letters of the Greek alphabet,[2] symbolizing eternity.

THE CROSS AS A CRUCIFIX

The crucifix typifies the triumph of Jesus Christ over death, and the redemption of mankind.

In the earliest years of the Christian era the figure of the suffering Saviour was not used, but instead the Agnus Dei (see *ante*).

[1] Which is in point of fact a monogram.　　　　[2] Rev. i. 8 and 17.

When Christianity was established as the religion of the state the imagination of the people envisaged our Lord as still living, ruling from the Cross as King, without any suggestion of grief or suffering. The body was in its natural healthy form, often fully robed and regally attired, but more usually clothed in the colobium; the eyes were open.

Fig. 188.
The Earliest Type of Crucifix, VII Century

Four nails secured the hands and feet, the latter supported by the suppedaneum or foot-rest.

As time went on various changes took place: thus in the late tenth century we find the eyes are closed, and in the thirteenth anguish is for the first time displayed. The early colobium gives place to a loin-cloth in the ninth century: and in the twelfth the number of nails has been reduced from four to three.

II CENTURY

No doubt the earliest extant representation of the crucifixion in art is the engraved gem (No. 43, BM.) which is possibly the work of the second century. Such gems were set in finger rings, and worn in secret during the era of persecutions.

IV CENTURY

In the same collection is a panel on an ivory box dating either from the last years of the fourth century or the beginning of the fifth.

VI CENTURY

In all probability it was at that time that the use of the crucifix began, so states Father Braun.

VII CENTURY

So early as the seventh century the Sixth Oecumenical Council in 680, and the Council of Constantinople in 692, had ordered: 'That, instead of the lamb, our Lord Jesus Christ shall be shown hereafter in His human form in images . . . so that we shall be led to remember His mortal life, His passion, and His death, which paid the ransom for mankind.' This ordinance does not, however, appear to have become very general until four or five centuries later.

An early form of crucifix is shown in Fig. 188; the colobium is girded but the girdle is unseen: in some crucifixes it is omitted. The neck-opening is strengthened by a fixed collar or band; the edges of the sleeves and bottom hem appear to have narrow bands. A gold cruciform nimbus surrounds the slightly bent head; the eyes are open and look lovingly down upon the suppliant. The hands and feet, the latter resting upon the suppedaneum, are each pierced with a nail. In this example the whole figure is of ivory or bone, and the cross wooden.

A very interesting Anglo-Saxon crucifix is carved upon the porch of Langford Church, near Lechlade. The figure wears a colobium and a girdle, the two hanging ends clearly shown.

Another early English carved-stone crucifix is to be seen at Romsey Abbey Church, Hants. Originally it was in the cloister, but at some period after the building of the south transept wall the crucifix was set on the outside. The figure wears a loin-cloth, but it is not possible, owing to some decay, to decide if the eyes are open or closed: the feet rest upon a suppedaneum. The work is undoubtedly Norman, of the latter part of the eleventh century.

About this time the crucifix was sometimes attached to the cross staff. See p. 138.

X CENTURY

An example showing the loincloth, but still retaining four nails, is given in Fig. 189, taken from a psalter of the late tenth century in the British Museum. The loin-cloth is evidently rectangular, and draped round the

Fig. 189. The Second Type of Crucifix, X Century

body: the folds hang in the characteristic manner depicted in illuminations of this period. The superscription in Latin reads: 'This is Jesus of Nazareth, King of the Jews.' By this time the figures of the Virgin and St. John stand on either side of the Cross: more and more persons were gradually included in the scene until eventually, toward the end of the fourteenth century, it had become a crowd.

XII CENTURY

An example of the stage of decoration reached in the twelfth century is shown in Fig. 190, which comes from Matthew Paris's illustration in his illuminated MS. in the British Museum.[1] The cross is probably of gold or silver gilt, and has extensive foliations at the terminals. The figure might also be of some precious metal, but was more

[1] 2 A. xxii, folio 221.

often of ivory.　The staff itself would be of gilt or some special wood, such as ebony or cedar.　The figure by contrast is very emaciated, and henceforth the eyes are closed in

Fig. 190. Later Type of Crucifix, XII Century　　　Fig. 191. A Standard Cross, XI Century

anguish.　Another alteration

Fig. 192.
A Standard Cross, XIII Century

of a slight though important detail took place during this century: three nails only were used, the two feet being secured by a single one, and the supporting block was sometimes omitted.

From the thirteenth and fourteenth centuries onwards the emphasis on the sufferings of the Saviour becomes more and more prominent.

Any of these forms of crucifix could of course be used as standards, fixed to a plain or ornamental base.　The same applies to an ordinary cross.　The standard or altar cross, presented by King Cnut to the New Minster, Winchester, is illustrated in Fig. 191, taken from *Liber Vitae* (1016–20).　The illumination is uncoloured, but the drawing in ink shows the cross of gold with a bevelled edge, or perhaps a silver fillet; the terminals appear to be moulded in ebony.

PLATE XIII (*see page* 127)

William of Wykeham in full XIV-Century Vestments

Fig. 192 is a much more elaborate altar cross of the thirteenth century of rather beautiful design. It is of goldsmith's work, set with jewels and pearls.

The cross of the resurrection was generally floriated or foliated at the extremities. There is an early and magnificent example in the mosaic of San Ponziano. Fig. 190 shows all four members treated in this manner.

THE PECTORAL CROSS

This was a small cross or crucifix used as a private ornament by bishops. It sometimes contained space within itself for a relic.

IV CENTURY

During the fourth century this custom of wearing round the neck a cross or reliquary spread to laymen, at first in the East, and later in the West.

Soon after the alleged discovery of the True Cross [1] in 326 by St. Helena (the first Christian empress), men and women wore around their necks particles of the True Cross enclosed in gold — so relates St. Chrysostom (*nat.* 344, *ob.* 407), Bishop of Constantinople.

The pectoral cross, shown in Fig. 193, is pronounced the earliest example extant. It was discovered about 1876 upon the breast of a corpse in the Basilica of St. Lawrence, outside the walls of Rome. No description of it is forthcoming, but from an illustration

Fig. 193. Early Pectoral Cross
After De Rossi

Fig. 194. Byzantine Pectoral Cross

it appears to be of black enamel on both front and back, and on them a design in gold or silver, perhaps niello. The crosses of white enamel bear inscriptions, on one side EMMANOVHA [2] (Emmanuel) on the transverse beam, and NOBISCVM DEVS on the upright. The whole cross is edged with fillet, which as well as the ring by which the cross is suspended is of precious metal. The reverse side, Fig. 193, has the same decorations, but the inscriptions are: on the transverse, MORS INIMICA TIBI, and on the upright, CRVX EST VITA MIHI.[3] A cavity in the centre is closed by a screw, and appears to have contained a relic.

[1] For a brief history of the True Cross see *Costume and Fashion*, vol. ii, p. 98.
[2] A Hebrew word meaning 'God with us,' from Matthew i. 23, itself quoting Isaiah vii. 14. 'Nobiscum Deus' is, of course, the Latin version.
[3] 'Death your enemy' and 'The Cross is my life.'

VI CENTURY

A reliquary in the form of a cross is mentioned, but not described, by Pope Gregory the Great (*nat.* 540, *ob.* 604), but it is quite likely that it was similar in shape to Fig. 193.

Fig. 194 is a pectoral cross of sixth-century Byzantine workmanship. The engraving from which this is taken suggests that it is made of gold, with the cross of coloured enamel outlined in silver.

IX CENTURY

Anastasius the librarian [1] wore an antique cross of the ninth century. There 'hung from his neck in front of his throat a cross of precious wood, containing relics of the saints that is called an encolpium.' This last was a small casket or little box, and as the Greek name implies was worn on the bosom by the most devout Christians.

Fig. 195.
Reliquary, IV Century

Fig. 196. St. Cuthbert's Pectoral
Cross, VII Century

Fig. 197.
The 'Canterbury Cross'

It usually contained a relic of some saint or else a passage from the gospels.

Reliquaries of this kind were sometimes made of gold, and some of these have been discovered at various times. One, dating the fourth century, is described as square in shape and furnished with a ring: on the front is engraved the monogram of Christ, as is shown in Fig. 195. Compare Fig. 187 of the fifth century.

An encolpium or reliquary is mentioned as being of gold with one side, obviously the front, formed of crystal, the other sides being enamel. This contained a second encolpium, in which fragments of the True Cross were arranged so as to form a pattern.

X CENTURY

The use of the pectoral cross was much more common amongst Eastern bishops than amongst those of the West, and it appears that there are only two English pectoral crosses in existence.

The one used by St. Cuthbert, which dates the seventh century and is now at Durham, is reproduced in Fig. 196; it is of gold set with enamel, mosaic, and jewels, the large red stone in the centre covering a small reservatory for a relic. This cross was discovered in the saint's tomb when opened in 1827, but lying on the breast *under* his episcopal vestments, as the pectoral cross had no significance at this time,[2] but was only a personal adornment.

---

[1] This Anastasius was probably the librarian of Pope Innocent IV (1243–54).
[2] The pectoral cross amongst the insignia of a bishop was unknown in England until after the Reformation.

The other is stated by Canon Dearmer to have belonged to St. Ælfeah (Alphege), who was Archbishop of Canterbury (1005–12): but efforts to trace it have failed unless it is the 'Canterbury Cross,' dug up in the main street of the city about 1860, and now in private possession.

Fig. 197 is a drawing of this cross which—although the pin is missing—has evidently been used as a brooch. It is about one and three-quarter inches across the arms, and in bronze, with a square boss in the centre. The arms are decorated with an unsymmetrical design of leaves and twining stems: in the centre of each is a silver triangle, engraved with a looped triangle filled with niello, a common design of the tenth century. It is tempting to imagine the archbishop losing his cross when taken prisoner by the Danes, who captured and burned the city in 1011.

XIII CENTURY

In the early years of this century Innocent III claimed the exclusive right of wearing a

Fig. 198.
Dedication Cross

Fig. 199.
Dedication Cross

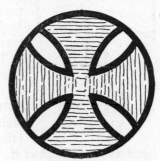

Fig. 200.
Dedication Cross, XI Century

pectoral cross, but this was not widely admitted, even in the West. There are numerous instances to the contrary, although no Western bishops attending the Council of Florence (1439) were allowed to wear crosses in the papal presence. In the East, however, the Greeks asserted and exercised their right to do so.

XIV CENTURY

It was not until the fourteenth century that the pectoral cross was acknowledged as a distinguishing episcopal ornament.

THE DEDICATION CROSS

Another purpose for which crosses were used in bygone ages, as also to-day, was that of consecration and dedication of a church. One often comes across them while visiting town and country churches. They are generally of the splayed Greek type, set within a circle as in Fig. 198, and painted a dull red on the white stone. They vary in number from one, usually to twelve, and sometimes lack the circle. They denote the part of the wall anointed by the chrism. Another slightly different kind is shown in Fig. 199.

At Radnage Church, Bucks., there are some very early (eleventh century, or possibly even earlier) dedication crosses; the best preserved show the cross constructed by four arcs of circles, as shown in Fig. 200. Only the lines are visible; the colour has vanished.

13. THE CROSS-STAFF

V CENTURY

From the fifth century onwards it was sometimes the custom for a cross to be carried in front of a religious procession, not only by the clergy, but also by lay-folk. These crosses would generally be of the Latin type, called *crux immissa*, Fig. 178; they might be also of the Greek type, Fig. 180.

They were constructed of wood or metal, and gradually became decorated, at first in a simple manner. Later the wooden frame would be covered with copper or bronze, and later still with silver or gold.

Fig. 201. Cross-staff of St. Gregory the Great, VI Century

An example of the use of a cross in procession comes from the year 597, when St. Augustine met King Æthelbert of Kent. This procession, we are told, was headed by a cross-bearer carrying a large silver cross; and by its side walked another monk bearing a picture painted on a board, the subject being Christ crucified.

The use of the staff or ferula surmounted by a cross was confined to archbishops, before whom it was carried in processions by their cross-bearers. On the other hand, archbishops are usually portrayed in paintings, mosaics, and sculpture holding a cross-staff in one hand (usually the left) as a sign of their episcopal office; and frequently, but not always, with a crozier in the other hand as the symbol of their pastoral care. When the occasion required the cross itself could be detached from the staff and fixed into a base to stand alone.

VI CENTURY

That the pope himself used a cross-staff is confirmed by a contemporary ivory diptych of St. Gregory I (the Great) (590–604), preserved in the treasury of the Cathedral of Monza.

It shows His Holiness holding in his left hand a staff or sceptre about three feet long, surmounted by a cross, like Fig. 201, except that the four members are all the same shape. It is the *cross patée*. In his right hand is held a sudarium, folded.

This pontiff is also represented in a drawing, pronounced to be contemporary, in which he holds a cross-staff in the right hand. Fig. 201 is a reproduction of the cross (of which three members only are symmetrical), surmounting the five-foot staff.

VIII CENTURY

As has been mentioned, the cross-staff was carried before popes from the sixth century; in this century its use began to pass from the pontiff to his legates, to archbishops and exarchs, patriarchs, and their deputies, and to metropolitans. By the eleventh century cardinals also had this privilege.

Ægbert, Archbishop of York, is represented with a cross-staff on one of his coins (732 or 734–66): this is probably the earliest example in England.

The precise date when the figure of the Redeemer, such as is seen in Fig. 188, was added to the archbishop's cross-staff, must be conjectural. However, Honorius of

Autun (*c.* 1130), writing retrospectively, gives us a clue. He says: 'The cross is carried before the archbishop to show forth the crucifixion of Christ.' This would, at first, no doubt, be a simple figure on a plain cross, but as time went on both figure and cross became more elaborate.

In its primary stages the figure was shown on one side only, being borne with the sacred image facing the archbishop. At about the beginning of the twelfth century it appeared on both sides, so that the eyes of the archbishop were fixed on one figure, those of the people on the other.

Fig. 202. Papal Cross-staff

IX CENTURY

It is recorded in *Ordo Romanus* that Charlemagne presented Pope Leo III (795–816) with a large processional cross of gold, which was stolen in the time of Pope Paschal I (817–24). Pope Leo IV (847–55) gave another in its stead, which was carried 'as was anciently the custom by a subdeacon, before the pope, in litany processions.'

It is likely that this cross closely resembles (if it is not identical with) the crucifix given by Charlemagne to Pope Leo III in 815, in which the figure wears an ample loin-cloth, showing the wound in the side. Four nails are used; the head is surrounded, as before, by a cruciform nimbus, but the eyes are closed.

It should be noted that the loin-cloth takes the place of the colobium from this time onwards.

It is not definitely known when the third transom was added to the cross-staff carried before the pope. The shape is shown in Fig. 202, the three transoms being of different lengths: it is entirely of gold and for the most part was without any decoration.

After the science of heraldry was introduced at the end of the twelfth century the papal cross-staff was sometimes used as an adjunct, but never incorporated in the armorial bearings of the pope.

X CENTURY

The cross-staff of simple and beautiful design, Fig. 203, is taken from the *Benedictional* of St. Æthelwold. It is the great masterpiece of the Winchester School, and was executed about 975–80, probably at Old Minster, Winchester. The cross would be made of some precious metal, most likely of gold, and is without any ornamentation except a fillet round the edge. The centre might be set with a jewel. The height appears to be about seven and a half feet over all.

Fig. 203. St. Æthelwold's Cross-staff, X Century

Fig. 204. Archbishop with Cross-staff, XIII Century

XII CENTURY

It is opportune to introduce here an archbishop in full vestments. Fig. 204 is a reproduction of an original drawing by Matthew Paris, who died in 1259.

Although this work is of the early years of the thirteenth century, the vestments must have been in use during the latter part of the twelfth. It is the illustration from which Fig. 190 also has been taken.

First of all the archbishop wears the usual alb: the embroidered hem and the sleeves at the wrists and the maniple are plainly seen, with the fringed ends of the tunicle above.

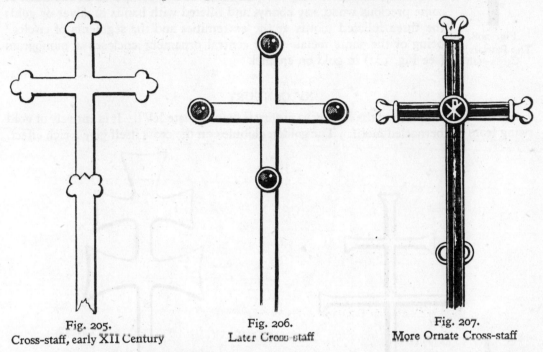

Fig. 205.
Cross-staff, early XII Century

Fig. 206.
Later Cross-staff

Fig. 207.
More Ornate Cross-staff

The dalmatic is embroidered or brocaded in a pattern of trellis-work enclosing motifs 'à pois,' and has a border set with jewels which is repeated on the amice. The chasuble is of plain coloured silk hanging in beautiful lines of drapery: the very narrow pallium seems to have been added as an afterthought.

Descriptions of the other items are given under their respective headings—the Mitre, Maniple, Ring, Buskins, and Gloves.

It must be repeated that the cross-staff did not supplant the crozier, nor did the archbishop ever carry it himself in processions. It was not a substitute for, but an addition to, the crozier, which was carried by his grace. Such cross-staffs would usually be about six feet high.

By the twelfth century ornament appears on the hitherto plain cross-staff, but at first it was of a simple nature.

In an illuminated MS. of the early years of the twelfth century there is depicted an archbishop's cross-staff, Fig. 205, which displays a slight innovation—the ends of the top and of the transoms are formed as trefoils. Fig. 190 shows a further development of this ornamentation. The cross is fixed to the staff by an ornament containing trefoil features. This design of a cross-staff is met with in several works of art of this period.

Fig. 206 is a little later in date, the entire cross being of plain metal or wood, gilded, or perhaps covered with plates of gold. The terminals of the three members, and of the base, could be of enamel, with some initial or other decoration in the centre of each disc.

An archbishop's cross-staff of the same period is seen in Fig. 207. This is much more ornate than the preceding, and is composed in the main of some precious wood, say ebony, and filleted with bands of silver or gold: the three foliated motifs at the extremities and the segments of circles [1] being of the same metal. The central ornament encloses a monogram (see Fig. 184) in gold on enamel.

Fig. 208.
The Patriarchal
Cross-staff

XV CENTURY

A beautiful cross-staff of the fifteenth century is seen in Plate XVI. It is entirely of gold rising from a tabernacled motif. The golden globules on the cross itself give a rich effect.

Fig. 209.
Hospitaller's Cross-staff, XII Century

Fig. 210.
Cross-staff, XIV Century

THE PATRIARCHAL CROSS-STAFF

Fig. 208 is the Patriarchal, or Primatial, also called the Benedictine, cross-staff. It is formed of an upright shaft crossed by two horizontal bars, of which the upper is the shorter, and represents the superscription board. This cross-staff was sometimes used by archbishops instead of the Latin cross.

[1] No doubt for holding the staff more firmly.

PLATE XIV (*see page* 160)
Canon Langeton, 1413, in Contemporary Procession Vestments

XII CENTURY

Of the following examples of this type of cross, the one shown in Fig. 209 is the earliest, as reckoned by the date of the illustration.

A slight elaboration of the simple original, Fig. 208, is met with in the order of the Knights Hospitallers of St. John of Jerusalem, which was founded in 1048, and which was for several centuries during the Crusades very powerful and wealthy. On his seal, dating about 1140, Prior Walter is represented kneeling in adoration before a patriarchal cross like that shown in Fig. 209. The total height is three times the width of the lower cross piece.

XIII CENTURY

Fig. 210 is a slightly varied form from one of the several illustrations in Queen Mary's psalter, which dates the beginning of the fourteenth century. There are some representations of this patriarchal cross with the ends either square or splayed in Matthew Paris's works, which evidences their popularity during at least the second half of the thirteenth century.

Fig. 211 is from a drawing by this artist and historian who gives such vivid pictures of his age. It is reproduced here to show how sacred and precious objects were venerated by covering or enveloping them and the hands with a piece of rich drapery as here, or with a portion of the bearer's sleeve or mantle.

The subject is St. Louis, King of France, mounted on a draped rostrum, and exhibiting to the people in 1241 a double or patriarchal cross in its original form, and saying 'Ecce Crucem Domini' (Behold the Cross of the Lord).

Fig. 211. St. Louis addressing the People, XIII Century

The patriarchal cross is frequently used as an adjunct to the armorial bearings of an archbishop, against all heraldic custom. A similar use of the papal cross, Fig. 202, is likewise without authority (see p. 139).

Archbishop's Cross-staff

We return now to the more usual form of cross-staff, the archbishop's or processional cross, Fig. 212. This is of the late thirteenth century, and is taken from the same New College window as Fig. 175. It is a good example of simple outline, reverting back in style to Fig. 206, but is much more elaborate in decoration.

This cross is apparently of gold, the centres of the discs being enamelled and set with pearls, and perhaps a precious stone in the centre of each. Fig. 212 is, perhaps, from an artistic point of view, the most beautiful in its dignity and simplicity, and the starting-point of gorgeousness to come.

I

XIV CENTURY

Paintings by the old masters exhibit a great number of ornate cross-staffs, some of them more sumptuous than others.

Fig. 213 is one of the less ostentatious, although rich in treatment, and dates the second half of the fourteenth century. It is in ebony, black or coloured enamel, and edged with a fillet of silver; the members are set with large pearls. On the sides of the

Fig. 212. Cross-staff in Stained Glass, XIV Century

cross smaller pearls are fixed. In the middle and at the terminals are silver quatrefoils, enclosing enamel of some contrasting colour. The boss, by which the cross is attached to the staff, is ornamented with a geometrical design in silver.

XV CENTURY

This is a period of highly ornamented cross-staffs.

Plate XVI, from the original painted panel in Ranworth Church, and depicting St. Thomas, presents an excellent example of goldsmith's work applied to a cross-staff dating the second half of the fifteenth century. It is entirely of gold, ornamented with many golden globules, and attached to a staff, also of gold, by four tabernacles.

Another beautiful cross-staff of very attractive proportions, dating late in this century, is given in Fig. 214. It is taken from a painting by Mabuse (1470–1534). Of gold, it is set with five large jewels and eight smaller ones. The four terminals suggest fleurs-de-lys. At its base where it meets the ebony staff are elaborate pinnacled one-tier tabernacles, enclosing figures of saints.

Ultimately the elaboration became decidedly overdone, as can be seen from the numerous examples of the period shown in contemporary works of art.

Fig. 213.
Jewelled Cross-staff, XIV Century

Fig. 214.
Cross-staff, late XV Century

14. THE HALO OR NIMBUS

HALO (ἅλως) is the Greek for a threshing-floor, which was circular in form, slightly raised in the centre, and kept scrupulously clean; it also applied to the disc of the sun and moon, and to a shield. Further, it refers to a circle of light, either white or prismatically coloured, seen round a luminous object, as is sometimes noticed surrounding a lamp in the darkness.

Nimbus is the Latin for a bright cloud, and a disc so called was adopted from the Greeks and employed by the Romans to set off the heads of divinities, thereby distinguishing them when they made their appearance on earth. The two names may be used synonymously.

A.D. IV CENTURY

It is difficult to state decisively at what date the earliest use of the nimbus in Christian art appears. The oldest catacombs yield no information, but there is slight evidence that its first appearance occurs early in the fourth century.

V CENTURY

In existing frescoes, mosaics, and sculptures of the fifth century several examples of the nimbus are to be found. As used in Christian art it is a disc, usually of gold, but

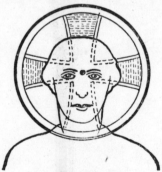

Fig. 215.
Nimbus shown Diagramatically

Fig. 216.
Early Nimbus from Byzantine Fresco

sometimes in colour, surrounding the head of a saint, an angel, or a sovereign, to impart a special dignity or sanctity, and as a symbol of honour. In some cases it is simply a ring of light with the background showing through.

It is possible that in the early days of art it was desirable to have a method of indicating which of the personages portrayed were saints, and so the nimbus was brought into use.

In the following drawings of nimbi it must be remembered that the lower member of the cross is, in the actual picture, hidden behind the head of the saint, as shown diagrammatically in Fig. 215. It will be seen that the centres of the Greek cross and of the disc coincide. Its position, shown by a dot, is between the eyes and level with the top of them, but this, however, was not invariably the case.[1]

[1] Gilbert French in his *Notes on the Nimbus* (1854) cites one or two examples in which he thinks the centre of the cross is not always in the centre of the disc, but below it. This may possibly be due to the faulty drawing of the artist. French also suggests that the three visible arms of the cross are intended to represent the Trinity.

In this same century we find in frescoes and mosaics, possibly for the first time, the nimbus charged with a cross (cruciform), used exclusively to surround the head of the Redeemer. Fig. 216 is taken from a contemporary Byzantine fresco at Rossano,[1] and shows Christ receiving homage from the evangelists. His head is framed by a golden disc, and on it is a cross which appears to be constructed of four arcs of a circle in double

Fig. 217.
The Infant Messiah, V Century

Fig. 218.
The Child Christ

lines of red or dull gold. This type of nimbus is frequently met with surrounding the head of our Lord during the following centuries.

Retrogressively, there are at least three very interesting representations of Him as a child, which are the central figures in the early fifth-century mosaic,[2] decorating the

Fig. 219.
Nimbus of Our Lord, VI Century

Fig. 220.
Nimbus of Our Lord, Early XIII Century

apsidal arch in the basilica of St. Maria Maggiore at Rome. One, the 'Presentation in the Temple,' shows the head surrounded by a disc of gold with a small Greek cross set outside the top, Fig. 217. In the second, 'The Meeting of Jesus and Affrodosius,' the same shaped cross occupies the space between the head and the top of the disc, Fig. 218. In the third, 'The Adoration of the Magi,' the Child is seated on a very

[1] Rossano is in southern Italy, west of the Gulf of Taranto.
[2] These mosaics were made by order of Sixtus III, Bishop of Rome (432-40).

gorgeous Byzantine throne, and robed in a tunica alba and himation (pallium): the nimbus is the same as in the second. All the angels in attendance are robed similarly, and have plain golden nimbi, but in all representations of the Virgin Mother in the mosaics and frescoes of this time her head is without a nimbus of any kind, as was often quite usual.

VI CENTURY

On the apsidal arch of the basilica of St. Vitalis at Ravenna our Lord is represented handing a crown to this first-century saint. The divine nimbus of gold is edged with pearls, and enshrines a Greek cross splayed like Fig. 219, the extremities of which are also studded with pearls. This same basilica contains examples of sovereigns being honoured with a nimbus, in the persons of the Emperor Justinian and the Empress Theodora. Each head is encircled with a plain gold nimbus edged with a white line.

VIII CENTURY

Henceforth the Greek form of cross became very generally depicted, but it was not always splayed at the ends, as is evidenced by the eighth-century fresco of the crucifixion in the Church of St. Maria Antiqua, Rome; here the ends of the cross are square.

XII CENTURY

Fig. 219 is the nimbus of our Lord in a fresco of this century; the ends of the cross of gold are slightly splayed.

In the figure of Christ in the mosaic at the Martorana, Palermo, in which He is placing the crown of the Two Sicilies on the head of Roger II, the nimbus is apparently of gold or silver, and the cross is the same shape as that shown in Fig. 219. In a similar mosaic in Monreale Cathedral, where William II of Sicily is being crowned, the nimbus is even more elaborate than that shown in Fig. 220. The disc is of gold outlined with pearls, and so is the coloured cross, which is set with many more jewels and pearls than heretofore.

XIII CENTURY

Fig. 220 shows the ends of the arms to be much more splayed than those in Fig. 219, and ornamented each with a precious stone in a gold setting and a pair of pearls. This is from a drawing of the dying Christ, dating from the first half of the thirteenth century.

From this time onwards the decoration of the cruciform nimbus became more and more elaborate, and resplendent with many jewels and pearls.

15. FLABELLUM OR MUSCARIUM, FAN

FLABELLUM, the Latin for a fan or fly-flap. The former is, and was from time immemorial, a useful accessory to costume and served many purposes: as an aid to coyness, affectation, and diffidence, and (especially in hot climates) for cooling oneself: the latter, a protection against unpleasant winged insects.

The fan was a necessity to the Assyrians, Persians, and Egyptians from remote times. At first fans were composed of palm or other broad leaves, then of feathers and the wings

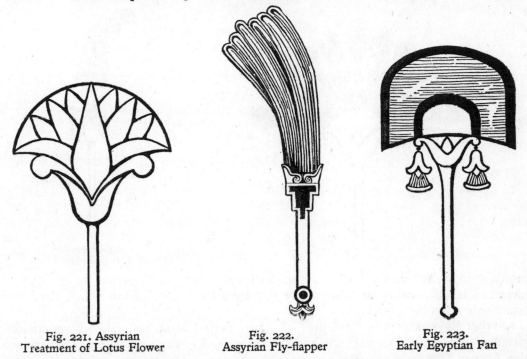

Fig. 221. Assyrian
Treatment of Lotus Flower

Fig. 222.
Assyrian Fly-flapper

Fig. 223.
Early Egyptian Fan

of birds. Later they were also made of linen, and in nearly all cases had handles either short or long, and always rigid.

As chronology relating to these early periods is still very uncertain, no dates are inserted until the classic Greek period.

EARLY TIMES. ASSYRIAN

Fig. 221 shows the conventional treatment of the lotus blossom or water-lily which grew abundantly in Assyria, Egypt, and the greater part of the East. Its form much influenced the art of these countries, and there is no doubt that the lotus so treated was the prototype of this particular shape of fan. Sculptures and many bas-reliefs show Assyrians and Persians of both sexes with such a lotus in the hand. It might be intended for the natural bloom, but sometimes its size suggests that it is a small fan.

149

The Assyrian fly-flapper shown in Fig. 222 is from a bas-relief, which represents King Ashurbanipal dining with his queen. It is made of shredded palm leaves fixed to an ornate handle, and two of them are held by officials standing behind the royal pair.

EGYPTIAN

An early Egyptian fan is given in Fig. 223. It is taken from a satirical papyrus [1] (No. 10, 1016) in the British Museum.

The shape is not too pleasing: and as parts of the original have been obliterated they have been supplied from other sources. This fan is probably composed of papyrus in its natural tones, and fixed on both sides of the curves to rigid borders, painted some

Fig. 224. Later Egyptian Fan

Fig. 225. Egyptian
Official Fan of Single Plume

bright colour, but shown black in the drawing. The handle is not more than 24 inches in length, and is attached to the flap by a lotus motif, from which hang two ornaments resembling tassels.

Another Egyptian fan or fly-flapper of a later period is likewise taken from one depicted on a papyrus, Fig. 224. It is clearly composed of feathers: ostrich feathers and also feather fans were importations from the Sudan. The feathers were not curled, but usually straight and rigid. Those of superior quality were curved at the top, and a single feather was carried by the Pharaohs and court officials as a sign of rank; Fig. 225 is that carried by Huy, Governor of Ethiopia under Tutankhamen (c. 1400 B.C.). The decoration of the feathers consisted chiefly of gilded quills and fronds dyed in zigzag horizontal bands of various colours—scarlet, blue, green, and gold.

In Fig. 224 the feathers are treated in this manner. They are fixed into a golden segment of a circle which might typify the rising sun or moon, and are supported by the usual lotus motif. When carried by slaves in attendance on important people the fan would have a long staff.

In the British Museum is a fan handle of normal length which is inscribed with the name of Nebseni of the city of Abydos, who was a priest of An-hur, the God of the Underworld.

[1] The date given by Sir Flinders Petrie is about 1150 B.C.

CLASSIC GREEK PERIOD

V CENTURY B.C.

At the end of the fifth century B.C. a fan modelled on the Egyptian was adopted by the Greeks. The materials of which these fans were made were much the same, papyrus being imported from Egypt.

II CENTURY B.C.

After the second century B.C. the new fabric—silk—was very popular among the wealthy for garments and accessories of all kinds. When used for fans it was stretched rigidly over a wire frame of leaf design. The handle varied in length.

Fig. 226 is a very characteristic Greek fan, shaped in wire and covered either with silk of some delicate colour, or with linen. The centre piece might be solid, studded with metal ornaments; it rises from a pair of metal volutes which are attached to the handle. This, as used by women, appears to be of any length from 15 inches to 4 feet. It should be noticed that the flap portion of this fan much resembles the honey-suckle motif so much used in Grecian art.

Fig. 226. Greek Fan,
II Century B.C.

Simultaneously feathers and wings of birds mounted back to back were attached to a 15-inch-long handle, and the proud feathers of the peacock were much favoured.

ROMAN PERIOD

IV CENTURY B.C.

Shortly after the introduction of the fan into Greece it found its way to republican Rome. It was a mere copy of the Greek.

I CENTURY B.C. AND LATER

Fig. 227.
Roman Fan for
General Use

During the empire the flabellum held in the hand was more elaborately decorated to suit the luxurious fancy of the ladies of imperial Rome. Large semicircular fans of feathers, especially of the peacock, fixed to poles anything from 6 feet upwards in length, were carried by slaves in attendance on these ostentatious nobles of both sexes.

Fig. 227 is a type of Roman fan not quite of the best, used by ordinary well-to-do people. The feathers of any bird are arranged without any attempt at symmetry. The handle of moderate length and simple design is of wood or metal.

I TO V CENTURIES

Christian Era

In the early years of the Christian Church the fan, or as it was more generally called the FLABELLUM, modelled on the Roman type, was introduced as a means of protecting the elements and numerous holy vessels from pollution caused by flies and other obnoxious winged insects.   Such a fan was also called a MUSCARIUM.

The following quotation from a liturgy of the fifth century testifies to the above: 'Two deacons, one on either side of the altar, are directed to hold fans formed of thin membrane of the feathers of the peacock, or of linen tissue, to drive away any little flying creatures, lest they should fall into the sacred vessels.'

Similar instructions are given under date 535.

Many churches did not possess a flabellum, possibly because one worthy of so sacred a function as purification might be too expensive or difficult to obtain.   As an alternative a napkin of superior quality was carried by a deacon, who, by shaking or rippling it, would scare away any offensive insects that came near the elements, the holy vessels, or the celebrant.   These napkins were often ornamented with 'divers colours of needlework on both sides,' and sometimes embellished with gold and pearls.

In old French the prefix *es*, a contraction of *en les*, was used when referring to any work of art in the sense of enhancement, and therefore ESMOUCHOIR meant a superior napkin.

Fig. 228. Flabellum, XII Century A.D. *After Viollet-le-Duc*

VI CENTURY

The Western Church does not seem to have used fans much earlier than this century.

As already mentioned these Roman fans were composed of peacocks' tail-feathers, of fine linen mounted on a circle of metal, or of radiating pleated parchment somewhat after the style shown in Fig. 228.   The latter was often coloured, and later painted and gilded with representations of saints or other sacred objects.   The handles were of metal, wood, or ivory, many of them appearing to be only about 3 feet long.

No further illustrations of the flabellum are available until we reach the twelfth century, but there are numerous descriptions, and a few of these are given here:

IX CENTURY

'A silver flabellum for keeping flies off the elements' is found in an inventory at St. Riquier, Abbeville, dating 831.   A flabellum similar to that shown in Fig. 228 was deposited in the treasury at Monza, and is assigned by an expert to the ninth century.

XI CENTURY

At the end of the eleventh century St. Hildebert, Archbishop of Tours (*c.* 1099), presented a fly-flapper to a friend.

XII CENTURY

See Fig. 228. Here at last we have an illustration.

XIII CENTURY

In an inventory at Salisbury dated 1214 occurs the entry 'Ornaments of the Church of Sarum: two flabella of subserica for purification.' See also Fig. 64.

An inventory relating to the Church of Amiens mentions 'a flabellum made of silk and gold for keeping off filthy flies.' This was given by a canon of the church about 1250.

In the Church of St. Faith, under the crypt of St. Paul's, London, there was (1298) 'a fly whisk of peacock's feathers.'

XIV CENTURY

Hamo Hethe, Bishop of Rochester (1319–52), gave to the cathedral in the year 1346 'a flabellum [muscarium] with an ivory handle.'

St. Chapelle possessed 'two flabella for purification purposes, and two French esmouchoirs ornamented with pearls' (1376).

XV CENTURY

John Newton, treasurer of York Minster, gave in 1413 a flabellum of silver weighing 5 oz., with the figure of Archbishop Henry Bowet (1407–23) wrought upon it in very fine enamel.

At the Abbey of St. Edmundsbury was preserved, 'j. muscifugium de pecok,' according to the *Compotus* dated 1429.

The churchwardens' accounts at Walberswick contain the entry 'for a bessume [1] of pekoks fethers, iv[d].'

FORM AND DECORATION

XII CENTURY

During the twelfth century the flabellum, or to call it by its French name, the 'esmouchoir,' took a circular shape as shown in Fig. 228. It was formed at first not as a square, but as an oblong, and pleated like a modern fan. For more practical purposes a disc with a circular hole in the middle was adopted later. Of parchment, or some other suitable material, it was pleated in radiating folds from its centre (on the principle of a modern lamp-shade) and measured about 12 inches in diameter. It was fixed between two upright supports, possibly of wood, their bases being the top of the handle, which was about 2 feet long. Around the outside edge there was sometimes an ornate border, either painted or worked, consisting of lines and scrolls of different colours and gold; similar scrolls might decorate the uprights. The handle was of ivory or it might be of silver.

Fig. 229. Deacon bearing Flabellum, XIII Century

[1] Obviously a fly-flapper: cf. the word 'besom' for a broom of twigs.

Fig. 230. Elevation of the Host, XIII Century
After Albert Way

A very simple flabellum is carried by the subdeacon, Fig. 64. The radiating folds are drawn exactly as they are shown in the original illuminated MS.; they suggest pleated parchment, linen, or silk stretched on a circle of metal.

There are several of these esmouchoirs scattered over France, and one is particularly worthy of a description on account of its decoration and beauty. This fan belonged to the Abbey of Tournus, and is now in the Cluny Museum. It has the same appearance as that in Fig. 228, and it is stated that the fan fully expands, meaning of course that it opens and shuts. Made of vellum, it is covered on both sides with paintings in gold and colours, arranged in concentric bands consisting of floral motifs and figures of saints. The narrow dividing bands are inscribed with hexameter and pentameter verses, setting forth its use and its oblation in honour of God and St. Philibert, who was the founder of the Abbey of Jumièges and died in 684. The 2-foot-long handle is of carved ivory, and round the pommel is inscribed: 'Johel me scae fecit in honore Mariae.'

Fig. 231.
Flabellum of the Eastern Church

XIII CENTURY

The public library at Rouen owned a thirteenth-century missal which once belonged to the Abbey of Jumièges; the deacon carrying a flabellum, Fig. 229, is taken from one of the illuminations. This circular fan is about 15 inches in diameter, or perhaps a little less. It is made with an outer rim, coloured red, and attached to a central disc of the same colour; from this spring wire spokes of gold between leaf-shaped motifs in green, the effect being that of an ornamented wheel. It is unlikely that it revolves on its hub, however. That the pole is of gilded wood, for lightness, is conjectural.

An illustration, Fig. 230, from an illuminated MS., a pontifical of the Cathedral of Rheims, shows a deacon waving a short-handled flabellum over the head of an officiating bishop who is in the act of elevating the 'hostia' or consecrated loaf. The fan is formed of a circular piece of plain parchment, necessarily strengthened with a wire rim. The bishop in mitre, chasuble, dalmatic, and alb, bows his head as he raises the element: this is stamped with a cross, the seal with which the bread in the eucharist is signed. The chalice, it will be noted, is covered with a cloth or chalice veil.

The vestments of the deacon are described on p. 49.

XIV CENTURY

The flabellum as an ornament of utility ceased to be used in the Western Church, except in a few cases, by the fourteenth century.

Although beyond the limit of this book two items of interest are given below.

Randle Holmes (1627–99), who published his *Academy of Armory* in 1688, lists among things pertaining to the altar at Dunwich 'a flap or fan to drive away the flies from the chalice.'

Even in our own time, at the coronation of Pope Pius XII in 1939, magnificent flabella, apparently of ostrich feathers, surmounting fans of heavy gold embroidery were borne near His Holiness.

In the Eastern Church a flabellum was in use which had a modelled head fixed to the end of a handle or long staff, see Fig. 231. The wings surrounding the face were in accordance with the description given by the prophet Isaiah (vi. 1, 2) of the seraphim above the throne of God. 'Each one had six wings; with twain he covered his face, and with twain he covered his feet, and with twain he did fly.'

16. THE COPE

The Lacerna, The Byrrus, The Pluviale, Cappa Nigra, Cappa Choralis, Cappa Magna.
Morse. Hood.

Ancestry of the Cope

THERE is a difference of opinion as to the origin of the cope. Some, including Father Braun, S.J., hold that it descends directly from the paenula; others, amongst whom is Canon Dearmer, consider that its origin is to be found in the lacerna or byrrus, or in both. The rival ancestors will now be described, and their differences noted: from the information given the reader may perhaps be able to come to a decision on the point.

The author inclines to favour the paenula, which has been already described under 'Chasuble': *see* page 56.

Fig. 232. Asiatic wearing the Byrrus

The *Lacerna* was a cloak like the Greek chlamys (see *Costume and Fashion*, vol. i, p. 45) but with two corners rounded off, in fact, almost semicircular, and similar to the paenula in shape, Fig. 6. It was introduced into republican Rome from Asia Minor by the voluptuous Lucullus, as an added protection against weather, for officers on his Bithynian campaign (74–68 B.C.) in the third Mithridatic War.

Of a light or heavy woollen material, usually red, it was worn fastened to the right shoulder, or in front by a fibula or clasp, and draped over the left arm. Sometimes a cucullus or hood was attached to it.

The fashionable upper classes of Rome were much taken with this cloak, and used it in different colours as a light wrap for summer evening wear. The young patrician, Fig. 5, is wearing the lacerna.

Simultaneously, its use in a thicker material continued in the army of republican and imperial Rome.

The *Byrrus*. Probably of barbaric origin, the byrrus was a cloak or cape to which a hood was attached. Usually of a brown or flame colour (hence its name), it was shaped like a curtailed paenula, and made of thick material such as heavy cloth or felt, and often of tanned or untanned hide.

Father Braun considers the byrrus, as well as the cope, to be a modification of the paenula.

Fig. 232 is from a fresco representing an Asiatic in a skin tunic open up the sides over a linen undergarment with long sleeves. A byrrus is fastened in front with a brooch, and is slightly draped over the left arm, showing the front edges rounded at the bottom. This Phrygian type of tunic and hood is met with in art, particularly in the mosaic of the Three Magi in the Basilica of St. Apollinare Nuovo, Ravenna.   The byrrus was an outdoor winter garment, worn in Rome before and after the Christian era by the lower classes and slaves: 'viles birri'=cheap cloaks.   The peasant in Fig. 73 is wearing a byrrus.   A byrrus of superior quality was used by better-class persons for the same purpose.

A.D. V CENTURY

By the fifth century the byrrus was worn by laymen and clergy alike, and we hear of even bishops wearing this cloak when out of doors.   By this time it is almost always referred to as a rather expensive item: 'pretiosi birri'= costly cloaks; and having a certain secular character. St. Isidore couples together the planeta and the byrrus, neither of which was allowed to monks.   The former was the more elaborate of the two.

By St. Augustine of Hippo's time (first quarter of the fifth century; he died in 430, aged 76) already the lacerna and byrrus were made of silk and other rich fabrics.

VI CENTURY

'Birrus albus' is mentioned in the sixth century, and was a white cloak or christening garment worn by the newly baptized.

It will be seen that between these two garments there was really no essential difference.   The outer garment or paenula worn by St. Cyprian at his martyrdom is called indifferently by both names, as is also the cloak of St. Augustine.

The lacerna tended to be of lighter material, a sort of dust cloak for summer use: whereas the byrrus was usually thicker and warmer.

Assuming then that the cope descends from the paenula we may now come to the vestment itself.

Fig. 233.
The Cappa Nigra, VI Century

The Cope Itself

During the earlier period of the Church's existence a black-hooded bell-shaped garment, known as a CAPPA NIGRA or CAPPA CHORALIS, was in use among the secular and regular clergy at choir services, and for outdoor processions.   Actually this garment is the paenula unfastened up the front, and already described in Section 5.   For its shape reference should be made to the diagram, Fig. 77.   It was a simple serviceable cloak, Fig. 233, used by the clergy to keep themselves warm in the cold churches which, before heating arrangements were installed, abounded in uncomfortable draughts.

It was also convenient as a rain cloak, and on that account was then referred to as a PLUVIALE.   When it had a hood attached, as worn by the Gallic monks, it was called a 'cucullus' (see p. 56); but in Italy, e.g. at Monte Cassino, it was termed a 'cappa.'

VIII CENTURY

Father Braun states that the garment in question became known as the COPE, and so a liturgical vestment, at the end of the eighth century; some authorities affirm that this happened in the century before, others say not until the ninth.

The late Latin 'cappa,' meaning originally a cap (deriving ultimately from 'caput' = head), has given us also 'cape,' which is a head-covering lengthened so as to cover the shoulders; and so eventually 'cope,' reaching nearly to the ground.

IX CENTURY

By degrees the higher clergy in western Europe embellished this previously unobtrusive cappa (which now reached to the feet) with much ornamentation, copes being made of rich plain fabrics beautifully embroidered. However, in Anglo-Saxon England this vestment retained its humble, sober character; for in a pontifical of the year 900 is represented a cope of plain cloth, the edges of the straight part fastened with an agrafe,[1] or tied with lappets—infulae. This last arrangement was, of course, a commonplace at the time.

Fig. 234. Orphrey on a Cope, Later Date

Those unfamiliar with the cope will find its general outline described, as paenula, under Chasuble, p. 56, where there is a diagram, Fig. 77, to show how it was cut.

Sometimes a small semicircle for the neck was cut in the centre of the straight edge, thus eliminating folds and fitting closer on the shoulders, a method not much used according to illustrations.

When a cope was made of a large-patterned damask with an upright design it was cut and sewn together as described on page 78; the diagram, Fig. 103, explains this method very clearly. It also shows the band of the orphrey, which edges the two fronts and surrounds the neck of the cleric.

Although Fig. 234 is drawn from a coin of a later date, it shows how this stiff band of embroidery forms a high collar effect at the back of the head.

X AND XI CENTURIES

Though the cope was generally worn in the Western Church during the tenth century, its use did not become universal until the eleventh; but even then, though its form was by this time standardized, the ritual connected with it still varied a good deal.

XIII CENTURY

It was not until early in the thirteenth century that the liturgical use became stereotyped.

The Syon cope, entirely covered with English needlework, and one of the most magnificent examples extant, is so well known through its frequent reproduction that a full description here is superfluous. All that need be said is that it dates the late thirteenth century, has the orphrey border on the straight edge, and fastens across the breast with

---

[1] i.e. jewelled brooch: see *Costume and Fashion*, vol. i, p. 284.

K

an embroidered rectangle called a morse. The surface is covered with interlacing barbed quatrefoils, filled with scenes from the life of our Lord, and with figures of saints: the intervening spaces contain seraphim. When the cope was worn all these figures would be upright. The wide orphrey along the straight edge contains armorial bearings in lozenges and circles. This cope belonged to the monastery of Syon at Isleworth, and at the demolition found a refuge in Lisbon: it now occupies a place of honour in the Victoria and Albert Museum.

Fig. 235. The Cappa Nigra,
XIV Century

XIV CENTURY

By the fourteenth century a slight change is noticeable in the cappa nigra or choral cope: this is shown in Fig. 235. It is from the brass dated 1383 to the memory of Nicholas of Louth at Cottingham, Yorks, who was an Augustinian canon. The cappa—which would, of course, be black in contrast to the white cappa of the canons of Prémontré—is here gathered or pleated into a narrow neck-band, resembling a collar, under the fur hood of the cape. The broad effect of the shoulders is due to this cape worn underneath. For a description of it see p. 174, and p. 176 for the white undergarment. The cassock underneath the surplice is invisible except for the sleeves buttoned at the wrists.

XIV AND XV CENTURIES

We see in Plate XIV a fully developed cope, although later in date; of rich material, and not so elaborately embroidered as the earlier Syon specimen just described.

The drawing, however, gives a good idea of what this vestment looked like when worn, and of its future appearance. The authority from which this drawing is made is the brass in Exeter Cathedral of the kneeling figure of Canon William Langeton, 1413, a scion of the House of Stafford. He is wearing processional vestments, which varied little from the earliest example (1382) down to the Reformation. The cope is made of velvet, which by this time was much used, but still very expensive. The border or orphrey would have a cloth of gold foundation, or possibly silk of the same colour, and is decorated with lozenges and discs alternating the full length. The discs contain the chrisma of rather unusual design (compare with Fig. 186) in purple on silver: the lozenges are red, with the Stafford knot worked in gold (see inset). A white fur cape with hood and stole-like ends (see Fig. 250) is worn under the cope, and below this a surplice over a purple cassock.

THE MORSE

The fastening of the cope at the throat evolved usually from an agrafe, and sometimes from two bands (lappets) with fringed ends. This method of tying was very usual,

PLATE XV *(see page 54)*

St. Laurence the Deacon in XV-Century Vestments

particularly with persons of importance, during the Carlovingian period, to fasten their mantles on the left shoulder.

XIII CENTURY

By the thirteenth century a rectangle of embroidery was sewn on one edge of the cope and fastened to the opposite edge by buttons and loops.   This was known as the MORSE.

Attached to the late thirteenth-century Syon cope is an elaborate silken morse ornamented with armorial bearings in lozenges and rectangles: the fastenings are elaborate Harrington knots (the same as frettes) of gold passement ending in loops for buttoning to the opposite edge.   Later the morse developed into a very beautiful piece of jewellery of excellent gold-smith's work.   That worn by William of Wykeham, Bishop of Winchester, and now in New College, Oxford, is shown in Fig. 236.   This is formed of the letter M in gold, the symbol of the Virgin, patroness of the diocese, surmounted by a crown, and is set with cabochon rubies, emeralds, and oriental pearls, in compartments outlined with granular work.   The vase in the centre is cut from a large ruby, from which spring three lilies, which are pearls backed by silver

Fig. 236.
William of Wykeham's Morse

foil, with cabochon emeralds set as leaves.   Standing in the open arches are the figures of the Virgin and the Archangel Gabriel, of gold in full relief, the wings being set with translucent green enamel.

THE HOOD

During the past centuries the hood or cucullus (Fig. 72 gives its original shape) of both secular and regular clergy had been a very general item of head-covering, either attached to or separated from the main garment.   This arrangement made it possible for special hoods of liturgical colours to be worn by the clergy during different seasons.

Such hoods, worn by the country folk and laity generally, were close-fitting; so when the clergy adopted them and found them rather small, a triangular piece of material, often beautifully embroidered, was substituted, sewn on to the cope at the back of the neck, this being now merely a token hood, for ornament, not use.

Some other head-covering was therefore necessary to protect a bald or tonsured head from the cold.   The skull-cap fulfilled this purpose.   Originating from the pilos, a round cap, Fig. 117, its descendants came to be known by various names, such as pillius, pileus, pileolus.   Many synods ordered the use of this cap as a substitute for the hood, and in one instance the synod of Bergamo, 1311, ordered the clergy to wear the 'bireta on their heads after the manner of laymen.'   This bireta proved very comfortable to men accustomed to being bareheaded in choir.

The round cap being made in four sections eventually developed into a square—the BIRETTA of the future.[1]

[1] A descendant of the pilos through the biretta is to be found in the more modern university 'mortar-board,' which dates back to the sixteenth century.

At a much later period (the sixteenth century) the flat piece of embroidery at the back of the cope, in imitation of the hood, assumed a different shape, becoming a semi-oval bounded at the top by the shorter axis. This was covered with even more gorgeous embroidery.

CAPPA MAGNA

A Cardinal's Attire

Another important cloak or mantle, a garment or vestment of state worn by prelates, was the CAPPA MAGNA. This was shaped as a complete circle with a hole for the head, and could be worn enveloping the whole person in front, as well as the back: the front portion was usually draped over one arm, or both. Its material was silk, generally lined with silk, either white or some colour, and not infrequently with fur. A hood of ample proportions was attached to, or separate from, the main garment, and usually worn thrown back squarely over the shoulders. Bishops wore the cappa magna of purple cloth, and cardinals a silk of rich scarlet, which had a tone of crimson in its shadows: by which the colour obtained the name of 'cardinal.'

XIII CENTURY

A useful fact to be remembered is that scarlet was not worn by cardinals until the middle of the thirteenth century.

Fig. 237 is a cardinal of the late thirteenth century wearing a cappa magna of scarlet silk lined with white. The large hood is obviously a separate item, and is broadly turned back over the shoulders. The cappa envelopes the left arm, and is draped over the right upper arm, leaving the hand free. More dignity was added to the appearance of this stately vestment by cutting it on the oval plan so that the back trailed along the ground.

Immediately beneath the cappa is worn a rochet of fine, almost transparent, white linen, reaching to just below the knees. The fairly loose sleeves are long, and ruck over the cassock sleeves, the ends of which, being unlined in this case, are turned back, forming what appear to be red cuffs. Under the rochet is the scarlet cassock of woollen material, buttoned up the front, the length all round reaching to the feet. At a later date the cassock was cut longer at the back, and formed a train, that of the cappa being dispensed with.[1]

The red hat was the distinguishing feature of the cardinal's attire. It descends from the *petasos* of the Greeks, which was awarded as a military honour, and used also as such by the Romans: it has a round crown with a fairly wide brim, an amalgamation of Figs. 119 and 120.

Pope Innocent IV (1243-54), at the First Council of Lyons, 1245, instituted that cardinals should wear a red *petasos*, to signify, says John Guillim fancifully, that they should be prepared to shed their blood and hazard their lives in the defence of ecclesiastical liberty.[2]

The cardinal, Fig. 237, wears this distinctive scarlet hat, which has a round crown and a wide turned-up brim. There does not appear to have been any definite rule regarding

[1] For a cardinal of the late fifteenth and sixteenth centuries see *Costume and Fashion*, vol. iii, p. 177, Fig. 227.

[2] In our own time this defence has been heroically manifested in the case of the Prince Primate of Hungary, Cardinal Mindszenty, 1949.

Fig. 237. A Cardinal of the XIII Century

the brim, whether it was up, down, or flat; however, illustrations afford some assistance
—at first it was turned up, and then down, but by the close of the thirteenth century it
was flat, see Fig. 238, and has more or less remained so ever since.

The hat is worn, in this case, over a scarlet coif, which fits closely to the head: this
would not be necessary when the hood was worn.

The single cord, by which the hat was supposed to be tied under the chin, was wound
round the base of the crown, knotted on each side, and passed *through* the brim, each
end finishing with a tassel. The arrangement of tassels varied. Bonaventura, the
renowned saint, doctor of the Church, and Cardinal Bishop of Albano (1231–74), in his
miniature [1] has, at the ends of the knotted cord, a triangle whence hang three tassels,
Fig. 238; whereas Henry Beaufort, Cardinal Bishop of Winchester (1404–47), has only
one at each end; but the brim of his hat is flat. Henceforward many more tassels
were added, to the limit of fifteen, arranged in pyramid formation as described on page
48, and shown in Fig. 239. By the fifteenth century custom had crystallized into
fifteen (five rows) for a cardinal, ten (four rows) for an archbishop, and six (three rows)
for a bishop and arch-abbot.

[1] MS. No. 213, Corpus Christi College, Cambridge.

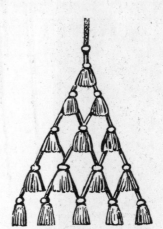

Fig. 238. Cardinal's Hat,
Later Type

Fig. 239. Tassels in Pyramid
Formation, XV Century

17. THE CASSOCK

THE origin of this garment is said by some to date back to pre-Christian times, and to be found in the costume of the Gauls—the barbarians of north-western Europe.

II CENTURY B.C.

This garment was known in the Latin tongue as CARACALLA, and described by Dio Cassius (c. 150–235) as a 'sleeved tunic made somewhat in the fashion of a corselet.' Fig. 240, a drawing made from the original bronze statuette in Vienne Museum, Isère, shows the caracalla worn by a Gaul, whose long hair and beard denote (according to the Roman idea) the barbarian. He wears a mantle of the lacerna type over a tunic—the caracalla—close-fitting to the thigh, open up the front, and slit behind. The long close sleeves, reaching to the wrists, are also barbaric, as are the behosed legs and sandals. The thrown-back hood—cucullus—was usually attached either to the mantle or to the caracalla.

The material of the caracalla, including its sleeves, and of the hosae, appears to be covered with squares, which may be of two or more contrasting colours; the sides of the squares would measure about 1¼ inches.

Fig. 240. Caracalla worn by a Gaul

A.D. III CENTURY

As a means of currying favour with his troops, the Emperor Marcus Aurelius Antoninus Bassianus (211–17) wore this short and sleeved barbaric tunic. He was celebrated for his eccentricities, and as might be expected the debased Roman nobles followed with alacrity the imperial example. In consequence the nickname 'Caracalla' was given to him.

After a time it tickled the emperor's fancy to lengthen this garment down to the ankles. It would then be cut as shown in Fig. 241, except that it was not so ample in the skirt: the result was referred to as a 'vestis talaris.' The populace in general, realizing that the emperor was responsible for the introduction of this outrageous garment, called it 'Antoniniana caracalla.'

All the same, this elongated version was widely adopted in Rome, in spite of its inconvenience to those accustomed to a short tunic: the populace must often have cursed Caracalla and all his monkey-tricks!

Under the Angevin kings of England a garment of this shape and reaching to the feet as shown in Fig. 241 became much used in the West. It corresponded in form with the older Turkish and Persian Kaftan, the exception being that the latter had long wide sleeves.

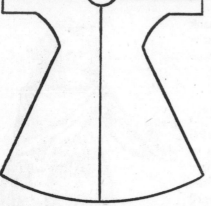

Fig. 241. Diagram of Caracalla

A similar robe was worn by Jews of the Orient, and called the GABERDINE or Galvardine; Jews of the Occident were compelled to substitute the wide sleeve for the closer one, such as western folk wore, as they were forbidden to engage in handicrafts of any kind. It was supposed that long full sleeves hindered manual labour.

V CENTURY

Early Church historians refer to the caracalla as worn by clerics, and in the middle of the fifth century it is described by St. Eucherius, Bishop of Lyons (434–50), as a kind of *short* tunic with sleeves and hood; so it is obvious that at this date the original shape was still in use, but at what period the clergy adopted the long garment as shown in diagram, Fig. 241, is not certain.

XI CENTURY

In medieval times, starting about the eleventh century, the caracalla, reaching to the ankles, came to be known in Italy as 'casacca,' and in France as 'casaque,' both signifying a long coat: and through these the name CASSOCK has descended into English. The shape remained the same as in Fig. 241, but the material was now usually black.

One is perhaps justified in hazarding the opinion that the cassock, having been used by the clergy since the fifth century, may now be considered a vestment.

Fig. 241 still gives the shape, and at this stage in its history it was made of black cloth. The chief purpose of the cassock was warmth; and being worn in cold churches, and also in the streets, it was usually lined with fur, in which case it was referred to as a 'pellicea,' or 'pellicia' [tunica]. These terms, and the modern form 'pelisse,' are derived ultimately from *pellis,* 'skin.' The cassock was worn *under* the alb, and was, in consequence, unseen. Very rich furs were used to line the caracalla when worn by the higher prelates: ordinary priests were not allowed these expensive furs, even if they could afford them; they had to be content with sheepskin.

XII CENTURY

Being a garment which opened up the front with a slit behind, it was fastened at first by the simple method of strings, although buttons were in use from classic times.

Fig. 242. Priest in Black Cassock, XIII Century

XIII CENTURY

A brass of a priest of the second half of the thirteenth century is shown in Fig. 242. He is clad in a black cassock lined with fur (which gives a rather bulky effect). The cut is the same as previously, but fuller in the sleeves and skirt on account of the fur lining. It is fastened up the front by six pairs of buttons below the waist: these may extend upwards, being perhaps covered by the hands. From an ornamental belt hangs an anlace or long knife in a sheath. This is rather unusual, but no doubt necessary, especially in isolated parishes. Over the shoulders and neck are the folds of a detached turned-back hood.

A narrow stand-up collar appears on cassocks seen in brasses late in this century, and in the next; but this, of course, is hidden when a hood was worn.

By degrees buttons placed very close together descend the whole length of the front: and at the back the slit was flanked by one, and later two, pleats let into the waist seam.

In more recent times, coloured cassocks became customary. The pope wore a white one; cardinals, scarlet; archbishops, bishops, and other prelates, purple. For ordinary every-day use both cardinals and prelates wore black cassocks, piped, buttoned, and girded with a silk sash (cincture) in scarlet and purple respectively. Plain black cassocks continued to be worn by priests and minor clergy.

The long cassock with train trailing on the ground, worn by prelates like Wolsey, dates from a later period, not before the early fifteenth century.

18. THE SURPLICE

XI CENTURY

THIS garment, a late modification of the alb, is to be traced with certainty no further back than the eleventh century, though some authorities affirm that it made its appearance a century earlier, or even during the fifth century.

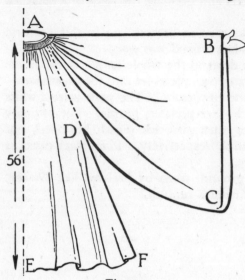

Fig. 243.
Half Diagram of Surplice, XV Century

However, it is first mentioned in a canon of Coyaca, Spain, 1050, and in an ordinance of Edward the Confessor (1042–66). Its name is derived from the fact that it was worn *over* the cassock—superpellicium—which became eventually SURPLICE.

XII CENTURY

The surplice of this period was made of white linen or cotton, and reached to the feet. In shape it was much like the alb. The sleeves, however, were wider and longer, and extended at least 10 inches *beyond* the finger tips, so producing folds along the arms. Around the open ends they measured about 30 inches, and where they joined the main garment they were about 32 or 34 inches. The neck-opening was circular for the head to pass through; sometimes there was a neck-band, continued down the front, fastened with buttons and loops. The surplice worn by the cleric, Fig. 233, answers to this description.

XIII CENTURY

The surplice so far had been only a choir vestment, but from now onwards it was deemed appropriate to be worn in the administration of the sacrament, and at other sacerdotal functions.

The subdeacon bearing the flabellum, Fig. 63, is wearing the surplice peculiar to the lower orders of the ministry. It is of more simple cut than that shown in the diagram, Fig. 243, which is later and more voluminous; but its shape is the same. At Lincoln in this century even servers were to be vested in surplices in order to add dignity to the service.

XIV CENTURY

By the commencement of the fourteenth century the surplice had become what it is to-day, the distinctive vestment of the lower grade of cleric, being used in choir and in processions, in fact, everywhere except as a eucharistic vestment. Even then the celebrant might wear a surplice under his alb.

The Augustinian canon, Fig. 235, is robed in the latest-shaped surplice, which is fuller than previously, and more closely related to that shown diagramatically in Fig. 243. Most likely the neck-band is gauged, but this is covered by the hood of his almuce.

XV CENTURY

During the fifteenth century certain developments took place in the shape of the surplice.

In the absence of any authentic diagram of its cut, one can only judge of its shape from illuminated MSS.: from the descriptions of shirts worn by the laity, which by this time reached a high standard of tailoring: and from existing surplices modelled more or less on the antique.   Fig. 243 shows one-half of a surplice founded on these sources.   Two linen rectangles, each 56 by 54 inches, are required for the main part of the garment. These are seamed up the sides DF, and form the back and front, the length AF, neck to feet, being the long side, allowing 15 inches AD for the arm-holes.   The top is drawn in parallel gathers to make a 24-inch circular neck-band 2 inches wide, see at A.

For each sleeve a rectangle 48 by 24 inches is needed: this is folded over to make a square, the bottom edges CD are joined, and 9 inches of the inner side is gauged into the neck-band, leaving 15 inches, AD, for the arm-hole to be joined into the main part.

If so much cannot be gauged in (and this depends on the size of the wearer) the lower edge, CD, must be correspondingly curved upwards.   All these measurements are approximate.   The neck-opening was treated in various ways, and was not always large enough for the head to pass through; then the surplice was open for a short distance in front, with a neck-band fastened with a button or two and loops.   Fig. 247 shows this method, and in addition has two cords with tasselled ends.

In the following century this vestment became shorter, as shown in Fig. 250; and eventually became so short that it reached only to the thigh, to the great detriment of its appearance.

It must be emphasized that the original twelfth-century surplice was a full-length garment, reaching to the ground, and that the gradual shortening did not begin until two or three centuries later.

The surplice is worn by the canon, Plate XIV, and also in Figs. 250, 233, 247.

19. THE TUNICLE

As has already been mentioned, the dalmatic was the characteristic vestment of the deacon as well as of the bishop.

VI CENTURY

By the sixth century the lesser clergy had taken into use a super-tunic, to be worn over the alb, which became known as the TUNICLE, because it was a smaller tunica.

IX CENTURY

It was in shape similar to the dalmatic, Fig. 62, slit up the sides, but narrower and longer in the sleeves, and usually made of woollen or linen material.

Fig. 244

Fig. 245

Background Patterns, XV Century

During this century the tunicle was simple in form, and was officially recognized as the distinguishing vestment of subdeacons, Fig. 229, in the celebration of the mass, and of clerks.

XII CENTURY

Its first appearance on a *bishop* seems about 1200: before this it was the dalmatic which was worn under the chasuble, and still earlier (ninth century) the under vestment was the alb.   In fact, it is often difficult to discriminate between a dalmatic and a tunicle, though the former is generally the shorter.

In cutting out such a garment the diagram of a dalmatic, Figs. 62, 67, 69, may be used according to the period.

XIII CENTURY

As time went on, bishops began to wear a more elaborate tunicle under the dalmatic: this was made of rich material, fringed on both sleeves, side slits and hem.

As long as these garments were both of the same length the tunicle was unseen: to overcome this the dalmatic was shortened by from 8 to 10 inches in order to display the bottom of the tunicle. This accounts for two rows of fringe appearing in illustrations (Plate XVI), one being at the hem of the dalmatic, and the other (of the tunicle) below it. This arrangement is well seen in Fig. 204, Plate XIII, and in Plate XVI.

XIV CENTURY

In certain churches there were detailed regulations concerning the lay-out of vestments, so that the prelate might vest himself with alacrity and ease. In connection with the Abbot of Westminster the rule to be observed on the subject of the tunicle is worth quoting. Instructions are given 'to lay ready the dalmatic with longest sleeves above the other [the tunicle],' which means that the tunicle had longer sleeves than the dalmatic: the term 'dalmatic' being applied to *both* vestments. *The Inventory of Westminster*, 1388,[1] mentions pairs of 'dalmatics.' Other churches had similar traditions.

In earlier times it had been the custom for priests to vest publicly in front of the altar, beneath which the vestments were kept. Few English churches before Perpendicular times possessed vestries.

On the rood-screen at North Burlingham Church, not far from Ranworth, is a representation of St. Thomas of Canterbury in fifteenth-century vestments, which illustrate an advanced stage of elaboration.

Plate XVI is a copy of this panel, apparently by the same artist as Plate XV.

The tunicle which the twelfth-century saint and archbishop is wearing is of dark purple, and is edged with a 2-inch fringe 'componée,' red, gold, and blue. His chasuble is of a light blue silk (of a shade known at the time as plunket[2] celestyne), with a Y-shaped orphrey of black and gold brocade. This is partly hidden by a golden (rather exceptional) pallium. At the edge of the chasuble is a narrow gold border with jewels in gold lozenge-shaped settings placed along it at intervals. Some of the other vestments and ornaments, e.g. the mitre, Fig. 137, p. 106; cross-staff, p. 141, are described under their separate headings. The dalmatic is identical with the tunicle.

The charm of the whole figure is enhanced by the background of soft brick-red, powdered with a pattern of palish pink flowers on golden stems and leaves. See, for similar patterns, Figs. 244 and 245.

[1] J. Wickham Legg, F.S.A., in *Archaeologia*, vol. lii, 1890, p. 193.
[2] Plunket is O.F. *plonquié*, lead-coloured.

20. THE ROCHET

IX CENTURY

THIS garment, another development of the tunica, was a tunic of linen, with close sleeves or sleeveless, and at first reached to the feet. It was quite plain, and has been referred to as an 'ungirt un-apparelled alb,' resembling in shape the tunica in Fig. 6. It *might* have the sides open or not; it was a convenient garment that could be slipped on easily, and was not infrequently worn by servers.

X CENTURY

In the tenth century English clerics were ordered by canon of King Eadgar (959–75) not to appear in church without this 'over-slip,' which was worn above the alb.

XII CENTURY

The word ROCHET is akin to the diminutive 'roccus,' meaning an overcoat: the equivalent of a smock-frock. The distinctive use of this garment did not come into force until the twelfth century. Possibly at this time this 'overcoat' was shortened, reaching to just below the knee.

XIII CENTURY

In 1215 the Fourth (twelfth oecumenical) Lateran Council, the greatest of the Middle Ages, ordered prelates, unless they were monks, to wear the rochet in public, whether in church or out of doors, under their other vestments. It was, however, a non-liturgical vestment, merely a mark of personal distinction.

At the end of the century the long sleeves of the rochet were full enough to ruck over the sleeves of the cassock; the sleeves of the latter were then turned back over those of the rochet to form cuffs of fur at the wrists.

Always of white linen, this garment was often made of very fine white lawn (chainsil), and later cutwork (lace [1]) was added to the lower hem; but it was exceptional, certainly in England.

In any case, the rochet is a garment of dignity, the prerogative of bishops, canons regular, and cardinals, and of others to whom the right to wear it may be specially granted. At this time it reached to just below the knees, and had moderately close sleeves.

The cardinal, Fig. 237, is wearing a rochet over his scarlet cassock.

[1] See *Costume and Fashion*, vol. iii, p. 48.

PLATE XVI *(see page 171)*

St. Thomas of Canterbury in full XV-Century Vestments

21. THE ALMUCE

ANOTHER reaction to the cold of medieval churches—especially in winter, or at night—as also a concession to the increasing desire of comfort, is to be found in the ALMUCE.

XIII CENTURY

This accessory first appeared in the thirteenth century, though there are traces of it early in the eleventh.

It was a cloak of various dimensions, from a cape to elbow level to a cloak reaching to the feet. A hood was attached to it as shown at A in the half diagram, Fig. 246: ABD, the front, is open, a button and loop are set at B to fasten it at the throat if required; AB is the portion which encircles the face. The distance AE is the back seam or fold. This diagram gives a short cape. If a longer cloak is needed, the radius from the centre C must be extended.

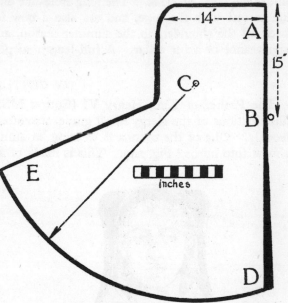

Fig. 246. Half Diagram of Almuce, XIII Century

XIV CENTURY

Fig. 247 shows the hood with the front portion turned back inside and rolled to form a pad over the head, the ends bunched to form an excrescence on each side. The hood could be fastened at the throat by a button and loop fixed inside it, and was finished off outside with a tuft or tassel of scarlet silk. This drawing is taken from an effigy of a canon of Sainte-Marie at Noyon, who died in 1353. Fig. 248 is a similar hood, with the cape thrown back off the shoulders: the side pads are obvious; and were probably achieved by small semicircular cushions sewn inside, a more convenient arrangement than that described in the first instance, Fig. 247. Both these examples are made of black substantial cloth, lined with white cloth, but more often with a white fluffy cotton cloth like short swansdown, known as 'carda' (sometimes made of silk), or with a coarse woolly Flemish serge called 'carised.'

Fig. 247. Hood of Almuce, XIV Century

The almuce was worn over the surplice as a choir habit or in processions by canons of the cathedrals, though in England it was also used by parish priests. It is suggested that the pads just described, so characteristic of the almuce hood, allowed the canon to rest his head more comfortably on the sharp-pointed carvings of his stall.

In place of the ordinary lining to the almuce, i.e. hood and cape, the more luxurious clergy used fur: this was sometimes of very superior quality—squirrel, sable, and even ermine; so it is not surprising that before long the lining of fur was displayed by being worn *outside*.   The Augustinian canon, Fig. 235, is wearing the almuce in this way under his cope or cloak.   The long stole-like ends of white fur which descend the front are in one with the cape, and are also a new feature.   The hood was usually turned back off the shoulders in the summer season, and when viewed from the front has the appearance of a fur collar.   A full-length surplice with wide sleeves is worn.

XV CENTURY

The Psalter of King Henry VI (Cotton MSS.), dating about 1433, contains many illuminations of the clergy of all grades assembled in choir: their vestments vary enormously.   One of the canons is wearing an almuce, the pads of which have developed almost into horns,[1] Fig. 249.   This is made of a dark-coloured cloth, lined with white;

Fig. 248. A similar Hood, XV Century

Fig. 249. Horned Hood, XV Century

the ample cloak of white fur is long enough to wrap around his knees, and the collar of the dark cassock and the neck-bands of the surplice are visible.   No longer was the erstwhile outer cloth of sober black, now that it was a lining to the fur; rich fabrics and gay colours were used instead.

An interesting excerpt from a statute concerning canons of the Church of St. Joan, Vienne, is worth quoting: 'From the Feast of St. Martin to Easter they wear the cappa nigra above the cassock (pellicium): and from Easter to the Feast of All Saints they wear the surplice (superpellicium) without the cappa, and on the head a grey cap (capellum), which they commonly call the almuce.'

The brass of Thomas Teylor, Fig. 250, Rector of Byfleet, Surrey, and a canon of Lincoln, was probably laid down in his lifetime, as the date 148– is left unfinished. Although a canon he is vested as a priest in a white fur almuce lined, one would expect, with some sober-coloured cloth.   The hood is thrown back, forming what looks like a fur collar.   The indentations of fur round the edge of the cape are an innovation, a type of ornament becoming very general during this century.   The long ends hanging down in

---

[1] That a prelate of the Church should appear wearing such an *outré* style of headgear in holy places may seem somewhat frivolous.   Not at all!   At this period women of all classes wore a head-dress constructed on similar lines.

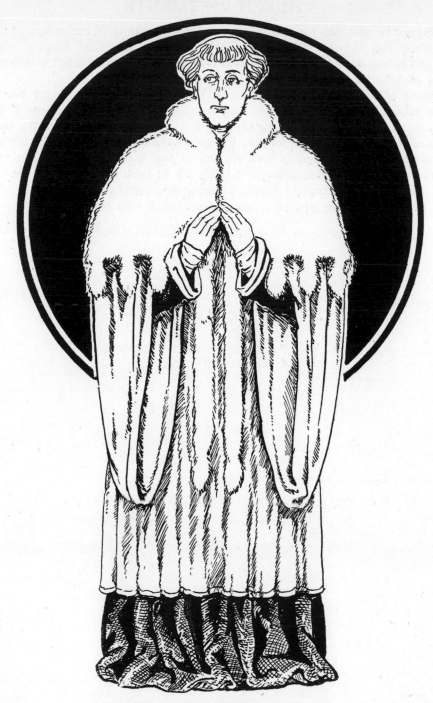

Fig. 250. Canon Teylor, 148–

front must not be mistaken for a stole: they are mere ornamental extensions of the cape, also of white fur. Under this Canon Teylor wears a shortened surplice with wide sleeves, and below this a black cassock with the sleeves turned back at the wrists. As a canon he would wear a white rochet in place of the surplice.

An almuce of white fur is seen in Plate XIV, worn by the canon under his cope.

In the succeeding century the two long hanging ends degenerated into a deep fur collar worn stole-wise, and even further into a mere scarf worn round the neck, and reaching to the waist and often longer: the hood vanished entirely. The almuce thus became a sign of dignity, and as such the colour and material varied—grey squirrels' fur for the highest rank, descending to a black silk or even cloth scarf for the ordinary clergy.[1] Its use disappeared in England during Elizabeth's time (1571).

N.B. The almuce must not, of course, be confused with the amice.

[1] This, it is needless to point out, is the origin of the scarf (tippet) of the Anglican clergy to-day.

22. THE CHIMERE

THIS garment was much used on the Continent since the early Middle Ages. It was a short sleeveless cloak or coat of sheepskin of Spanish origin, so it is said, called the 'zamarra.' This is the origin of the garment known as the simar (see *Costume and Fashion*, vol. iii, pp. 18–19), worn by royalty and the gentry at the end of the fifteenth and during the sixteenth century. Also of the 'chamarre' (see Fig. 282, p. 243 ibid.). This is an old French word, and both it and the Spanish zamarra derive ultimately from the same root, from which we obtain the English term CHIMERE.[1]

XII CENTURY

By the twelfth century the chimere was still a short cloak, descending to below the knee, and open up the front where it was usually buttoned. At the sides there were slits for the arms from 18 to 24 inches in length. The garment was cut as a semicircle, the straight edge AD being gathered into a narrow neck-band: later, a portion at the ends of the diameter ABCD was left ungathered to form hanging lapels, see Fig. 251.

It was about the same period that the chimere was worn by bishops of the western Church as an outdoor garment, for riding and other purposes; but it was not reckoned as a vestment. At first it

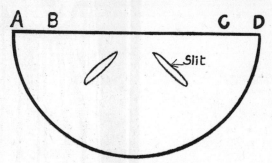

Fig. 251. Diagram of Chimere

was made of black silk, but later in colours—scarlet, purple, or blue, and probably lined if required for warmth. Fig. 252 is an archbishop or bishop of the twelfth century in full convocation robes, wearing the chimere in purple silk, and beneath it a white rochet over a scarlet cassock. Thrown back on to the shoulders is a scarlet hood lined with white.

As with vestments, alterations were made in some details of the chimere as the centuries passed.

XIV CENTURY

The early fourteenth-century bishop, Plate III, appears to be wearing a chimere of the latest shape. The slits for the arms are open down the whole length. As usual it is worn over the cassock, the hood being thrown back. He wears the pileus. In fact, if a bishop wore a chimere, it was only as an outdoor garment which he would wear over his rochet on the way to church: during our period, the limit of this book, it never became a vestment.

[1] This name is used for two other garments: the sleeved cassock, worn under a sleeved rochet; and a sleeveless upper garment, generally worn open in front, but sometimes closed by folding forward the lapels.

Fig. 252. Stephen Langton, Archbishop of Canterbury,
in full Convocation Robes, XII Century

THE MOZZETTA

XV CENTURY

The fur cape worn by Pope Sixtus IV, Fig. 151, with a hood worn under the tiara, is known as the MOZZETTA. This was short, about elbow length, and fastened up the front by buttons: and was made of cloth, silk, or velvet, and lined with fur, usually white. (It will be noted that the pontiff is wearing his mozzetta with the fur outside, a very common proceeding.) Popes, cardinals, and bishops of a later date wore it in scarlet or purple. The word is Italian, a diminutive of *mozza*, itself deriving from medieval Latin *almussa*, which has given us almuce. Similarly the immediate ancestors of the mozzetta certainly seem to have been the almuce and chimere.

23. THE TONSURE AND HEADGEAR

THE TONSURE
(Latin, *tondeo*, I clip)

THE ecclesiastical tonsure is the shaved part of the head, and this practice of shaving the whole or part of the hair was from very early times a necessary preliminary to the monastic life of holy orders. The tonsure is, of course, much older than this, for Egyptian priests shaved their heads: it is probably from them that the first Christian monks derived the practice. In the fifth century the clergy copied the monks. The shaving or clipping of the head was done in three different ways. They are as follows:

The Roman. The head was shaved on the top, leaving a circle of hair to grow round it like a crown surrounding the head of a king, or in a symbolical sense resembling the Crown of Thorns encircling the Head of Christ.

Fig. 253. The Tonsure of St. Peter

Fig. 254. The Tonsure of St. James

This coronal tonsure is also known as the tonsure of St. Peter, Fig. 253, and was in use in the early churches of Britain, Italy, Spain, and Gaul.

The Eastern or Greek tonsure had the head completely shaved, and is referred to as the tonsure of St. Paul.

The Celtic tonsure, worn in the early Scottish churches of Great Britain and Ireland, was made by shaving the head in front of a line drawn from ear to ear over the top of the head, and is called the tonsure of St. James, Fig. 254.

The tonsure was prescribed by canon law in very early Christian times: it was imperative for all clerics to be tonsured, and this was very solemnly done before ordination by a bishop in the case of the clergy, an abbot performing the same ceremony for a monk entering a monastery.[1]

The ceremony of tonsuring for the reception of the minor and major orders appears to have been much the same as at the present day: the bishop or other prelate clips the hair in front, behind, over each ear, and on the crown of the head of the candidate kneeling before him, and then invests him with a surplice. Until this was accomplished a layman could not be admitted to the clerical state.

[1] The monastic tonsure differed very considerably in the various orders, a subject with which this book is not concerned.

These regulations concerning the hair of the clergy were inspired by the abhorrence of the prelates of the Church for the long hair so prevalent among fashionable men at various periods. Special injunctions forbade *long* hair to be worn by any officers of the Church: this is also St. Paul's opinion (1 Corinthians xi. 14).

HEADGEAR WORN BY CLERICS AND LAYMEN IN CHURCH

A.D. I CENTURY

'Every man praying . . . having his head covered dishonoureth his head. . . . For a man indeed ought not to have his head veiled, forasmuch as he is the image and glory of God.'[1]

V CENTURY

Basing his opinion on the above, St. Augustine of Hippo prohibited the wearing of headgear by men at divine service. He also forbade monks and other men to cover their shaven or unshaven heads when they were preaching or praying.

VIII CENTURY

As previously mentioned on page 71 men removed their head-covering, if they were wearing any, during divine service.

IX CENTURY

Reference has already been made (on page 71) to the fact that the men who formed part of St. Æthelwold's congregation were bareheaded during communion. Whether they were covered in church before and after this is a question: all the women appear to be veiled, according to the manner which had been customary from the earliest Christian times.

X CENTURY

In the tenth century we have the authority of Simeon, Archbishop of Thessalonica, to the same effect, who says: 'Every bishop and priest of the East, with the exception of the Patriarch of Alexandria, says mass with his head bare, because the Apostle St. Paul wished that, to honour Jesus Christ, we have our heads bare while praying.'

Hats in Church

It is a common belief that in former times men kept their hats on in church. This was certainly true at some periods, and for certain parts of the service (e.g. during the sermon and reading of the lessons): from time to time, however, courageous clerics inveighed against this practice as being irreverent, especially during prayers. The universal doffing of hats dates in modern times only from the early nineteenth century.

XIV AND XV CENTURIES

In the fourteenth century it would have been out of the question for fashionable noblemen to remove their elaborate headgear, in church as in the presence-chamber: and it would have been equally impossible to put it on again under such circumstances.

[1] 1 Corinthians xi. 4, 7.

What they certainly did, in order to show reverence and respect, was to push it back in such a manner as to uncover a little of the forehead. With the simpler headgear of the latter part of the fifteenth century it became easier to remove them as an act of courtesy, and a good deal of elaborate etiquette arose in this connection which must have had its effect upon manners in church. Nevertheless the Coventry tapestry shows Henry VII at prayer with his hat on. In the same century we find Bishop Peacock of St. Asaph (1444–50) claiming that there is no scriptural authority 'that a womman chuide were upon her heer [hair] and heed eny cover-chief of Lynnen threde or of silk,' her long hair being sufficient covering.

These examples are sufficient to show that there is much more in the matter of 'Hats in Church' than is commonly supposed.[1]

[1] What has been written above may throw light on the present-day custom in regard to wearing the biretta during the mass and divine office. When the clergy and choir are seated they cover, but uncover when standing or kneeling.

24. RINGS AND GLOVES
THE FINGER RING OR ANULUS

NOTE. To avoid mistakes fingers are numbered separately from the thumb: 1 (fore), 2 (middle), 3 (third), 4 (little) finger.

RINGS were universally worn amongst the ancients, as ornaments, as seals, and to denote rank: they were made of precious metals (or even bronze or iron), and were set with jewels or semi-precious stones, often engraved with initials, monograms, and symbolic devices.

A.D. II CENTURY

Clement, Bishop of Alexandria [180–212 (or 220)] advises all Christians to wear their rings upon the little finger of the left hand so as not to impede their work , and to engrave them with Christian symbols.

III CENTURY

The first bishop who is known to have worn a ring seems to have been St. Caius of

Fig. 255. The Roman Benediction   Fig. 256. The Greek Benediction

Rome (283–96), one (now lost) being found on his finger when his tomb was opened in 1622.   The chief use of such a ring was, as in the case of the laity, for sealing a document, the owner's name or monogram being engraved on it.

IV CENTURY

Thus Eusebius of Emesa (310) had a ring engraved with the monogram of Christ [chrisma?] on one side, and with his own name on the other.

V CENTURY

St. Augustine of Hippo, so he says, sealed a letter to Bishop Victorinus with a gem engraved with a man's profile.

VI CENTURY

Clovis, King of the Franks, recognized the letters of the Gallican bishops only if authenticated with their signet rings.

183

VII CENTURY

In England, St. Birinus of Dorchester (Oxon, 634–50) and St. John of Beverley (*ob.* 721) also possessed rings which were found in their tombs—but none of these had hitherto any definite ecclesiastical character.

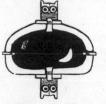

Fig. 257. The
Episcopal Ring,
XII Century

In this century, however, bishops began to receive a ring—symbolical of their marriage to the Church—at their consecration: this is clear from a statement by St. Isidore of Seville at the Fourth Council of Toledo (633); the relevant finger was, according to the *Ordo Romanus*, the third finger of the right hand: in spite of the fact that at any rate English medieval bishops wore a ring on the middle joint of the second, so that it might be visible in giving the blessing or benediction. This was given in the Latin manner by bending the third and fourth fingers of the right hand down on to the palm, the first and second fingers being upright as in Fig. 255.[1]   In the Greek use the thumb touches the first knuckle or tip of the bent third finger, the upright fingers being the first, second, and fourth, as shown in Fig. 256.

Thenceforward the examples of episcopal rings are numerous, e.g. the ring of Arnulphus, Bishop of Metz, contained a milk-white carnelian, bearing a fish in a basket: this is now one of the treasures of the cathedral.

IX CENTURY

Another still existing early ring is that of Eahlstan, Bishop of Sherborne (824–67), which is in the Victoria and Albert Museum: the design contains his name, a cross, and fabulous animals.   A third, alleged to be St. Cuthbert's, but more probably St. Frithestan's (see p. 90), was found when the tomb was opened: a massive gold ring set with a cabochon sapphire.   In fact, existing episcopal rings can be studied in most of the museums in Great Britain and on the Continent.

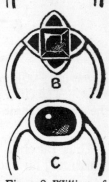

XII CENTURY

Fig. 257 shows a gold episcopal ring of the twelfth century: it is set with a large uncut sapphire, joined to the shank by two dragons' heads.

XIII CENTURY

The pope's ring—a gold ring with a design of St. Peter fishing from a boat, together with his name—does not seem to be earlier than the thirteenth century: the first mention appears to be in a letter of Clement IV (1265).   This ring was placed on the pope's finger immediately after his election, and was used by him as a seal.

XIV CENTURY

In this century we have an English example in the practice of William of Wykeham.   The effigy in his chantry at Winchester has bare hands, and there is a ring on the third finger of the right hand, see Fig. 257; the left hand has rings on the third and little fingers: see Fig. 258, A, B, C.

Fig. 258. William of
Wykeham's Rings

---

[1] At the present time the pope alone gives the blessing in the manner shown in Fig. 255.

It is not possible to tell whether any of these rings is an episcopal ring or not: they are certainly modest for so great a churchman, and of the simple design approved at the time.

XV CENTURY

Fig. 259 shows an ecclesiastical ring of the fifteenth century or probably earlier, set with a sapphire. The shank is octagonal: the edges are bevelled and engraved. The jewel would be either square or round, the claws branching out to hold it.

In this same century bishops used to wear rings above gloves, and are so represented in pictures: there are usually several rings, including a thumb ring. The degree of elaboration may be judged from Fig. 260, which is set with a square amethyst, the heavy gold shank and bezel being richly enamelled with scroll-work.

Fig. 259. Ecclesiastical Ring, XV Century

Fig. 260. Bishop's Ring of the XV Century

Bishops' rings were often designed so as to contain a relic, such as a fragment of the True Cross. A ring of this kind of the late fourteenth or early fifteenth century was found in the river Thame in 1944, and is now in the Ashmolean Museum, Oxford: it has been pronounced one of the finest medieval rings in existence. It has a box bezel with movable lid, so that it is evidently intended to serve as a reliquary: and on it is set a large amethyst in the form of a patriarchal cross. On the lid and around the sides is an inscription, and under the bezel a representation of the Crucifixion.

What has been said about bishops' rings applies very largely to those of cardinals and abbots: such a ring is nowadays worn on the third finger of the right hand, and as a sign of respect for his high office his ring is kissed by any cleric of inferior rank.

THE GLOVE

In 1923 when the tomb of Tutankhamen was opened a glove combining finger and thumb stalls with a sleeve-like gauntlet was discovered—the oldest glove in existence. Obviously the Egyptians of the early XIV century B.C. understood the craft of the glover.

The glove in its original form was a piece of hide laced round the hand, and often round the forearm as well, leaving the fingers free, with a hole for the thumb. This was in use among the lower classes of the Greeks. In fact the first gloves were working gloves, as they would not—in Mediterranean countries—be generally required for warmth. A refined edition called 'manica,' which had separate fingers, was used by the more wealthy citizens of Rome in pre-Christian times, probably for ornament.

The European custom of wearing gloves appears to have begun in Germany, where a bag of skin to cover the fingers, with a separate 'thumb,' was devised: such gloves were made of finely dressed skins with the fur inside or out, and ornamented outside in various ways. The Anglo-Saxon 'glof' was a glove of this kind: in England during the Norman period, gloves (called 'muffola') were rare and costly, and it was not until the twelfth century that a glove with separate fingers was introduced there. Such early

Fig. 261.

The Glove, XII Century

Fig. 262.

Glove worn by King Edward I

Fig. 263.

William of Wykeham's Glove, XIV Century

Fig. 264.

Another Knitted Silk Glove, XV Century

examples were sufficiently loose round the wrist to allow the hand to pass through with ease. A small cuff covered the wrist, and a band of gold or embroidery covered the join, see Fig. 261, and on the back was an ornament of some kind, usually in a circle. The very early fingered gloves worn by Pope Gregory, Plate VI, are obviously red.

As with rings, so with gloves: bishops, like other people, at first wore both, without any ecclesiastical significance. Thus an early inventory (831) of the Abbey of St. Riquier includes two pairs of gloves, one of skin ornamented with gold, and one of linen. Riculfus, Bishop of Helena (*ob.* 915), left in his will a pair of gloves, apparently of great value. The Cluny Museum preserves the white silk gloves of Ingon, Abbot of St. Germain-des-Prés (1025). All of these were most probably bag-gloves, without fingers.

XII CENTURY

As a Church vestment there is no mention of gloves until the twelfth century, the usage being recognized by Pope Innocent III about 1200. It would appear that the liturgical use of gloves was introduced by French bishops: at first, as in the case of hats, it was a sign of reverence to remove gloves in church—but later they were worn so that nothing sacred should be touched with the bare hands. In the absence of definite examples of early date an attempt has been made to reconstruct an ecclesiastical glove from twelfth-century examples, Fig. 261.

Ecclesiastical gloves, like others, were made of skins, silk, wool, linen, or a knitted fabric, and were usually white to suggest purity: on occasion coloured gloves (green or violet) were worn, and by the fourteenth century this had developed so as to follow the scheme of liturgical colours. They were often richly embroidered in gold and silk, chiefly on the backs and cuffs, and round the fingers. In days of luxurious dress clergy below the rank of bishop had from time to time to be restrained from wearing gloves.

XIII CENTURY

There was at first no real difference in material or design between the gloves of bishops and those of the nobility, or even royalty: Fig. 262, though actually belonging to King Edward I (1272–1307), will serve as a thirteenth-century example. The orange and black embroidery on the little finger, simulating a ring, will be noticed.

An ecclesiastical glove would certainly have a typical Christian device, such as a cross or chrisma, on the back. A gold plate on the back of a glove, displaying such a symbol or set with a jewel, was called a 'monial'—an example is to be seen in Fig. 261.

XIV CENTURY

In fact on William of Wykeham's gloves (1366–1404) this design is the IHS monogram surrounded by the sun 'in glory.' These gloves are still preserved in New College, Oxford: they are of crimson purl-knitted silk, and have two circles of gold embroidery round the base of each finger. The chief design consists of crimson octagons separated by green squares, the whole on a white ground: a fringe of crimson surrounds the edge of the cuff, see Fig. 263. Fig. 264 shows a silk glove of similar design: it is of fifteenth-century date, and is preserved at St. Sernin de Toulouse.

A panel on the sculptured sarcophagus
dating the IV century in the Lateran shows
the monogram of Christ inscribed in the
circle of a victor's wreath of bay or olive,
and elevated on a cross which forms its
upright P.   Two soldiers resting on their
shields are placed beneath its transom on
which perch two doves.

INDEX

Principal references are italiciezd

189